ROTTEN MOVIES WE L✳VE

ROTTEN MOVIES WE L*VE

CULT CLASSICS, UNDERRATED GEMS, AND FILMS SO BAD THEY'RE GOOD

The Editors of Rotten Tomatoes
Foreword by Paul Feig

RUNNING PRESS

PHILADELPHIA

Running Press
Hachette Book Group
1290 Avenue of the Americas, New York, NY 10104
www.runningpress.com
@Running_Press

Printed in Canada

First Edition: October 2019

Published by Running Press, an imprint of Perseus Books, LLC,
a subsidiary of Hachette Book Group, Inc.
The Running Press name and logo is a trademark of the Hachette Book Group.

The Hachette Speakers Bureau provides a wide range of authors for speaking events.
To find out more, go to www.hachettespeakersbureau.com or call (866) 376-6591.

The publisher is not responsible for websites (or their content)
that are not owned by the publisher.

All images courtesy of Everett Collection.

Print book cover and interior design by Josh McDonnell.
Infographics pages 56-57, 112-113, and 174-175 by Courtney Kawata,
Yerania Sanchez, and Francis Navarro.

Library of Congress Control Number: 2019938509

ISBNs: 978-0-7624-9605-1 (paperback), 978-0-7624-9606-8 (ebook)

FRI

10   9   8   7   6   5   4   3   2   1

CONTENTS

FOREWORD

Nobody sets out to make a bad movie.

I don't think any studio executive or commercial filmmaker has ever said, "You know what would be fun? Let's make a terrible movie. One that audiences will really hate and laugh at in all the wrong ways and make merciless fun of; one that lets critics practice their comedy writing skills as they see just how brutal they can be in their tearing down of our film. That would be the perfect use of many, many millions of dollars of our money and really great for our reputations."

No, bad movies aren't made on purpose—they just sort of slowly happen. Scripts are developed in earnest. A screenwriter has a spark of inspiration that they then sequester themselves away for months to develop. A studio reads it and takes a shine to something, whether it's the overall idea, a character they like, or the entire script. They see something commercial in it, something that they're pretty certain will draw people out of their homes, into their cars, and down to the local multiplex, where they'll pull out their hard earned cash and plunk it down to spend two hours sitting in the dark having the time of their lives watching the end result of whatever drew the studio and the filmmakers to the script in the first place. A production crew is put together and actors are cast. The movie goes into production and there are problems and fights and disagreements along the way, and maybe people are fired and maybe the film is taken away from the director after the studio doesn't like the director's version and the final cut is finished by committee. Or maybe everything goes swimmingly.

Then enter the audiences and the critics.

Audiences don't have any horse in the race when it comes to the success of a movie. The only thing they're rooting for is to not waste their money on a bad or unsatisfying experience. As filmmakers, we can all sit around and high-five each other about how great we think our movies are and how cool our shots were and how we were right to make it way over two hours long because how could we possibly lose any of those perfect moments we spent so much time shooting and editing. But audiences don't care about that. Some will watch the movie in the spirit in which we intended and really look deeply into its hidden meanings. Others will sit there going "This is dumb," or "This is boring," or "Look at how weird that actor's hair is," or focusing on any of the myriad things that those of us who make the movies just assume people are going to go along with.

And then there are the critics. Most of us assume that the critics will love our movies. We're pretty sure they'll get exactly what we were going for and appreciate the way we did it. We know *they'll* watch our films in the spirit in which we made them. They'll laud our successful moments. They'll forgive our shortcomings. They'll judge our work in the context of the audience for which it was intended. They'll be fair and kind and understand how hard it is to make a movie with all the compromises and politics and challenges we have to deal with along the way.

Then the reviews come in and they're terrible. Then opening weekend comes and nobody shows up. Then the finger pointing starts. The script should have been better! The director should have listened to us! The studio gave us bad notes that they demanded we follow! They ruined the movie! Our vision was compromised! The critics were too hard on us! The audience didn't get it! We were ahead of our time!

Some of these things may be true. They may all be. Or we could all have been delusional. Whatever the cause, we are now sitting with something none of us ever wanted or could have predicted we would have.

A bad movie.

None of the movies in this book are bad movies. Some weren't great but tried their best to be. Some were amazing but nobody realized it because they were expecting something else. Some just got better the more we watched them.

I like to say the biggest hurdle to getting people to like your movie is simply getting them used to the idea that it exists. They go into the theater with a set of expectations based on the trailer and the poster and the word of mouth they've heard, and if the movie is different from the image they had formed in their minds, they then spend the whole time watching it through a different lens—a lens of disappointment, of confusion, of longing for it to be the thing they wanted it to be. So when it ends, they say, "I didn't like that." And then, for them, it is a "bad movie."

But movies have a way of rehabilitating themselves. Many are like wine. They get better with age. Thanks to DVDs and streaming services and cable TV, you'll come across a movie you saw once and didn't like, but you'll start watching it again anyway, and since you know what's coming, you'll find yourself enjoying it more the second time. You'll start to appreciate the characters and the performances. You'll start to see the humor in it when originally you saw the movie as taking itself too seriously. Or, many times, you'll stumble across a movie you'd heard was bad and have read scathing reviews about and then you'll watch it to make fun of it and end up loving it instead.

That's the beauty of movies. Once they're finished, they're set in stone. They don't change. They present themselves as earnestly as they did the day they opened. And they're always ready and waiting to entertain you, to plead their case for being worthy of your time even long after everyone who worked on the film is gone.

That's why those of us who make movies do it in the first place. So, before you denounce any of our work as bad, give it a second chance. Just like so many of the movies you're going to read about in this book, it may deserve another lease on life.

Making movies is hard. But watching them doesn't have to be. It should be fun. Hopefully this book will help more people realize that.

Paul Feig
Director of movies that some people think are good and some people think are bad

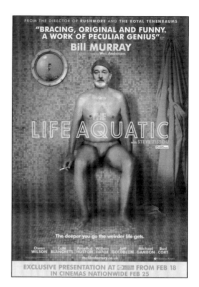

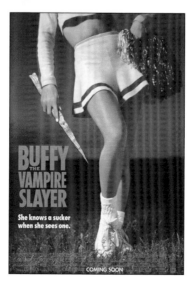

INTRODUCTION

When you work at Rotten Tomatoes, you don't just tell people what you do for a living—you *admit* it. Or *confess* it. Sometimes, depending on the type of person you're speaking to, you take a big step back, away from the line of fire. Because you know what's coming next.

For me, what comes next usually involves *The Greatest Showman*, the mega-hit musical from 2017 starring Hugh Jackman that audiences love but that our Tomatometer deems Rotten. "How could you call that a *bad* movie?" an Uber driver once barked at me. "Do you even have a soul?!" Or, upon confessing what I do, I might suddenly find myself confronted with an animated defense of Michael Bay's *Bad Boys*, a movie whose Rotten 42% score was enough to once prompt a partygoer to lecture me for ten minutes about the out-of-touch-ness of our critics. Another time, a *Step Brothers* fan told me bluntly, upon hearing where I worked, that "we're not going to be friends." (The movie has a Rotten Tomatometer score of 55%; just five more points and we might have been besties.)

If they happen to bring up *Venom*, I just make a run for it.

I rarely get a word in during these exchanges, but when I do, I tell them this: I hear you. All of us at Rotten Tomatoes do. The Tomatometer*—which shows the percentage of critics who like a movie or TV show enough to recommend it—can drive us crazy, too.

Sometimes we're with it all the way, allowing it to guide us to the latest well-oiled blockbuster or point the way toward an underground masterpiece we wouldn't have otherwise discovered. But other times, it knocks the wind out of us. We feel your pain when an upcoming film we're *dying* to see gets a Rotten score (which is anything below 59%), and it can totally lay us out when we discover that a movie we've loved for years has been wearing the big green splat all this time. When I first found out that critics at the time mostly hated my favorite Christmas movie, *Home Alone 2: Lost In New York* (Rotten at 32%!), I had to ask: *Do they even have souls?*

Exchanges and discoveries like these brought us to the subject of our very first Rotten Tomatoes book: *Rotten Movies We Love.* Why did we decide to start with a tome in honor of the Rotten and not the Fresh? Because we understand your passion (we're fans, too). As much as we love movies that score 90% or higher, we, like you, also love movies that don't always connect with critics or movies whose virtues are best revealed with age. We love dumb comedies, and we laugh at any and *all* fart jokes. (At least I do.) Our desks are covered in toys and postcards and other tchotchkes from critically maligned films that would become cult classics. And we love a well-executed jump scare, regardless of whether it adds value to the story. Some of us—though not many—even loved *The Greatest Showman*.

In this book, we make the case for *why* we love these "Rotten" movies. For digestion's sake, we've grouped this list of 101 Rotten movies into seven

*For more on the Rotten Tomatoes lingo, see the Glossary on page 214.

XIII

categories, each of which hint at the reasoning you'll find within: popular favorites that dominated the box office or found love on TV and in home entertainment (but not with critics); weird and wonderfully Rotten sci-fi and fantasy; rare Rotten films from Fresh and famous directors; movies that were panned at release but found a cult following; underestimated titles that were doing a little more than reviewers gave them credit for at the time; oft-dismissed sequels we think deserve a second look; and dumb-fun flicks that just make us laugh, scream, or get our hearts racing.

Some movies straddle multiple categories: *Rocky IV* was a box office smash, a sequel dismissed far too quickly, and a super-interesting critique of US nationalism during the Cold War (really); *The Cable Guy* was a severely underestimated satire that still pulled off some big stupid laughs on its way to becoming a cult classic. *All* have inspired enough passion in the Rotten Tomatoes' staff for us to stand up, turn toward the Tomatometer, and declare our love for the green stuff.

A Note on Our Scores

Tomatometer scores are dynamic: as more critics review a movie and their reviews are added to our system, a movie's score can change. This is most common with new movies, which see bursts of new reviews added when they hit theaters, and then again when they hit the home entertainment market. But it also happens with older movies; it might be that there's a sudden new wave of interest in an older movie (a sequel is released, the director's next movie comes out), or that we onboard a bunch of new critics whose reviews for that movie weren't included in the score. Which is all to say, the scores in this book are accurate at time of press—and they might have changed slightly since then.

Passion is an appropriate driver for our first book, as it was passion that got Rotten Tomatoes started some twenty-one years ago. Cofounder Senh Duong had grown up a big fan of Chinese actors/ass-kickers Jackie Chan and Jet Li, and when Chan released his first big US crossover film, *Rumble in the Bronx*, Duong wondered what critics would make of it. The Berkeley undergrad was searching for reviews of Chan movies he loved—among them *First Strike* and *Twin Dragons* (both of which would be Rotten when the site eventually launched)—when the idea for a review aggregator came to him. He founded the site a few years later, on August 18, 1998, with two other Berkeley students, Patrick Y. Lee and Stephen Wang.

The idea was simple: create a pool of critics who meet a set of criteria (professionals with experience and an audience); collect their reviews when a movie is released; and calculate the percentage of reviews that recommend the movie. That percentage would be its "Tomatometer" score.

Rotten Tomatoes has evolved a lot since those early days in the Bay Area, but that basic calculation remains the same. We're bigger now, of course, and we cover TV. (Want a Tomatometer score for every episode of *Game of Thrones*? We got you.) We also put on live shows where you can debate critics in the flesh, and we produce a ton of original content—everything from celebrity interviews to the thing you're holding in your hand right now.

We've also updated how we source and approve the people who contribute to our critic pool, with a big refresh in 2018 that made it easier for freelance critics, those working in newer media (think YouTubers, podcasters), and those speaking to underrepresented groups to join the ranks. Our Tomatometer hasn't changed, but the opinions that contribute to it have evolved with the times.

Critics have been as core to our evolution as

our own passion for movies; it's their Fresh or Rotten opinions on which the RT foundations stand. We couldn't celebrate Rotten movies we love without asking some critics to tell us theirs. And so, mixed in with our own selections of fantastic Rotten films, you'll find impassioned defenses of Rotten films from some of the world's most talented and thoughtful reviewers. They're names you know and names you should make a point of seeking out.

The incredible Leonard Maltin, whose yearly movie guides have been helping us decide what to watch since 1969, endorses what some consider one of the worst movies ever made, *Bela Lugosi Meets a Brooklyn Gorilla*. It was an embarrassment for the legendary Lugosi but an enduring source of pleasure for the veteran critic. *Rolling Stone*'s David Fear, meanwhile, asks us to take a second look at *The Usual Suspects* writer Christopher McQuarrie's directorial debut *The Way of the Gun*, arguing that it's so much more than the Tarantino rip-off most dismissed it as back in 2000. UK magazine *Empire*'s editor-in-chief, Terri White, sets the page on fire in a wonderful and galvanizing new look at 1996's teen-witch flick *The Craft*, which itself attempted to set the patriarchy alight. And *Time Out New York*'s Joshua Rothkopf proves that Will Ferrell can put a smile on even the most seasoned of critics' faces—if he lands those fart jokes *just right*. Rothkopf's ode to the unrelenting and totally winning stupidity of *Step Brothers* is a delight.

One critic even pitches a tent in support of *The Greatest Showman*, albeit in a much more reasoned manner than my hostile Uber driver. In a true highlight, Kristen Lopez wrestles with the P. T. Barnum bio-musical's problems (primary among them a glossing-over of the circus impresario's treatment of those with disabilities) even as she finds herself won over by its charms (those songs, that glitz, that glam!). Lopez, who herself is disabled, brings a fascinating perspective, contemplating what to do with a piece of cinema you love when you know it's been made without *you* in mind.

Lopez's moving piece gets to the heart of why we're putting this book out into the world. "Fresh" and "Rotten" are really just starting points. There's a lot that goes into those scores—thousands of opinions, millions of words spoken and written, thoughtful curation, and eventually some pretty simple math. But they can't account for things like audience sentiment and the way culture and perceptions of a movie might change over time. In the end, though, that big green splat and that perfect-looking red tomato are there as much to guide your viewing choices as they are to start a conversation about what you've just seen.

Fresh or Rotten isn't the final word on a film; it's often the first word, a kickoff to a debate about whether the critics got it right or wrong, and—in these pages particularly—whether time might have changed the answer to that question. And it's an invitation to tell us what you think. The more voices join the conversation, the more fun and dynamic that conversation is; the experience of watching a movie is enriched by the thoughtful and insightful discussion that follows.

We hope this book gets you talking.

Joel Meares

Editor-in-Chief, Rotten Tomatoes

PEOPLE'S CHOICE

Box Office Slayers and Household Names

We still haven't met a critic who would call Michael Bay their favorite filmmaker (though famously contrarian critic Armond White has come close, calling him a "real visionary"). Bay is considered by most professional movie watchers a maker of a kind of anti-cinema, a man with little feel for narrative and humanity but a whole lot of eye for tits and ass and big 'splosions. His credits run green with Rottenness—Nic Cage action flick *The Rock* is his single Fresh film as a director—and yet people *love* his work (*real* people, that is, not those dark-dwelling critics). His recent string of *Transformers* films has pulverized the global box office, and his 1990s output includes some of the decade's most cherished movies (*Armageddon*!). When it comes to Michael Bay, the people have spoken—and they've drowned out the critics. The director's

buddy-cop classic, *Bad Boys*, is among the films celebrated in this chapter, which is devoted to movies that made serious bank at the box office, despite Rotten reviews, and that have become audience favorites over the years. They're the movies that still have people screaming for sequels (*Space Jam*, *The First Wives Club*), that play perennially on cable (*The 'Burbs*, *The Holiday*), and movies about which our dear readers write frequently to us to ask, How the f—k can that be Rotten? (*Twins*, *Teen Wolf*). Sometimes, they demand we simply let go and enjoy the populist ride—and sometimes they're more complex than meets the eye, as critic Monica Castillo argues of Disney blockbuster *Maleficent*. This is decidedly *not* the case with *Bad Boys*, but hey, that's part of why we love it.

EVERY WHICH WAY BUT LOOSE 1978

 **37%**

Directed by James Fargo
Written by Jeremy Joe Kronsberg
Starring Clint Eastwood, Sondra Locke, Geoffrey Lewis, Beverly D'Angelo, Ruth Gordon

Critics Consensus

Clint Eastwood shows off his brawn and sensitive charm, but this gonzo comedy fails to entertain by playing loose with its dramatic elements and volleying uninspired gags every which way but funny.

Synopsis

Philo Beddoe is a brawler whose best buddy, Clyde, happens to be a mischievous orangutan. When Philo falls for country singer Lynn Halsey-Taylor, he finds he's gotta fight—with the cops and a buffoonish biker gang—for what he loves.

> **" FEW CRITICS AT THE TIME APPRECIATED THE PURE JOY OF WATCHING EASTWOOD ACT OPPOSITE A CHARISMATIC ORANGUTAN. "**

Why We Love It

Upon its release, *Every Which Way but Loose* became a sudden hit, the most successful film Clint Eastwood had ever made, and it still holds a spot in the top 250 highest-grossing films of all time (adjusted for inflation). Yet so few critics at the time appreciated the pure joy of watching Eastwood act opposite a charismatic orangutan, with one even wondering if Eastwood was playing a joke on them to see how low he could go. Everyone had told him not to take the part, apparently, but he went ahead with it anyway. After a string of gritty hits like *The Gauntlet*, *The Enforcer*, and *The Outlaw Josey Wales*, the actor was the consummate "man with a gun," but he had plenty of fun early in his career in more whimsical pictures like *Paint Your Wagon* and *Kelly's Heroes*. Maybe he yearned for a more challenging role or a return to lighter fare. Whatever ultimately drove Eastwood into the arms of an orangutan, it resulted in exceptional fun.

Eastwood's got comic chops, and it's partly because he takes his comedy *very* seriously. Throughout the film, there's no indication the actor thinks Philo's deep friendship with a primate is anything but real, which only makes this story that much more bizarre and watchable. This is a future Academy Award winner confessing his deepest secrets to his orangutan. "When it comes to sharing my feelings with a woman, my stomach just turns to royal gelatin," Philo whispers in the dark to his hairy buddy. It's genuinely touching.

Also in the film: Ruth Gordon as Ma swats Philo good with a broom, while Sondra Locke—romantic partners with Eastwood at the time—sparkles as a small-time con woman. (Eastwood hadn't had such dynamic female costars since 1970's *Two Mules for Sister Sarah*, in which Shirley MacLaine matched him wit for wit.) Add in a clownish gang of bikers bedecked in Nazi regalia summarily having their asses handed to them again and again, and this is as screwball as you can get, a seeming throwback to 1938's *Bringing Up Baby*. Its heart is in the right place.

PROBLEM CHILD 1990

0%

Directed by Dennis Dugan
Written by Scott Alexander and Larry Karaszewski
Starring John Ritter, Amy Yasbeck, Jack Warden, Gilbert Gottfried

Critics Consensus

Mean-spirited and hopelessly short on comic invention, *Problem Child* is a particularly unpleasant comedy, one that's loaded with manic scenery chewing and juvenile pranks.

Synopsis

In this black comedy, wannabe dad Ben Healey adopts an adorable seven-year-old boy, only to find that said child has a penchant for terrorizing anyone who crosses his path.

Why We Love It

Just months before *Home Alone* would premiere and immediately become Christmas canon, Dennis Dugan's bad-kid slapstick comedy *Problem Child* would become an improbable box-office success and a frequent punching bag for critics, who couldn't foresee that audiences were hungry for darker fare. The late 1980s and early '90s had offered a slew of men-with-feisty-children comedies, including *Parenthood*, *Kindergarten Cop*, and *Uncle Buck*, but the gloss of the John Hughes era had died with Reagan, and '90s moviegoers were outgrowing their popped collars.

Writers Scott Alexander and Larry Karaszewski had originally envisioned their script as an adult black comedy parodying the avalanche of heartwarming kiddie-friendly flicks. When the studio told them it was the wrong direction, that they needed to appeal to both children and adults, writers and director undertook a frantic overhaul of the script and footage, with extensive reshoots. What they were left with reportedly made the writers cry at the cast screening, as they were now worried their names would be associated with a muddled monstrosity that seemed far too black for children and far too light for adults. Surprise, surprise: kids couldn't get enough of this story about a near-psychotic child who befriends a serial killer who, in one scene, actually has sex with the kid's mom while the father is contemplating murdering his new adopted son. Whew!

Dugan would go on to team up with another comic crudester embraced by the juvenile nineties, Adam Sandler, and *Problem Child* would spawn a moderately successful sequel that would feature a vomit extravaganza etched into the memories of any kid brave enough to view the whole thing—Alexander and Karaszewski later said they intended it to be a John Waters film for children. While critics called the original film and its sequel "tasteless," kids yearned to emulate this little demon and give their parents some hell. Alexander and Karaszewski say that it took those childhood fans to grow up and become movie executives themselves for the pair to find good work again.

BOOK CLUB 2018

 **54%**

Directed by Bill Holderman
Written by Erin Simms and Bill Holderman
Starring Diane Keaton, Jane Fonda, Candice Bergen, Mary Steenburgen

Critics Consensus

Book Club only intermittently rises to the level of its impressive veteran cast; fortunately, they're more than enough to entertainingly bring pedestrian material to life.

Synopsis

Four lifelong friends look to spice up their lives and select the erotic novel *Fifty Shades of Grey* for their book club. As they finally begin opening up about their hopes and fears, the women individually take giant leaps to achieve happiness.

Why We Love It

The four actresses who headline this movie don't immediately scream "big box office" to studio execs, which is why they work less frequently than their younger twenty-something analogs in the industry. (Except Mary Steenburgen, because, well, she's in everything.) Watching *Book Club* only underscores how deprived audiences have been of their talents.

With a so-so script played out on overly lit sets that only wish they could be Nancy Meyers's kitchens, *Book Club* is a breezy two hours of women talking, laughing and drinking *so much* white wine. A good chunk of the movie's considerable box office came from women thirty-five years and up: the older of the crowd wanted to see their lives reflected back to them, and the younger of the crowd wanted reassurance that love and fun doesn't end at some predestined date. *Book Club*, in its simple message that older women are people too, is life affirming.

Jane Fonda, Diane Keaton, Candice Bergen, and Steenburgen all took their roles for less money and frills than any of them are worth—or used to—specifically so they could work together and commit to film a story about aging women and their evolving attitudes towards sex and love. Their camaraderie in *Book Club* comes off as authentic and spontaneous, as though Fonda just happened to call up her old buds for a wine-and-bitch session. Nobody's playing against type here: Fonda's a feisty, powerful, vain version of herself, and Bergen's performance could have been ripped from the reboot of *Murphy Brown*. But that's also the appeal—after so many years of playing characters, now they're just playing themselves.

And while critics mostly shrugged, there were those who recognized the film as the simple pleasure—and the small surprise—that it is. *The Atlantic*'s David Sims wrote that despite the "green-screened view of a romantic sunset that looks like stock footage from a karaoke video" here and there, the film is "a delightfully tacky summer romp that feels destined to become a classic in basic cable reruns." And Leah Greenblatt at *Entertainment Weekly* called *Book Club* "some kind of small Hollywood miracle" for letting older women "live" on-screen.

The movie's writer, Erin Simms, says executives asked her to make the characters younger, which she called a "non-starter." Based on real conversations and events she had with the older women in her life, she took a chance bringing this story to the screen, and with a box office ten times the budget, the film proves that even the mundanity of older women's lives is bankable with the right actors in place.

COCKTAIL 1988

 5%

Directed by Roger Donaldson
Written by Heywood Gould
Starring Tom Cruise, Elisabeth Shue, Bryan Brown, Kelly Lynch

Critics Consensus

There are no surprises in *Cocktail*, a shallow, dramatically inert romance that squanders Tom Cruise's talents in what amounts to a naïve barkeep's banal fantasy.

Synopsis

In this romantic drama, a hotshot flair bartender meets the woman of his dreams but must contend with both her wealthy family and his own competitiveness to keep it all from falling apart.

Why We Love It

Cocktail may have an outdated storyline in which women are objects and prizes to be won, but if anything can transcend the trashiness of the script, it's the charisma and easy, relaxed chemistry between Tom Cruise and Elisabeth Shue. Secondarily, what really stands the test of time—and what altered the drinking habits of Americans across the country—were the numerous thrilling scenes of Cruise flipping, tipping, and tossing liquor bottles in intricately choreographed flair routines that became so popular, people flocked to a chain restaurant called T.G.I. Friday's to see the real flair bartenders in action. (The restaurant's founder, Alan Stillman, claims to have been the inspiration for Cruise's character Brian, though writer Heywood Gould based it on his own life.)

Gould's original script played more like an anti-*Wall Street* drama containing layers and depth about the meaning of money, class, and age—and if you squint, you can still see a little of that in the film. But Disney chose to soft-sell that aspect, sensing the country's Reagan-era hunger for wealth and power was on the way out the door but not quite dead yet. By nixing the sociopolitical elements, director Roger Donaldson allowed for more time spent behind the bar, watching Cruise and Bryan Brown's Doug Coughlin perform their own routines to cross-generational party songs like "Hippy Hippy Shake."

Writing for the *LA Times*, Sheila Benson said, "The pairing of old-hand Brown and young-hand Cruise may have been meant to remind us of Cruise and Paul Newman; if so, think of this as 'The Color of Counterfeit Money.'" What the partnership—and the movie—lacked, according to Benson, was a moral compass, noting that early press screenings had people "hiss[ing] and hoot[ing]" at Cruise's character Flanagan's more vacuous decisions (of which there are plenty). But even Benson conceded that if there were a draw for *Cocktail*, it was Cruise's "twinkling, twinkling, twinkling" self, as he flipped bottles behind the bar.

According to Cruise, to prepare for the role, he interviewed thirty-five bartenders to get the tools of the trade and only broke five bottles in the process. He'd already shown in *Top Gun* that he'd be willing to immerse himself in his character so much as to attain a license to fly. *Cocktail* may just be a romantic drama, but it's also the foundation for Cruise's subsequent career of physically demanding roles and deep research, which would lead him to perform all of his own spectacular stunts in the *Mission Impossible* films.

HOCUS POCUS 1993

 33%

Directed by Kenny Ortega
Written by Neil Cuthbert and Mick Garris
Starring Bette Midler, Sarah Jessica Parker, Kathy Najimy

Critics Consensus

Harmlessly hokey yet never much more than mediocre, *Hocus Pocus* is a muddled family-friendly effort that fails to live up to the talents of its impressive cast.

Synopsis

Three witches of Salem are burned at the stake, vowing to return to steal the town's youth. Three hundred years later, they do, and send one unlucky kid on a goose chase to save his sister and Salem.

Why We Love It

Until newspapers and magazines start employing children to critique some films, adult critics are gonna have a hell of a time predicting what will land with the kids and how exactly it will weasel its way into their hearts. In the case of *Hocus Pocus*, which features a child actually dying on screen in the first ten minutes, some older folks found the film's willingness to go dark a bit perplexing. Gene Siskel called the film "dreadful," while Dennis King, writing for *Tulsa World,* said, "With the rather ghoulish deaths of children depicted, it's certainly too strong for very young moviegoers. The sights of kiddy corpses here are enough to scare the bejabbers out of most pre-schoolers." Kids, meanwhile, gobbled up the fatalism in this bonkers Disney picture.

In the film, the witches are so diabolical that their evil deeds take on a whimsical tone. Sarah Jessica Parker's Sarah Sanderson may resurrect her dead boyfriend as a zombie in an attempt to capture and murder a little boy, but she's also, like, super-relatable to boy-crazy girls. Bette Midler's Winifred Sanderson dresses like a buck-tooth clown with bright red rat lips and a blazing red muff of hair on her head—this is a multi-award-winning and Oscar-nominated actor we're talking about. Yes, Winifred performs a Broadway-ish rendition of "I Put a Spell on You" in a school gymnasium to compel all the adults in town to dance until they drop dead, but she was so cartoonishly wicked that the character endeared herself to kids, who immediately adopted Winifred as a Halloween costume. And then there's character actress extraordinaire Kathy Najimy as Mary, the ride-or-die sister who's perpetually attempting to keep the others' dramatics to a minimum while simultaneously appeasing their desires. She's evil, yeah, but who can't identify with a woman constantly put upon to keep things chill?

Aaron Wallace, writer of the book *Hocus Pocus in Focus*, pointed out the curious mix of "spooky meets kooky that imprinted on a young generation." Those grown-up kids once used a Reddit AMA to coax Midler to perform her "I Put a Spell on You" routine in full costume at one of her concerts, likely baffling some of her older fans. Today, the cult status of this box-office bomb has soared, spawning costume contests and a legion of die-hards who've sparked enough interest that Disney greenlit a remake.

THE HOLIDAY 2006

 48% | Written and directed by Nancy Meyers
Starring Kate Winslet, Cameron Diaz, Jude Law, Jack Black

Critics Consensus

While it's certainly sweet and even somewhat touching, *The Holiday* is so thoroughly predictable that audiences may end up opting for an early check-out time.

Synopsis

Two women—one a London wedding columnist, one an Angeleno who makes movie trailers—swap houses for the holidays when they both find they need to escape some tangly romantic situations at home. Each gets more than they bargained for from the house swap when some new and even more tangled romantic situations arise in their new cities. Romance, cuteness, and cashmere ensue.

> **THE MOST NANCY MEYERS OF NANCY MEYERS MOVIES.**

Why We Love It

For many thinking moviegoers, enjoying a Nancy Meyers movie requires much suppression of self and sense. Got hang-ups about class? Consumerism a turnoff? Have a Bechdel test on hand? You'll need to abandon those, all ye who enter. But the Meyers-verse can be like Las Vegas—if you accept what it is and go in with the right frame of mind, there are sugary pleasures to be had.

In movies like *It's Complicated* and *Something's Gotta Give*, those pleasures are rarely derived from story or character—the sugar highs are found in ogling mammoth kitchens with continent-sized marble islands at their centers and the expensive, pillowy beige knits in which Meyers's leads live their

lives. It's about drinking in the Nancy Meyers aesthetic and fantasy. *The Holiday* might be the most Nancy Meyers of Nancy Meyers movies, marrying her trapped-in-a-West-Elm-with-no-way-out aesthetic to the sentimentality of Christmas and featuring not one but two too-good-to-be-true Nancy Meyers–style romances.

The two women at the center of the dual love plots seem to spend much of their time marveling at the fact they're *in* a Nancy Meyers movie. When British Iris (Kate Winslet) arrives at the L.A. manse of Amanda (Cameron Diaz), she plays stand-in for the audience, bouncing on the plush California King as if it's too good—and too huge—to be true; when Amanda arrives at Iris's uber-British cottage to set up shop, even the grinchy Angeleno is charmed by the too-perfect Christmas village ornament she's going to call home for the holidays.

While characters in other Meyers movies take for granted their ludicrously well-appointed lives, the characters here can't believe the luxury, on one hand, and the quaintness, on the other, of their vacation lives. Even the men are too good to be true. Diaz's Amanda is offered a perfectly lit Jude Law (as a caring single dad, no less), and Winslet's Iris is served Jack Black, whose only discernible personality trait here is his need to make her smile.

There is substance in this heaping cup of very sweet hot cocoa, though. And that comes courtesy of Eli Wallach, as an elderly neighbor and super-knowledgeable Golden Age screenwriter who befriends Iris and becomes her tour guide through L.A. and its history. Winslet and Wallach are electric in a way that makes you wish the director had done away with the love stories and made a buddy comedy. It's this thread that gives the movie its heart and makes Meyers's Christmas confection more than just empty holiday calories.

BAD BOYS 1995

 **42%** | **Directed by** Michael Bay
Written by Michael Barrie, Jim Mulholland, Doug Richardson
Starring Will Smith, Martin Lawrence, Téa Leoni, Joe Pantoliano, Marg Helgenberger

Critics Consensus

Bad Boys stars Will Smith and Martin Lawrence have enjoyable chemistry; unfortunately, director Michael Bay too often drowns it out with set pieces and explosions in place of an actual story.

Synopsis

Two Miami cops—one a slick playboy, one a frenzied family man—chase down a stolen cache of drugs as they try to protect the only witness to a related murder. A moment of mistaken identity means they must do it all as they pretend to be each other.

Why We Love It

Michael Bay's first feature film carries many of the Michael Bay hallmarks that audiences would come to know over his next twelve. There are slow-motion action shots—and lots of them (the final sequence is 50 percent "Will Smith running in slow-mo with his shirt unbuttoned"). There's that certain Michael Bay sheen to the people and backdrops (this is Miami as shot through an Instagram filter). There's an incredibly anxiety-inducing score (this one courtesy of Mark Mancina, fresh off of *Speed*). And then there's that Bay-level testosterone that's pumping through every frame.

Seriously, if this movie didn't have three men's names attached to the screenplay, you'd be forgiven for thinking it had been written and directed by a hard-on. Every guy in *Bad Boys* is called a "bitch," calls someone a "bitch," or defends themselves by insisting they're not a "bitch." The worst thing in the world—in *this* world—is for someone to think you're gay. And no woman is allowed on screen without the camera first leering at her for an uncomfortably long stretch of time. (And they're not allowed to wear much, either—Téa Leoni's skirts make Megan Fox's *Transformers* outfits look positively Amish.)

Snip all of that away—along with the generically European bad guy and his inconsequential paint-by-numbers scheme to get rich or die trying—and *Bad Boys* is actually, at its heart, a screwball comedy in an action film's clothing. And it's a good one, too, thanks largely to the chemistry between Martin Lawrence and Smith. They're dynamite together, trading profanity-peppered insults or singing the *Cops* TV series theme as they drive through Bay's filtered Miami ("Bad boys, bad boys, what ya gonna do-o-o?"). And they're even better when their characters navigate the mundane-seeming moments of the life-swap subplot: as when the smooth Mike Lowrey (Smith) is forced to play it cool while a witness's dog craps on his rug, not realizing the rug is Lowrey's, or when the mouthy Detective Burnett (Lawrence) play-acts suaveness as he impersonates his partner (Lawrence's delivery of "Mike *Loow*rey" is as hilarious and quotable ever).

You can't help but wonder what the duo would be able to do with stronger material. We might get the chance to see in the third installment in the franchise, *Bad Boys for Life*, set to release in 2020.

STEPMOM 1998

 **45%**

Directed by Chris Columbus
Written by Gigi Levangie, Jessie Nelson, Steven Rogers, Karen Leigh Hopkins, Ron Bass
Starring Julia Roberts, Susan Sarandon, Ed Harris, Jena Malone, Liam Aiken

Critics Consensus

Solid work from Julia Roberts and Susan Sarandon isn't enough to save *Stepmom* from a story whose clumsily transparent manipulations fatally undermine a potentially affecting drama.

Synopsis

Isabel is the eponymous stepmom, a young New York photographer adjusting to her new boyfriend's two kids and the impossible standards set by his ex-wife, Jackie. When the family receives tragic news, the dynamic is thrown off, and new bonds start to form.

Why We Love It

Might Christmas Day 1998 have been the most maudlin date in American box office history? We're willing to bet a sack full of toys that it was. It was the day, after all, that two of the 1990s' most relentless tear-jerkers hit theaters, going head-to-head and sob-for-sob for the country's movie moolah. Robin Williams's (very Rotten) *Patch Adams*, about an overbearingly joyous Doctor-slash-Clown, would win the box office—despite Roger Ebert saying the "shameless" film "extracts tears individually by liposuction, without anesthesia"—and yet the weekend's number-two film, *Stepmom*, is the one that remains the more fondly remembered.

We're not crying just thinking about it, *you are*.

Chris Columbus's film is in many ways a by-the-books schmaltz fest. It has a family fractured by divorce (Ed Harris and Susan Sarandon play the divorcees, Julia Roberts the new woman in his life). It has two adorable children struggling with that divorce (Liam Aitken and Jena Malone, excellent as a bratty teen who eventually comes around to her stepmom-to-be). It has one of those infectious scenes of people dancing around their house in their pajamas to a bouncy hit song ("Ain't No Mountain High Enough"). And it has a midway cancer twist that's aimed with ruthless precision at the tear ducts of any soul-carrying viewer in its path.

But *Stepmom* has something else going for it, too: a little more bite than critics perhaps gave it credit for at the time. That mostly comes down to Sarandon, who is wonderfully icy as Jackie in early scenes, eyeing Roberts's career-focused Isabel with fierce territoriality even as she pretends to play nice. As the two come to bond, Sarandon loosens, but only a touch. During the film's climax, if you can call it that, Jackie and Isabel have dinner, sharing their fears for the future (dying Jackie worries the kids will forget her; Isabel is sure she will never compare to their "real mom").

Sarandon's big Bette Davis–esque eyes convey a thousand things here and in the film's final shot: kinship, hope, and love, yes, but something like envy lingers, too. As it would. She is sitting across from, and then next to, the woman who—likable and capable though she may be—will get to finish the life she started.

SPACE JAM 1996

 **43%**

Directed by Joe Pytka
Written by Leo Benvenuti, Steve Rudnick, Timothy Harris, Herschel Weingrod
Starring Michael Jordan, Wayne Knight, Theresa Randle, Bill Murray, Charles Barkley

Critics Consensus

While it's no slam dunk, *Space Jam*'s silly, Looney Tunes–laden slapstick and vivid animation will leave younger viewers satisfied—though accompanying adults may be more annoyed than entertained.

Synopsis

This part-animated, part-live-action film sees the Looney Tunes recruiting Michael Jordan to help them win an intergalactic basketball match that will save them from enslavement on an alien planet. Bill Murray, for some reason, is along for the ride.

Why We Love It

Space Jam has lived the life of a film much older than its tender twenty-three years. It was a corporate union between the NBA and Warner Bros. that became a blockbuster that become a beloved VHS favorite and eventual cult classic—a nonsensical little slice of pure nineties for the kids who grew up on Acme antics and at one time or another just wanted to "be like Mike." When those '90s children became 2000s grown-ups, *Space Jam* went through its academic reassessment phase—some have called it a masterpiece, a crowd-pleasing yet subversive melding of genres, while the guys at Honest Trailers have quipped it is "the *Citizen Kane* of live-action-animated hybrid basketball movies."

We are now somewhere in the backlash phase, where headlines like "Millennials are wrong: *Space Jam* is bad" and "Nostalgia Has Tricked Us Into Thinking *Space Jam* Wasn't a Cynical Money Grab" are common. But with respect to the AV Club and *HuffPost*, which respectively published those two bubble-bursters, we'd like to kick off the backlash to the backlash, and we think we have a slam-dunk case.

First, all major family-targeted, animated, or partly animated movies are designed to sell toys and live for eternity on the home entertainment market. It's about the money, not the art, even for Disney and those heart-breakers at Pixar. Warner Bros. tapping into our mid-nineties obsession with the NBA to make its moolah was cynical, yes, but it was undeniably smart. It was also indicative of why *Space Jam* is such a joy: the movie gives the audience *exactly* what it wants. That includes a surprisingly charming Michael Jordan bouncing and shooting and dunking *a lot*; a bunch of sassy Bugs Bunny one-liners (the inside jokes about royalties and Disney do fall a bit flat); and a blowout finale in which monsters do some seriously hokey on-court battling with Jordan and our Looney Tunes heroes. As a bonus, we get a multi-platinum soundtrack that features Seal, Monica, Coolio, and Salt-N-Pepa.

The movie also smartly refuses to give us the stuff we didn't ask for: things like a compelling story arc or rounded characters or any of the parent-pleasing cleverness that would invade kids' flicks in the 2000s. Its critics may ding it for lacking some of these elements, but the film's simple fan-focused pleasures are why we're still talking about it decades later. It spoke directly to the kids, and those kids haven't forgotten it.

A LeBron James sequel is apparently in the works, with *Black Panther* director Ryan Coogler producing. Cynical cash-grab? You betcha. Will we be there opening night? Absolutely—sporting our finest new Air Jordans.

I, ROBOT 2004

 **56%**

Directed by Alex Proyas
Written by Jeff Vintar and Akiva Goldsman
Starring Will Smith, Bridget Moynahan, Alan Tudyk, Bruce Greenwood, James Cromwell

Critics Consensus

Bearing only the slightest resemblance to Isaac Asimov's short stories, *I, Robot* is a summer blockbuster that manages to make the audience think, if only for a little bit.

Synopsis

A mystery arises when a robotics scientist apparently commits suicide. The homicide detective called to the scene has a history with the dead man and investigates a robot exhibiting unusual programming.

Why We Love It

Will Smith lays on the charm in a futuristic setting as robot-skeptic Detective Del Spooner, whose unique history as a former patient of James Cromwell's Dr. Alfred Lanning lands him in the center of the investigation of Lanning's murder. Isaac Asimov's Three Laws of Robotics prevent robots from harming a human, but all evidence in Lanning's death points to Sonny, an NS-5 by U.S. Robotics Corp. who refers to Lanning as his "father," rather than "maker," and exhibits unheard-of emotional responses.

Critics seemed so caught up on the film's faithfulness to Asimov's source material that they perhaps forgot to have fun while watching Alex Proyas's take on it. And it's a helluva lot of fun. If Smith's natural swagger, Bridget Moynahan's stiff resolve, and Alan Tudyk's moving performance as the robot suspect weren't enough, you've got solid effects, killer action sequences, and an unusual twist.

The effects, in particular, are worth the watch, and the film was deservedly nominated for an Academy Award in 2005 for Best Achievement in Visual Effects. The robots appear simultaneously fluid in their motion and firmly mechanical. Roger Ebert compared the robot swarms to *Starship Troopers*'s insects, functioning much like video game targets. (Gamers will likely not have a problem with that.)

"You can't even be mad at them, since they're only programs," Ebert wrote. "Although, come to think of it, you *can* be mad at programs; Microsoft Word has inspired me to rage far beyond anything these robots engender." It's exactly that rage that the film attempts to tap into, a frustration with day-to-day technology that stubbornly refuses to yield to its human user. (In this case, though, the malfunction is technological malfeasance rather than user error.)

I, Robot also gifted us with a number of great catchphrases spoken amidst all the action and technical spectacle: "You are the dumbest smart person I have ever met in my life," "Somehow, 'I told you so' just doesn't quite say it," "[*Sneeze*] Sorry, I'm allergic to bullshit," and one designed for limited use: "This relationship just can't work. I mean, you're a cat, I'm black, and I'm not going to be hurt again."

There are, admittedly, some glitches in this system. However, emotionally investing in sci-fi already requires setting aside reality, so is it really so difficult to believe that Dr. Lanning—the smartest smart person Detective Spooner knows—can't figure out how to stop rogue A.I. without killing himself?

> **CRITICS SEEMED SO CAUGHT UP ON THE FILM'S FAITHFULNESS TO ASIMOV'S SOURCE MATERIAL THAT THEY PERHAPS FORGOT TO HAVE FUN WHILE WATCHING.**

HELLO, DOLLY! 1969

 **43%**

Directed by Gene Kelly
Written by Ernest Lehman
Starring Barbra Streisand, Walter Matthau, Michael Crawford, Marianne McAndrew, Danny Lockin

Though Streisand charms, she's miscast as the titular middle-aged widow in Gene Kelly's sluggish and over-produced final film as director.

Synopsis

New York City matchmaker and life fixer Dolly Levi travels to Yonkers on assignment to meet wealthy Horace Vandergelder. He has one job for her, but she has other business in mind, and soon Dolly, Horace, and a crew of potential young lovers are spending the day in the big city courting, dancing, and enjoying the mischief Dolly has made.

Why We Love It

In *Hello, Dolly!*, the bickering between title matchmaker Dolly Levi and curmudgeonly love interest Horace Vandergelder feels more authentic than their eventual romance, and with good reason: the actors portraying them—Barbra Streisand, twenty-five while filming, and Walter Matthau, *many* years older—despised each other. He couldn't stand that Hollywood's latest bright and uppity young thing, fresh off of the success of *Funny Girl*, would deign to ask for reshoots; she couldn't stand his lack of refinement (it's alleged she once presented him with a bar of soap for his "sewer mouth"). When it came time to shoot the characters' wedding scene, the cameramen are said to have had to find angles that made it look like the two lovers' lips were touching because, well, these two were definitely *not* going to be touching lips that day.

Director Gene Kelly had his hands full. And it wasn't just bickering thespians (Matthau also stopped talking to costar Michael Crawford). He was overseeing a mammoth production—the $25 million budget was more than three times that of Fox's *The Sound of Music*. It was shot on multiple locations and under the weight of almost crushing expectations: the Broadway musical, starring Carol Channing, had opened just a few years earlier to incredible acclaim, and beyond that, the studio needed *Dolly* to be a hit (it had been nearly half a decade since *The Sound of Music*). Perhaps that weight contributed to the leadenness that critics perceived in the end result, with many calling the 146-minute film a bloated, relentlessly opulent bore. Audiences weren't so hot on it either: the movie barely recouped its budget. Later, it would be cited as one of the final nails in the movie musical's coffin.

As far as failures go, though, this is a lavish one, and one imbued with enough pleasures that the film has drawn significant audience affection in the fifty years since its release. Streisand is primary among those pleasures. Though she *is* admittedly miscast—Dolly Levi is supposed to be middle-aged—she's also beguiling, peppy, and lends the film her impeccable voice. The songs, too, with music and lyrics by Jerry Herman, are so sensational that Kelly could have been asleep at the director's chair and you'd still be tapping your feet leaving the theater. He wasn't, though: Kelly and choreographer Michael Kidd do fine work, particularly during an extended waiters' dance at the Harmonia Gardens restaurant.

The Harmonia is host to the film's other big highlight, when Louis Armstrong cameos as the restaurant's band conductor and duets with Streisand for the title song (his recording of the track had been a hit after the stage play's debut). Streisand looks ecstatic to be singing with the jazz legend, all wide smiles and twinkling eyes as they twirl arms and trade lines. It's clear that no love needed to be faked there.

54%

Directed by Robert Stromberg
Written by Linda Woolverton
Starring Angelina Jolie, Elle Fanning, Sharlto Copley, Lesley Manville, Imelda Staunton, Juno Temple, Brenton Thwaites

CRITIC: Monica Castillo

Monica Castillo is a writer and critic based in New York City. Her work has appeared in the *New York Times*, *The Washington Post*, NBC News, the *Village Voice*, RogerEbert.com, Remezcla, *Variety*, *Vanity Fair*, and NPR.

Disney has remade several of its most beloved animated classics with live-action casts and computer-generated animation over the past decade. The studio started with Tim Burton's adaptation of *Alice in Wonderland* in 2010, before moving on to *Cinderella* in 2015 and *Beauty and the Beast* in 2017. The Disney Princesses of those films were given a modern-day makeover with scripts that played up their independent personalities and strength in the face of their stories' villains, but the movies' central narratives remained largely unchanged from the hand-drawn films that inspired them.

Robert Stromberg's *Maleficent* is an outlier in this sense: it follows the familiar story beats of its source, the 1959 animated film *Sleeping Beauty*, but turns its focus away from that classic's titular princess. *Maleficent* instead follows its namesake villainess in a sympathetic look at the other side of the fairy tale.

Long before Aurora fell into a cursed sleep, a young Maleficent (Isobelle Molloy) flew among the fairies of the forest. She was their protector, and when a young boy trespassed, she swooped in to handle him. Only, instead of chasing him away, she befriended the young man, a sign of the peace that was possible between the two kingdoms of man and fairies. Unfortunately, it was not a lasting union. Years later, the now adult Stefan (Sharlto Copley) makes a violent appeal to the king for a chance at his throne. He tricks Maleficent (Angelina Jolie), using their friendship as a way to get close enough to drug her and cut off her wings to prove he is a worthy successor for the crown.

Of all the decades of Disney villainy I've witnessed, I can't recall any scene quite so disturbing as this one. It plays out essentially as a date rape of the movie's protagonist; a part of Maleficent's body and identity is forcibly taken from her by someone she felt safe with. What happens next is perhaps

> ## "A SYMPATHETIC LOOK AT THE OTHER SIDE OF THE FAIRY TALE."

even more fascinating than this initial betrayal: the fairy tale becomes a story about surviving trauma, finding forgiveness, and developing the strength to heal.

It's pretty clear that Maleficent is justified in her anger, and it's what she does with it that forms the film's narrative arc. As she broods on her betrayal, the free-flowing earthy robes she wears early in the film give way to darker fabrics and leather, and she transforms into the Maleficent that audiences will recognize from the Disney classic, complete with the twisted horns and sharp-edged cheeks. Her wardrobe becomes her armor, and her view of love turns cynical.

When news of Aurora's birth reaches her, she's upset that Stefan has not only moved on from her and started a family but that he's written her out of his life entirely. As in Sleeping Beauty's prologue, Maleficent dramatically bursts into King Stefan's court to curse his child so that before her sixteenth birthday—the age when Maleficent kissed

Stefan—she will prick her finger on a spindle and fall into a sleep that can only be broken by true love's first kiss. Maleficent chooses these terms precisely because she, like many who have had their hearts or bodies broken by love, no longer believes true love exists.

So rarely do protagonists in Disney movies get to be so righteously angry at the world or at love. Yet here the title character is given the room to mourn and act out in anger—and then to grow. As her heart softens over time, Maleficent becomes protective of the little girl she first wished to harm. But by then, the damage has already been done, and she can no longer undo the curse she cast. She's become a complicated character capable of both good and evil, a subtlety rarely given to a Disney villain.

Maleficent's ending is markedly different from the 1959 film. In that version, she is slain by the prince on his way to wake his princess; in the 2014 movie, Prince Phillip is practically irrelevant. Much like the ending of 2013's Frozen, in which a sisterly bond breaks a curse, it's Maleficent's vow to protect Aurora, coupled with a gentle forehead kiss, that takes the place of the traditional "true love's kiss." After so many Disney movies emphasizing romantic love, it feels refreshing to see the definition of love extended to include its many different kinds.

Not every critic was charmed by *Maleficent*, and that's fine. It has its faults, especially in the characters of the three fairy godmothers, whose juvenile antics and banter make them a chore to endure. It doesn't help that some of the other fairy creatures look like cast-off Jim Henson puppets. Yet the film remains a singular entry in Walt Disney Pictures' output, a movie I doubt could have existed at any other time in the studio's history.

Perhaps one of the reasons *Maleficent* does so well by its central character is the number of women who helped flesh her out from the sketches of *Sleeping Beauty*. Linda Woolverton wrote the screenplay, and Anna B. Sheppard designed costumes to reflect Maleficent's emotional journey from fairy to warrior. (By contrast, all eight writing credits on the animated film are male.) Jolie's influence is felt throughout the film, too, and her performance comes across as deeply felt and sympathetic. So far, she's the only star of this era's Disney remakes to share a producer's credit. It was a smart move for Jolie. Despite the film's tepid critical reception, *Maleficent* earned an astounding $758 million at the worldwide box office and a sequel, *Maleficent: Mistress of Evil*, is set for late 2019.

Maleficent shows us a world in which characters cannot be easily labeled as "good" or "evil."

> ## "MALEFICENT CHOOSES THESE TERMS PRECISELY BECAUSE SHE, LIKE MANY WHO HAVE HAD THEIR HEARTS OR BODIES BROKEN BY LOVE, NO LONGER BELIEVES TRUE LOVE EXISTS."

A king can do bad things, an enemy can become a friend, and it's never too late to learn forgiveness. It's a story that challenges Disney's once codified worldview while still playing with its magic. It's a misfit movie among tales of princesses and talking animals, and still the only remake—so far—to imagine what drives a character to become a Disney villain.

Rotten Tomatoes' Critics Consensus Angelina Jolie's magnetic performance outshines *Maleficent*'s dazzling special effects; unfortunately, the movie around them fails to justify all that impressive effort.

THE FIRST WIVES CLUB 1996

 **49%** Directed by Hugh Wilson
Written by Robert Harling
Starring Goldie Hawn, Bette Midler, Diane Keaton, Maggie Smith, Sarah Jessica Parker

Critics Consensus

First Wives Club is headlined by a trio of comedic dynamos, but the script lets them down with tepid plotting and a fatal lack of satirical bite.

Synopsis

When a college friend commits suicide, three divorced women reunite and join forces to honor her memory by getting revenge on the husbands who kicked them to the curb for younger women.

Why We Love It

Pity the poor *First Wives Club* fan. Almost from the moment the hit comedy was released, rumors of a sequel have swirled. There have been scripts written, scripts rewritten, and scripts trashed, and the three lead actresses have said—multiple times!—they're game. Netflix even became involved at one point, or so it was reported. And yet here we are, more than two decades later, still wondering what became of Elise (Goldie Hawn), Brenda (Bette Midler), and Annie (Diane Keaton) after they burst through the doors of their newly minted club and down the cobblestone streets of New York, declaring they were young, and they loved to be young; free, and they loved to be free.

Perhaps it's been wise to leave such a beloved film untouched. (And yes, to all the grumpy critics who dismissed it as fluff upon its release, who moaned about the stereotyping of the husbands and the younger women who stole them, and who wanted a little more bite to the script: the film is almost universally beloved today.) We wouldn't want, after all, to discover that the lightning-in-a-bottle chemistry between Midler (brash and frumpy at once), Keaton (buttoned-up and nervy), and Hawn (a wonderful mess as a struggling starlet) had somehow been lost. Nor that the film's rousing message of female empowerment might have dulled with age, or that writer Robert Harling, here adapting Olivia Goldsmith's book of the same name, might no longer be able to conjure such deliciousness as Elise's riposte: "I *do* have feelings: I'm an actress—I have *all* of them!"

And lord knows how they'd top the sight and sound of Midler, Keaton, and Hawn, each suited up for war in white, belting out Lesley Gore's "You Don't Own Me." Twice.

Turns out there's a perfect reason for the lack of sequel to this *near*-perfect film (even *we* wish the subplot about the women's shelter felt less throwaway), or, at least, a reason perfectly in keeping with the spirit of the movie. In 2017, Hawn told *Total Film* magazine that the three women had been offered the same paycheck for a sequel as they had been given for the original—no bump whatsoever—a deal almost unheard of for the stars of a hit film. Certainly unheard of for *male* stars of a hit film. "It was such an insult," Hawn said. "It wasn't about the money, it was about the respect."

In a boss move worthy of a member of the First Wives Club, Hawn turned down the offer and did *The Banger Sisters* instead.

THE 'BURBS 1989

 53% | Directed by Joe Dante
Written by Dana Olsen
Starring Tom Hanks, Bruce Dern, Rick Ducommun, Henry Gibson, Carrie Fisher, Corey Feldman

Critics Consensus

The 'Burbs doesn't completely waste its engaging premise, its likable leading man, and Joe Dante's unique brand of weirdness, but it's still a mixed-up genre exercise that isn't quite as dark or as funny as it could have been.

Synopsis

Ray Peterson just wants to spend his week of vacation relaxing at home, but when his mysterious new neighbors begin acting suspiciously, he's roped into a covert operation to discover exactly what they're up to.

Why We Love It

Movies about the dark secrets of suburbia are a dime a dozen, but few of them have engaged the topic as playfully as The 'Burbs. That shouldn't be too surprising, considering the man at the helm is Joe Dante, who tangled with similar themes and achieved great results in Gremlins. The 'Burbs is only slightly less sinister, but its goofy charms are nearly on par with those of Gizmo's Christmas adventure, and it's a perfect fit for someone of Dante's talents and stylistic instincts.

Tom Hanks plays Ray Peterson as the sort of credulous everyman he's now famous for portraying so effectively, but his career was still on the rise when The 'Burbs hit theaters in 1989. He was a star, to be sure, but his breakout hit Big had only come out the year before, and he was still a few more years away from A League of Their Own, Sleepless in Seattle, and the two films that would earn him Best Actor Oscars, Philadelphia and Forrest Gump. You can see flashes of his brilliance here in the way that he slowly transforms Ray from a normal family man into an obsessive armchair sleuth, all with that trademark twinkle in his eye.

Hanks isn't the only big name to play his role to perfection, though. Bruce Dern is all ice and steel as military vet Mark Rumsfield, while Carrie Fisher brings a voice of reason to proceedings as Ray's wife, Carol. Coming off a string of hits that included The Goonies, Stand by Me, and The Lost Boys, Corey Feldman adds some teenaged recklessness, and Henry Gibson, who worked with Dante on Innerspace, plays his ambiguous villain role with just the right amount of irony to keep you guessing.

> IF IT PROMPTS A DOUBLE-TAKE THE NEXT TIME YOU SEE YOUR NEIGHBOR LUGGING A HEAVY TRASH BAG TO THE CURB, IT'S DONE ITS JOB.

It's a bit too easy to pick apart the film and say it's a horror-comedy that doesn't commit enough to either genre. But doing so misses the point. Every street has that one house that's a little run down and vaguely menacing, or neighbors who are a little peculiar, and every child has wondered what mysteries lie behind those closed doors, waiting to be discovered. This is pure fantasy wish fulfillment in that regard, and if it prompts a double-take the next time you see your neighbor lugging a heavy trash bag to the curb, it's done its job.

TEEN WOLF 1985

44%

Directed by Rod Daniel
Written by Jeph Loeb and Matthew Weisman
Starring Michael J. Fox, James Hampton, Susan Ursitti, Jerry Levine, James MacKrell

Critics Consensus

Though Michael J. Fox is as charismatic as ever, *Teen Wolf*'s coming-of-age themes can't help but feel a little stale and formulaic.

Synopsis

A regular teen's life is turned upside-down when he discovers he comes from a long line of werewolves, and his very public transformation into one alters the course of his high school career.

Why We Love It

Michael J. Fox's biggest hit in 1985 was a little movie about a high schooler who travels back to 1955 in a DeLorean and helps his nebbish father woo the girl of his dreams. His second biggest hit in 1985 was another comedy about a high schooler with an unusual dilemma, and it opened just a month and a half later. While *Back to the Future* went on to become the top grossing film of the year and an enduring classic, *Teen Wolf* quietly took its place as an also-ran, remembered only by those who connected with it as adolescents. (We prefer to pretend *Teen Wolf Too* never existed.)

Teen Wolf wears its metaphors on its sleeve—scratch that, they're emblazoned across the entire back of the jacket—which is likely to induce a few eyerolls in adult viewers, but it is entirely appropriate for its target audience. Imagine you're a twelve-year-old witnessing Scott Howard's (Fox) struggles. Patches of hair growing in unusual places? Check. Dramatic vocal changes? Check. Romantic entanglements, parental squabbles, and general anxiety?

Check, check, and check. The fact that *Teen Wolf* is essentially an after-school special filtered through the lens of *The Munsters* isn't a bug—it's a feature.

At the time, Fox was at the height of his popularity as the ambitious, conservative Alex P. Keaton on NBC sitcom *Family Ties*. His remarkable affability is a big reason *Teen Wolf* works as well as it does, and certainly the only reason audiences don't give up on Scott when he switches to full-on "bro" mode as the Big Wolf on Campus.

There's also a lot of genuine sweetness to be found in the relationships he maintains with his loved ones. His bestie Boof, played by Susan Ursitti, is awkward and adorable, and there's real catharsis when they end up together. James Hampton plays Scott's widowed father as an encouraging and supportive anchor, and his scenes with Fox are some of the film's emotional highlights.

Back to the Future is the superior movie, but *Teen Wolf* was made for just a fraction of the budget (just over $1 million), and it did well enough upon release to inspire a short-lived animated series and the aforementioned sequel before it disappeared into the pop culture ether for decades. Eventually, it sparked enough nostalgia to spawn a well-received TV adaptation in 2011 that ran for six seasons. It's tempting now to wonder if it might have been better received by critics if it hadn't inevitably suffered from comparisons to *Back to the Future*, but we think there's more than enough room in our hearts for both.

TWINS 1988

 **44%**

Directed by Ivan Reitman
Written by William Davies, William Osborne, Timothy Harris, Herschel Weingrod
Starring Arnold Schwarzenegger, Danny DeVito, Kelly Preston, Chloe Webb, Marshall Bell

Critics Consensus

Though it offers a few modest pleasures for undemanding viewers, *Twins* leans too heavily on the wackiness of its premise to overcome its narrative shortcomings.

Synopsis

Two fraternal twins are separated at birth; one of them grows up to lead a life of petty crime, while the other becomes a physical and intellectual prodigy. When the latter learns of his brother's existence, he journeys to Los Angeles to find him and, together, search for their mother.

Why We Love It

Twins is one of those comedies whose primary conceit is readily apparent in the poster: a stalky, balding Danny DeVito leans against a towering, upright Arnold Schwarzenegger, both of them sporting identical suits, shades, and smiles. It's an effective visual gag that writes itself, so to speak, and absent any other compelling angles, it easily could have made *Twins* feel like a feature-length *Saturday Night Live* sketch (we're looking at you, *It's Pat*). To be fair, that's exactly how a lot of critics felt about the film, but this is no one-trick pony.

By the time he joined *Twins*, Schwarzenegger had already established himself as an action icon in movies like *Conan the Barbarian*, *The Terminator*, *Commando*, and *Predator*, and he channeled that same charisma into what was to become the first of several successful starring roles in comedies. As Julius, the guileless brother raised on a remote island, Schwarzenegger adds a layer of fish-out-of-water naivete that works fairly consistently in conjunction with the street smarts of DeVito's Vincent and registers some of the film's biggest laughs. He readily accepts that Vincent is his twin brother, takes everyone's word at face value, and oh, by the way, he's also a thirty-five-year-old virgin. DeVito is perfectly cast as the cynical foil to Julius's wide-eyed wonder, but that's kind of what he's known for. Schwarzenegger's rock-solid comedic timing is a revelation, even if some of the jokes don't fully land.

Aside from the chemistry between the film's leading odd couple, *Twins* is also surprisingly heartfelt for a high-concept caper. Vincent's initial distrust of Julius and eventual redemption are fairly paint-by-numbers, but damned if it isn't sweet to watch how they gradually come to rely on each other. And when a missed connection with their birth mother is revealed, it's impossible not to feel their loss.

Ivan Reitman, one of Hollywood's preeminent comedy directors at the time, was still riding high off the success of *Ghostbusters* when he took on *Twins*, and it's hard to imagine there was any expectation that the latter would be as well received. The film brushes up against some high-falutin' ideas about eugenics and nature versus nurture without really exploring any of them, and it features a misguided subplot involving a stolen car with a trunk full of valuable contraband. But *Twins* proved to be an enjoyable diversion that made Arnold Schwarzenegger a bankable comedy star, and he and Reitman would go on to make two more together, *Kindergarten Cop* and *Junior*.

YOUNG GUNS 1988

 41%

Directed by Christopher Cain
Written by John Fusco
Starring Emilio Estevez, Charlie Sheen, Kiefer Sutherland, Lou Diamond Phillips, Terence Stamp, Jack Palance, Terry O'Quinn

Critics Consensus

Young Guns rounds up a posse of attractive young leads, but this cheerfully shallow Brat Pack Western ultimately has too much hat and not enough cattle.

Synopsis

After his cattle rancher and mentor is killed by a rival's enforcers, a young William H. Bonney—a.k.a. Billy the Kid—and his band of hotheaded gunslingers set out for justice, only to end up on the wrong side of the law themselves.

Why We Love It

By the time the late 1980s rolled around, Westerns were no longer a hot commodity in Hollywood. They were still being made, sure, but most of the titles were small films that generated little to no fanfare; it wasn't until *Silverado* and Clint Eastwood's hugely successful *Pale Rider* came out in 1985 that studios began to take interest again. *Young Guns* was no prestige picture, by any means, and it didn't have much on its mind other than telling a good, old-fashioned tale of revenge, but it did wrangle some of Hollywood's hottest young stars, put guns in their hands, and let them loose to swagger all over the western frontier.

For fans of the Brat Pack era, this was a chance to see Emilio Estevez, Charlie Sheen, Kiefer Sutherland, and a few other impossibly handsome dudes bounce off each other in one of the most testosterone-fueled settings put to celluloid, and all of them were at the top of their game. Estevez had just come off of *The Breakfast Club*, *St. Elmo's Fire*, and *Stakeout*, among others; Sheen had *Platoon*, *Wall Street*, and a memorable bit part in *Ferris Bueller's Day Off*; Sutherland had just appeared in *Stand By Me* and *The Lost Boys*; and Lou Diamond Phillips had impressed in both *La Bamba* and *Stand and Deliver*. This was a who's who of up-and-comers, and their sense of camaraderie was palpable even as they jostled each other for the spotlight.

The combination proved irresistible and audiences ate it up, but critics found the whole enterprise shallow, limply crafted, and more than a little pleased with itself. It also didn't help that the film hung expectations on a familiar piece of folklore only to buck historical accuracy in favor of delivering a cheeky action flick starring cocksure twenty-somethings. But a lot of the film's shortcomings are forgivable purely for the fact that its leads are so fun to watch, and they do make you care about their characters more than you might the old, grizzled cowboys of other Westerns. There's a rather effective message of loyalty and brotherhood throughout the proceedings that adds weight behind every barbed one-liner, every exchange of gunfire, and over time, the Regulators begin to look like the most die-hard "pals" you could ask for (just ask Warren G). If nothing else, *Young Guns* helped a new generation discover what the genre could offer on the big screen, all because people were attracted to the idea of six rising stars teaming up to play Wild West outlaws.

> "THIS WAS A WHO'S WHO OF UP-AND-COMERS, AND THEIR SENSE OF CAMARADERIE WAS PALPABLE EVEN AS THEY JOSTLED EACH OTHER FOR THE SPOTLIGHT."

SAN ANDREAS 2015

 51% | Directed by Brad Peyton
Written by Carlton Cuse
Starring Dwayne Johnson, Carla Gugino, Alexandra Daddario, Paul Giamatti

Critics Consensus

San Andreas has a great cast and outstanding special effects, but amidst all the senses-shattering destruction, the movie's characters and plot prove less than structurally sound.

Synopsis

A series of devastating earthquakes hits California, and one man from the Los Angeles Fire Department is on a mission to save his family and the survivors of the worst tremors the world has ever seen.

> " *SAN ANDREAS*, FOR AS OUTLANDISH AS IT IS, EXUDES A KIND OF REALNESS AND BELIEVABILITY THAT'S ALL THE MORE THRILLING. "

Why We Love It

Big. Dumb. Fun. Every disaster movie—from *The Poseidon Adventure* and *The Towering Inferno* up to *Deep Impact* and *Volcano* and beyond—must possess a few key elements: a hero dad, an expert whose warnings are unheeded, and an ensemble cast of stars giving just enough of a performance to get that fat paycheck. *San Andreas* hits every mark, but its towering achievement is in its destruction set pieces. The satisfaction you get from watching towering monuments crumble beneath people's feet is a bit of a sick thrill. Though *San Andreas* isn't available to watch in 3-D anymore, the special effects are just as breathtaking on a television.

Viewers have become numb to CG effects—it's nearly impossible to find a recent movie that doesn't use them at all. But as *San Andreas*' effects supervisor Colin Strause has said, "CG for the sake of CG is always a mistake." Strause and his team used the film's $100 million budget to construct and then blow up structures the old-fashioned way, then used the actors' green-screen footage to insert them in the shot. So many big-budget films appear so artificial that it's like they're on another plane of existence, but *San Andreas*, for as outlandish as it is, exudes a kind of realness and believability that's all the more thrilling.

And despite working with dialogue that's at times as basic as it gets—"I'm gonna get you out of there!"—Dwayne Johnson seems especially committed to this role, with real fear and anxiety flashing across his face; Johnson later said the practical effects better helped him envision his character and his emotions.

Strause told *Variety* the experience was like working on a "big budget indie," saying that he would sometimes be provided "one little pothole and a couple of bricks," and the rest was all imagination and ingenuity. Look closer as the world in *San Andreas* burns, and you might find a few surprises.

THE GREATEST SHOWMAN 2017

 **55%**

Directed by Michael Gracey
Written by Jenny Bicks and Bill Condon
Starring Hugh Jackman, Michelle Williams, Zac Efron, Zendaya, Rebecca Ferguson, Keala Settle

CRITIC: Kristen Lopez

Kristen Lopez is a freelance pop culture critic whose work has appeared on rogerebert.com and in the *Hollywood Reporter*, and *The Daily Beast*. She is the co-creator and host of the feminist film podcast *Citizen Dame*.

When the first trailer dropped for *The Greatest Showman*, a musical biopic exploring the life of famous huckster P. T. Barnum, my eyes did the mother of all rolls. I've spent several years as a disabled film critic writing on and educating readers about the representation of people like me in movies. The prospect of a jubilant tale about the man who infamously declared "there's a sucker born every minute" and exploited—and *owned*—people with disabilities wasn't too thrilling.

But something amazing happened when I eventually *watched* the movie. The lights went down, the speakers released a pounding series of foot stomps, Hugh Jackman emerged as our top-hat–donning impresario, and I had a ball. He starts singing about the "fire" and "freedom" of the circus as various members of the cast prepare to enter the ring, and when the chorus kicks in and fire shoots into the air, he asks the audience, "Tell me, do you wanna go?" And I did.

What makes *The Greatest Showman* work is how perfectly and unashamedly it pays homage to studio-era musicals—films like *The King and I*, *My Fair Lady*, and *West Side Story*, in which lavish production value and memorable songs compete and eventually overcome sometimes repellant social commentary, the exploitation of minority characters, and historical fact. Like those classics, *The Greatest Showman* triumphs over its inherent issues. It's wrong and dated but also enchanting.

Barnum's story has been told before, most memorably in 1952's *The Greatest Show on Earth* (even more Rotten than *Showman* at 45%). Charlton Heston played Barnum in that film, but it's hard to watch his performance, with his gravelly voice and perpetual sneer, and believe that he is the man charismatic enough to coin the term "show business."

Jackman is certainly up to the task. He has the right matinee idol mien to convince us that Barnum really was just a down-on-his-luck guy who never caught a fair shake from anyone because he was poor. Jackman's persona works even when the character is being a terrible person, something the film does occasionally allow for. As Barnum quests for legitimacy at the expense of his performers—shutting them out and making them sit in the back of a theater—the actor imbues him with such likability

> ## "IT'S WRONG AND DATED BUT ALSO ENCHANTING."

and passion for the stage that we don't pause for a second when the rest of the characters start singing about how *others* are mistreating them.

There is no framing device (à la *Chicago*) or justification for why these people are singing. They have songs in their hearts—courtesy of *Dear Evan Hansen* and *La La Land* songwriting team Benj Pasek and Justin Paul—that need to be exorcised.

Keala Settle's bearded woman, Lettie Lutz, has the strongest voice, so it's understandable that her song "This Is Me" was nominated for the Oscar (it was ultimately beaten out by *Coco*'s more somber "Remember Me"). The rest of the actors sing powerfully, too, and in cases where they can't (sorry, Rebecca Ferguson), the movie isn't afraid to embrace that studio-era technique of hiring someone else to sing for you! #BringBackDubbing.

The big numbers offer a heavy dose of spectacle and dance, compliments of choreographer Ashley Wallen. We're not talking a little hair-tossing or some light arm movements, but full-body regimented choreography. *The Greatest Showman* needs to be applauded for having tight, precise dance numbers at a time when musicals often don't bother or over-edit their choreography into a blur. Whether it's Jackman and Zac Efron dancing on a bar or Efron and Zendaya swinging in the air on a trapeze, there's technique and talent here. The latter number, performed to the song "Rewrite the Stars," never fails to dazzle me, even on a small screen. You see the sweat and skill in every frame.

You're probably asking, "What about how the people with disabilities are represented?" I won't lie: it's as bad as most movies about disabilities

Hollywood puts out today. The film has an upbeat message about inclusion, yet the message doesn't include ableism—the "oddities" that populate Barnum's show are never allowed to become fully fledged characters. But movies aren't made with me in mind; in order to enjoy cinema at all, I often cast aside problems that pop up regularly, and so it is with *The Greatest Showman*. I know others in my position take different approaches and that my enjoyment becomes especially complicated when these problems are about people I advocate for and champion in my career. Where is the line between allowing myself to enjoy a film and my compulsion to condemn it? It's a tricky question I don't always have an answer for. I allow myself to be seduced by the whiz-bang and opulence, knowing that the movie's goal is to blind me to the real problems it has.

P. T. Barnum said there was a sucker born every minute, and I'm that sucker. But as Jackman's Barnum says, people stare at the odd and macabre because it's fascinating, and *The Greatest Showman* is compelling because it, itself, *is* odd and macabre. Could this movie have explored ableism in a way that was nuanced and new? Giving Lettie Lutz more screen time, a character arc, and the ability to tell Barnum when he's being a sonofabitch would be a start. It might have shown that people with differences have a voice. But to do that would mean shaping a story that didn't want to simply glamorize

> ❝ **I ALLOW MYSELF TO BE SEDUCED BY THE WHIZ-BANG AND OPULENCE, KNOWING THAT THE MOVIE'S GOAL IS TO BLIND ME TO THE REAL PROBLEMS IT HAS.** ❞

the self-made man. When Hollywood has been bad at disability for years, it's hard to expect more.

In the end, this is the film we have—one that mythologizes a phony and puts ableism into a corner. But I enjoy it every time. How can you resist fire, freedom, trapeze acts, and Jackman's broad grin? Even if it's not always a comfortable surrender.

Rotten Tomatoes' Critics Consensus *The Greatest Showman* tries hard to dazzle the audience with a Barnum-style sense of wonder—but at the expense of its complex subject's far more intriguing real-life story.

SO BAD THEY'RE GOOD

Incomparably Weird Sci-Fi and Fantasy

You won't find *Plan 9 From Outer Space*—celebrated as the "worst film ever made" in Harry and Michael Medved's *The Golden Turkey Awards*—in the pages of this book, but its spirit hovers over this particular chapter like a chintzy flying saucer bobbing at the end of two very visible wires. Here we celebrate the "so Rotten it's good," the "WTF were they thinking?" and the "let's just do a bunch of edibles, press play, and get very, very *weird*." These are the worst of the worst: bizarre ideas that met questionable filmmaking and resulted in the unforgettably terrible. Of course, no genre does *terrible* quite so well as sci-fi, and it's been doing it since the dawn of film, hitting a particularly Rotten golden age in the 1950s. During that period, Leonard Maltin, the man to whom America has turned for movie advice for almost forty years, first became

> **LET'S JUST DO A BUNCH OF EDIBLES, PRESS PLAY, AND GET VERY, VERY *WEIRD*.**

entranced with Bela Lugosi, which would lead him to the singularly awful *Bela Lugosi Meets a Brooklyn Gorilla*, a slice of sci-fi weirdness that would be the low point of the *Dracula* star's career and yet hold a lasting allure for Maltin. In the following chapter, Maltin writes of the film's strange pull, even to this day. Elsewhere in this chapter you'll find robots—both sex- and battle-ready—and Sean Connery in a wedding dress. We allowed some fantasy into the chapter's sci-fi mix, including a bizarre first attempt at adapting Tolkien as well as the appallingly enjoyable *Masters of the Universe*, which introduced He-Man to the movies by way of a cheap *Star Wars* rip off. We'd love to tell you exactly *why* we mixed the genres, but that would require thoughtfulness, logic, and sense—none of which you will find in the next set of pages.

CHERRY 2000 1987

 **40%**

Directed by Steve De Jarnatt
Written by Michael Almereyda
Starring Melanie Griffith, David Andrews, Tim Thomerson, Pamela Gidley

Critics Consensus

Despite a strong supporting cast and some memorable moments, *Cherry 2000* mostly plays like *Mad Max*'s sillier, less exciting younger sibling.

Synopsis

A corporate worker leaves Anaheim behind for desert wasteland with a bounty tracker as he seeks a replacement for his rare sex robot. But maybe he'll find something more along the way.

Why We Love It

Las Vegas has turned to sand. Unemployment is down to a cool 40 percent. And the CDC can wipe a little thing called love off their list of reportable diseases. Welcome to 2017—the future! It's a place where adults have taken consent to an extreme end. Nightclubs employ lawyers to contract sexual encounters between two (or more) people, ironing out all the details down to when, where, and how long. Two pumps is fine, three's over the limit!

But if you're tired of that mechanized song and dance, how about something mechanical? In this society, it's normal to shack up with a companion android, who will fawn over your every move and who looks, talks, feels, and frisks like the real thing.

That's what Sam Treadwell did. He's got a Cherry 2000, the fairest and rarest of them all. But when a soap suds snafu destroys Cherry, Sam (David Andrews) is called to the eastern desert with her memory chip in hand, where rumors whisper of a lost manufacturing plant deep among the dunes. To navigate the harsh environment and roving gangs, Sam hires bounty hunter E. Johnson, played here by Melanie Griffith as a cross between tough, intuitive cowgirl and lovey-dovey ingénue. Soon they'll encounter the malevolent and cheerful Lester, who dresses his murderous cult members in pastel khakis and leads with positive reinforcement lines like, "Keep the sun out of your eyes and be yourselves!"

Cherry 2000's premise is out there, but there's enough visual wit and story surprises to keep the viewer going—if only to see how committed the movie is to its own weirdness (it's like *Buckaroo Banzai* on benzos). It builds a world addicted to pleasure and gratification that ensnares men and enfeebles their masculinity. The cities are awash with twenty-first-century digital boys like Sam, a soft yuppie who's obviously had it easy for way too long and who never accomplishes anything particularly amazing. The woman gets the work done. He may be the main character, but he's not really a hero, or

> IT BUILDS A WORLD ADDICTED TO PLEASURE AND GRATIFICATION THAT ENSNARES MEN AND ENFEEBLES THEIR MASCULINITY.

outsider, or the tragic figure these sci-fi stories usually call for. Sam Treadwell is simply another victim of a warped society, comfortably trapped in his own reality. Yet you come to root for him, to see where his demented quest leads. This is nothing you'd expect from a typical movie protagonist. But then, sci-fi isn't here to be normal, is it?

I COME IN PEACE (DARK ANGEL) 1990

 31%

Directed by Craig R. Baxley
Written by Jonathan Tydor and David Koepp (as Leonard Maas Jr.)
Starring Dolph Lundgren, Brian Benben, Betsy Brantley, Matthias Hues

Critics Consensus

At first glance, a movie about a cop battling outer space drug dealers seems too good to miss; unfortunately, *I Come in Peace* botches its killer premise and settles for routine action scenes.

Synopsis

Detective Jack Caine is a loose cannon. His new partner, Larry, is an FBI agent who plays it by the book. Sound like every buddy-cop movie out there? It is, until you throw in an outer space drug dealer running amok, harvesting endorphins from his human victims. Time to raise some Caine.

> "SOMETIMES YOU NEED A MOVIE WHERE EVERYTHING JUST EXPLODES. CARS. BUILDINGS. POLICE EVIDENCE. EVEN THE PEOPLE."

Why We Love It

Sometimes you need a movie that doesn't take itself seriously. And with a seven-foot extraterrestrial thug (with hair that's half Billy Ray Cyrus, half George Costanza) who comes to Earth to steal our endorphins for re-sale on the cosmic black market? This movie knows it's ridiculous. Brian Benben's FBI agent even points out how convenient it is that the alien speaks English. The acting is questionable and so is the dialogue, which is in keeping with the plot that develops in between the action. And speaking of . . .

Sometimes you need a movie where everything just explodes. Cars. Buildings. Police evidence. Even the people. And not those CG explosions that blockbusters feed us these days. We're talking gratuitous pyrotechnics on over-cranked cameras so you can see the contours on those slow-motion large-scale fireballs; explosions that make you think about how much easier it was for movies to get insurance back then.

Sometimes you also need to see some old-fashioned stunts. And this movie's are a cut above. Plenty of fist fights, car chases, defenestration, and dudes outrunning objects that are spontaneously combusting. The director shares the same last name with several people on the stunt team; turns out they're father, son, and uncle. A lot of families drive each other crazy, so this appears a healthy outlet.

And sometimes you need a steady dosage of stupid one-liners over the course of ninety minutes. "I come in peace," the jacked alien-man says before he fatally pumps his victims' veins with heroin. "And you go in pieces, asshole" is Caine's delicate riposte. Or how about the movie's centerpiece quip, delivered in Dolph Lundgren's steely mumble: "Fuck you, spaceman!" Already, you're thinking of two times previously in your life when that phrase would've proven useful.

Sometimes you just need a movie like *I Come in Peace*.

ZARDOZ 1974

 **48%** | Written and directed by John Boorman
Starring Sean Connery, Charlotte Rampling, Sara Kestelman, John Alderton

Critics Consensus

Zardoz is ambitious and epic in scope, but its philosophical musings are rendered ineffective by its supreme weirdness and rickety execution.

Synopsis

In 2293, Exterminator Zed sets out to learn the truth about Zardoz, his clan's patriarchal god. Arriving in the settlement of the Eternals, he uncovers a secret so shocking, it could end human existence forever.

Why We Love It

Just because a film presents itself as an incoherent mishmash of ideas doesn't mean you should skip it.

One would have to look to Alejandro Jodorowsky for a genre movie as audacious and bizarre as *Zardoz*. Hot off the success of *Deliverance*—and his failure to realize *The Lord of the Rings* for United Artists—director John Boorman turns his lens to a vision of humanity's twisted future. He presents us with a time when mankind is divided into the Brutals, who live in a wasteland growing food for their superiors and indulging in primal violence, and the Eternals, who live in "The Vortex" and bicker about philosophy as they slowly succumb to an advanced state of apathy.

All of that is just set dressing, though—the real story centers on an Eternal trying to reunite the mind, heart, and genitals of humanity and create a new and better version of the species.

Or maybe it really is just about that shot of Sean Connery in a wedding dress. (If you don't know it, Google it *now*.)

To try to describe *Zardoz* is, in some ways, to miss the point (and damn difficult, as you can see). It is the dream of a stoned hippie after reading too many sci-fi novels—a thing meant more to be experienced than processed. Characters disappear for large portions of its runtime. Philosophical ruminations are abandoned in favor of shocking visuals. Sexual freedom appears to be advocated despite a return to a patriarchal norm by the film's baffling final dissolve. Any traditional metric of quality is too parochial a concern for *Zardoz*.

At the center of the madness is Connery, who holds onto the film for dear life in a bid to escape the shadow of James Bond. He gives what would become his standard Connery performance in a film he barely comprehends, but the audience is too busy trying to piece together the last inexplicable set piece to notice.

"ONE WOULD HAVE TO LOOK TO ALEJANDRO JODOROWSKY FOR A GENRE MOVIE AS AUDACIOUS AND BIZARRE AS ZARDOZ."

And yet the confusion is a net positive. The film is both brainy and dumb all at once. It will leave you a little bit nauseous and, like, wondering what it all means, man.

THE LORD OF THE RINGS 1978

 **50%**

Directed by Ralph Bakshi
Written by Chris Conkling and Peter S. Beagle
Starring John Hurt, Anthony Daniels

Critics Consensus

Ralph Bakshi's valiant attempt at rendering Tolkien's magnum opus in rotoscope never lives up to the grandeur of its source material, with a compressed running time that flattens the sweeping story and experimental animation that is more bizarre than magical.

Synopsis

In the Third Age of Middle-earth, a party of Hobbits, Men, Dwarves, and Elves sets out to destroy a ring of power sought by its creator, the Dark Lord Sauron, and end a generations-long conflict.

Why We Love It

While outclassed in every way by Peter Jackson's twenty-first-century *The Lord of the Rings* trilogy, Ralph Bakshi's ambitious adaptation of the J.R.R. Tolkien epic offers key storytelling choices for future filmmakers—and a lesson in how easily fantasy films can go wrong.

Convinced he could deliver high-quality animation for an adult audience, Bakshi decided to make the film via the rotoscoping technique—that is, shoot the film in live action with minimal sets and costumes so the animators could use the motion of the actors in the finalized footage. The process offers lifelike animation when done correctly. *The Lord of the Rings* pulls it off infrequently, with overly caricatured movement dominating the performances. Additionally, the characters rarely look part of the world realized by the background paintings, and the voice-acting suggests an uninterested ensemble rushed into the recording booth. Bakshi himself boldly claimed he was uninterested in the details—Tolkien fans would fill in the gaps, he said—leading to an astonishing lack of consistency from sequence to sequence; there are whole scenes in which the live-action reference footage is tinted with the animated cell colors and inserted into the final film to save time and money.

The result is a production that is fascinating to watch for all its miscalculations.

Its more legitimate significance in the post-Jackson era may come from several choices that Bakshi and writers Chris Conkling and Peter S. Beagle made at the scripting stage. Like Jackson's first film, this one removes much of Frodo's journey from Hobbiton to Bree, getting the Fellowship of the Ring on their quest as quickly as possible. That brevity may not pay off once the film shifts to material from *The Two Towers*, but it indicated the best way to start *The Lord of the Rings* as a cinematic adventure.

Watching *The Lord of the Rings* now is much more an academic pursuit than it was in 1978, but it reveals the difficulty filmmakers face when attempting to adapt beloved fantasy epics. It also offers a curious contrast to the modern conception of Middle-earth.

ROBOT MONSTER 1953

36%

Directed by Phil Tucker
Written by Wyott Ordung
Starring George Nader, Claudia Barrett, George Barrows

Critics Consensus

Its titular baddie is a guy in a gorilla suit with a head that looks like an oversized television antenna. In other words, it's practically the dictionary definition of a grade-Z classic.

Synopsis

In a postapocalyptic future, the last remaining family on Earth tries to outsmart Ro-Man Extension XJ-2, a computer intelligence supervising the end of the human race.

Why We Love It

Robot Monster is one of the great sci-fi camp classics of the 1950s. While 3-D exhibition was its calling card then, it is notable now for its awesome and era-defining cheese factor. And sometimes, you're in the mood for fromage.

Let's skip to the end. It turns out that everything that happens in *Robot Monster* is just the dream of a child wandering in a park. *Or is it?* The film's final shot—showing the title creature emerging from one of the famous caves at L.A.'s Bronson Canyon—commits the most hackneyed of storytelling conventions ever devised: the it-was-all-a-dream fake-out. Nonetheless, those who appreciate *Robot Monster* forgive the film this terrible decision because, ultimately, the film is already so silly, the pre-credit awfulness is totally on brand.

As one of the cheapest sci-fi movies ever made—the film reportedly cost $50,000 to produce—the bulk of the film consists of the human family arguing with Ro-Man (George Barrows) over a video phone. When the action moves away from these scenes, we are treated to shots of characters wandering the scrub-covered hills around Bronson Canyon. Spare no expense!

The movie might have disappeared entirely if not for the low-budget genius of Ro-Man himself. The creature is little more than Barrows's own gorilla suit with a diver's helmet on his head instead of the gorilla mask. The obvious off-the-shelf costume gives Ro-Man a charm he might not otherwise have. You can't help but chuckle at the sight of him casually bounding around the canyon, even as you know what he's there for.

The situation only becomes more outlandish when Ro-Man decides he has feelings for Claudia Barrett's Alice and openly wonders if the "hu-man" can love a Ro-Man.

That mismatch is the key to understanding why *Robot Monster* endures: it is a nuclear disarmament treatise disguised as a monster movie for kids. It cannot help but botch its tone, miss its mark, and yet still thoroughly entertain. Add a score by Elmer Bernstein, who would go on to be nominated for fourteen Oscars, and you get a very silly monster movie painfully unaware just how silly it is.

MANNEQUIN 1987

 19%

Directed by Michael Gottlieb
Written by Edward Rugoff and Michael Gottlieb
Starring Kim Cattrall, Andrew McCarthy, Meshach Taylor, James Spader, Estelle Getty

Critics Consensus

Mannequin is a real dummy, outfitted with a ludicrous concept and a painfully earnest script that never springs to life, despite the best efforts of an impossibly charming Kim Cattrall.

Synopsis

An Ancient Egyptian princess would rather explore the world and find true love than be in a boring arranged marriage. The gods hear her plea and turn her into a muse who ends up possessing the form of a department store mannequin, where she meets an intriguing window dresser.

Why We Love It

Plenty of young, idealistic kids have run from arranged marriages in movies before—but how many of them did it by faux-mummifying themselves in a sarcophagus? Kim Cattrall as Emmy, the headstrong young Ancient Egyptian, desperately wishes for a life outside of the one she knows. So, while she's arguing with her mother about the possibilities that life could hold for her, she asks the gods to take sides, and *poof*—she disappears. Even in Ancient Egypt, parents just don't get it.

When we next catch up with Emmy, she's a department store mannequin being created/ogled by sexually-unthreatening-but-still-dreamy Jonathan (Andrew McCarthy). It's unclear what scarab beetles the gods were smoking to create this wild ride, but it remains one of the most creative rom-com "meet cutes" in movie history. He's fired for spending too much time creating her, but he can't ignore how having her in his life made him feel like a real artist. The stars align, and he gets a shot at creating window dressings starring his muse, which brings him fame and fortune and causes nearly every other character in the movie to participate in weird department store espionage to try to stop him from making windows pretty.

In a film full of wild hyperbole—Emmy hang-gliding in the department store after hours, a security guard (G. W. Bailey) sic'ing his bulldog on Jonathan while he's on the clock dressing windows—there is still a small, grounded message within. Emmy is a creative, resourceful woman who wants to express herself, and she found a partner who's driven to do the same. Sure, he takes all the glory because she freezes whenever someone else looks at her (a twisted representation of the male gaze?), but you can't have it all.

Speaking of which, Meshach Taylor is an accomplice in all this, playing a gay window dresser named Hollywood. Watching the film in modern times highlights a certain dichotomy: Hollywood's flamboyant sunglasses are simultaneously an outdated exaggeration of homosexuality as well as an inarguably fierce accessory. But hey, it's all about the conversation.

"THIS WILD RIDE . . . REMAINS ONE OF THE MOST CREATIVE ROM-COM 'MEET CUTES' IN MOVIE HISTORY."

MASTERS OF THE UNIVERSE 1987

 **17%**

Directed by Gary Goddard
Written by David Odell
Starring Dolph Lundgren, Billy Barty, Frank Langella, Courteney Cox, Meg Foster

Critics Consensus

Masters of the Universe is a slapdash adaptation of the He-Man mythos that can't overcome its cynical lack of raison d'être, no matter how admirably Frank Langella throws himself into the role of Skeletor.

Synopsis

Hoping to save the planet Eternia from destruction by an evil empire, He-Man faces off against Skeletor in the weird, far-away environs of . . . suburban California.

Why We Love It

What do you get when you combine a *Star Wars* knockoff, budget woes, plot holes galore, a young Courteney Cox, flagrant product placements, and enough body oil to make Rambo blush? This pop-culture curio, which proved the death knell to the He-Man character—at least until an upcoming reboot—albeit a so-bad-it's-good final blow that deserves some kind of special mention in the ironic-stoner film canon. Up until *Masters of the Universe*'s release, He-Man was having one hell of a run in the 1980s, existing as a toy first (a toy *first*, people), then a series of comics, then an animated TV show, before making the jump to the big screen. For a certain generation of kids, the pull quote calling *Masters of the Universe* "The *Star Wars* of the '80s" on the poster was reason enough to give it a whirl. (Spoiler alert: It wasn't the *Star Wars* of the '80s.)

Speaking of, let's address the Death Star in the room: so much of this movie reeks of ripping off the biggest film franchise ever, from the font on the opening title card (with a booming horns score to boot) to Skeletor's soldiers (Darth Vaders without the capes) to Gwildor (a jocular Yoda lite played by screen vet Billy Barty) to . . . too many other things to mention here. The aping doesn't stop there. To get from space to La La Land, it also features a car that jets you off to another dimension—the film lifts liberally from *Back to the Future*'s playbook. There's some nonsense about changing the past to keep your family together. The character played by Cox, in her second film role, has a boyfriend with a band who's pumped to—you guessed it—play the big high school dance. And even James Tolkan is in this thing, pretty much in the same "fuck you, McFly" mode as he was as *Back to the Future*'s Mr. Strickland, only this time as a detective.

But *Masters of the Universe*'s charm lies in its preposterousness. As a sort of greased-up Conan the Barbarian, Dolph Lundgren's He-Man runs around modern-day California with a black Speedo, blond mullet, and a thick Swedish accent. (Worried producers initially planned to dub all of his lines but eventually decided against it.) Frank Langella, as He-Man's nemesis Skeletor, brings his A-game acting chops to a movie that really doesn't deserve it. And the big face-off fight scene between hero and villain is so underwhelming that learning it was shot hastily after the movie had already run out of money is not at all surprising. It's a car crash of a cash grab, for sure, but if you're not down to laugh along to this buoyantly fun fiasco well past midnight, we don't think we can be friends.

BELA LUGOSI MEETS A BROOKLYN GORILLA 1952

 **29%**

Directed by William Beaudine
Written by Tim Ryan
Starring Bela Lugosi, Duke Mitchell, Sammy Petrillo, Charlita, Muriel Landers

CRITIC: Leonard Maltin

Leonard Maltin is best known for his long-running reference book *Leonard Maltin's Movie Guide* and its companion, *Leonard Maltin's Classic Movie Guide*. He appears regularly on Turner Classic Movies, teaches at the USC School of Cinematic Arts, hosts the podcast *Maltin on Movies* with his daughter Jessie, and holds court at leonardmaltin.com.

When I'm asked about my guilty pleasures, I often name this ultra-low-budget movie but hasten to add that I don't feel guilty about enjoying it. It is, by any rational measure, a terrible film. To someone not steeped in B-movies of this era, it might seem like an incoherent message from Mars. But for some strange, perverse reason, its mere existence makes me happy.

The seventy-four-minute movie features a bargain-basement Martin and Lewis trapped on a jungle island with a mad doctor played by Bela Lugosi. If those ingredients don't intrigue you, I suggest you move on right now.

Bela Lugosi was a Big Deal to me. Like many Baby Boomers, I came of age when the classic Universal horror pictures were first released to television. Seeing *Frankenstein*, *Dracula*, and their various spouses and offspring were key moments in my life as a film buff. Forrest J. Ackerman's magazine *Famous Monsters of Filmland* sealed the deal, as it did for other Boomers like Stephen King and Steven Spielberg. It took impressionable readers behind the scenes of classic horror films and heightened our appreciation of such genre giants as Lon Chaney,

Boris Karloff, and, of course, Bela Lugosi.

I'd watch any movie he was in. That included a lot of junk as well as some unexpected gems like *Abbott and Costello Meet Frankenstein* (1948), in which he played it straight and proved he still had

> ## "TO SOMEONE NOT STEEPED IN B-MOVIES OF THIS ERA, IT MIGHT SEEM LIKE AN INCOHERENT MESSAGE FROM MARS."

what it took to be a potent and persuasive Count Dracula. Just four years later, Bela's career was on the skids when he accepted an offer from fledgling producer Jack Broder to appear in a much lower-rent comedy called *Bela Lugosi Meets a Brooklyn Gorilla*.

Most lists of so-bad-they're-good movies from this era cite Ed Wood's immortal turkey *Plan 9 from Outer Space*, which also features Lugosi. I love that one, too, but I have a special place in my heart for the earlier production. Maybe it's the combination of Bela and a carbon copy of my favorite comedian at that time, Jerry Lewis.

The title itself is irresistible—apparently the brainchild of Broder's young son. The cast includes Charlita, a beautiful woman with a figure made for sarongs; Ramona the chimp (reportedly played by the same simian actor who was Cheetah in the Tarzan films); rotund Muriel Landers, a singer and comedienne who later worked with The Three Stooges; and the comedy team of Duke Mitchell and Sammy Petrillo.

Remember, Dean Martin and Jerry Lewis were the hottest act in show business, appearing on TV's *Colgate Comedy Hour* and starring in a series of hit movies for producer Hal B. Wallis. Mitchell and Petrillo were unabashed clones of Dean and Jerry: a romantic crooner and a monkey-like, anything-goes comedian. This was fine for desperate nightclub owners who wanted a novelty attraction but lawsuit-bait for a moviemaker. Associate producer Herman Cohen told researcher Tom Weaver that Jerry Lewis had a heated meeting with Broder, and Wallis followed up to rattle the cage. (Broder would have been happy to accept a check from Wallis to burn the negative, but that transaction never came to pass.)

The storyline has Mitchell and Petrillo, using their own names, as performers who wind up on the jungle island of Kola Kola after stepping out of a plane by accident. On the secluded isle, they encounter two amorous women, one of them the daughter of the tribal chief. When she gets a look at them after they've cleaned up, she does a "take" and Petrillo says, "Lady, you got us mixed up with two other guys." Indeed. They also meet a mad scientist in residence named Dr. Zabor, who is conducting experiments involving the evolution of apes into men. The chest-pounding animal is played by Steve Calvert, who purchased his customized gorilla suit from the legendary Ray "Crash" Corrigan.

Duke falls in love with the chief's daughter, while Sammy is pursued by her heavyweight sister. ("Fat women" were a staple of lowbrow comedy back then.) Lugosi doesn't show up until twenty-one minutes into the picture, and when the stars meet him, they can only think of the vampire who bites people's necks. "Watch out for bats!" exclaims Petrillo.

The only problem with this purported comedy duo is that they aren't funny. At all. While the toothy Petrillo inevitably summons up thoughts of Jerry Lewis, he is merely loud and obnoxious. He has all the superficial moves but none of the innate feel for comedy that made Jerry a sensation. Duke Mitchell is an adequate singer, but he'd never be mistaken for Dean Martin. The other secret of Martin and Lewis's success was that Dean had superb comedy chops.

For a quickie feature made for $100,000 and shot at the General Service Studio in Hollywood, where *I Love Lucy* was filming next door, *Bela Lugosi Meets a Brooklyn Gorilla* looks pretty good. Veteran cameraman Charles Van Enger, who started in the silent era, knew what he was doing, and so did director William Beaudine, whose career showed great promise in the 1920s but never took off. Instead, he became one of the most prolific B-movie makers in Hollywood. He has literally hundreds of features, shorts, and TV episodes to his credit. He'd worked with Lugosi several times before, including on a pair of Bowery Boys comedies for Monogram Pictures. (On the set of one such endeavor, Beaudine looked around late one night, saw the exhaustion on the faces of his cast and crew, and muttered aloud,

> # "THE ONLY PROBLEM WITH THIS PURPORTED COMEDY DUO IS THAT THEY AREN'T FUNNY. AT ALL."

"You'd think someone was *waiting* for this!")

Even Duke Mitchell's featured songs aren't as cheesy as one might expect. Broder bought the rights to a pop standard, "Deed I Do," along with an Americanization of a Latin hit, "Too Soon," and hired young Dick Hazard to arrange and conduct them. Hazard had a long career as a pop and jazz composer and arranger.

The screenplay is credited to ex-vaudevillian Tim Ryan, who appeared in and wrote many B pictures, with additional dialogue supplied by frequent collaborator Edmond Seward and Leo "Ukie" Sherin, a comic crony of Bing Crosby who also served as dialogue director on the set.

Call it a curio, an oddity, a one-off, even a dud. All of those descriptions accurately describe this movie, which was retitled *The Boys from Brooklyn* a short time after its initial release. But it retains a strange pull for me, just because someone had the nerve to make it.

Rotten Tomatoes' Critics Consensus *Bela Lugosi Meets a Brooklyn Gorilla* . . . and many viewers won't be able to help wondering why.

1994 THE ROTTENEST YEAR EVER

The year of *Street Fighter* was also the year with the lowest Tomatometer average for its movies. Here, we connect the splats between some of the worst films of cinema's worst year.

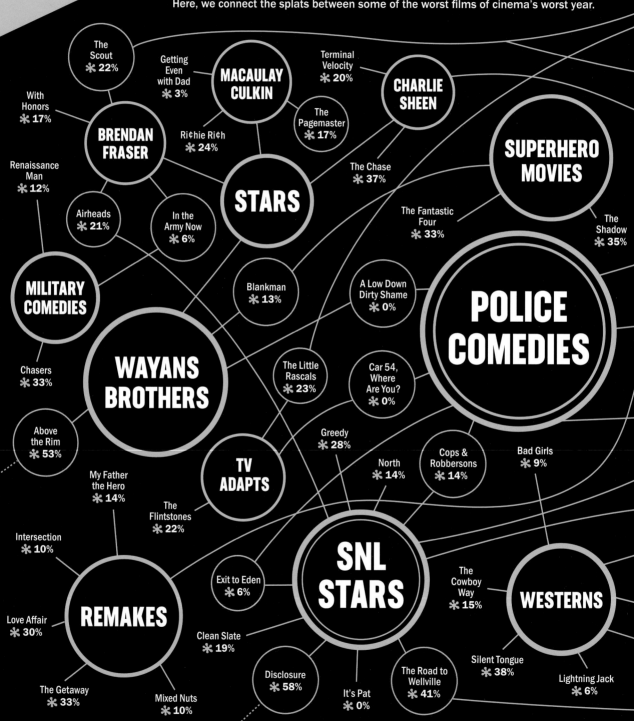

The Scout ✳ 22%

Getting Even with Dad ✳ 3%

MACAULAY CULKIN

Terminal Velocity ✳ 20%

CHARLIE SHEEN

With Honors ✳ 17%

BRENDAN FRASER

Ri¢hie Ri¢h ✳ 24%

The Pagemaster ✳ 17%

SUPERHERO MOVIES

Renaissance Man ✳ 12%

STARS

The Chase ✳ 37%

Airheads ✳ 21%

In the Army Now ✳ 6%

The Fantastic Four ✳ 33%

The Shadow ✳ 35%

MILITARY COMEDIES

Blankman ✳ 13%

A Low Down Dirty Shame ✳ 0%

POLICE COMEDIES

Chasers ✳ 33%

WAYANS BROTHERS

The Little Rascals ✳ 23%

Car 54, Where Are You? ✳ 0%

Above the Rim ✳ 53%

TV ADAPTS

Greedy ✳ 28%

North ✳ 14%

Cops & Robbersons ✳ 14%

Bad Girls ✳ 9%

My Father the Hero ✳ 14%

The Flintstones ✳ 22%

Intersection ✳ 10%

SNL STARS

Exit to Eden ✳ 6%

The Cowboy Way ✳ 15%

WESTERNS

Love Affair ✳ 30%

REMAKES

Clean Slate ✳ 19%

Silent Tongue ✳ 38%

Disclosure ✳ 58%

It's Pat ✳ 0%

The Road to Wellville ✳ 41%

Lightning Jack ✳ 6%

The Getaway ✳ 33%

Mixed Nuts ✳ 10%

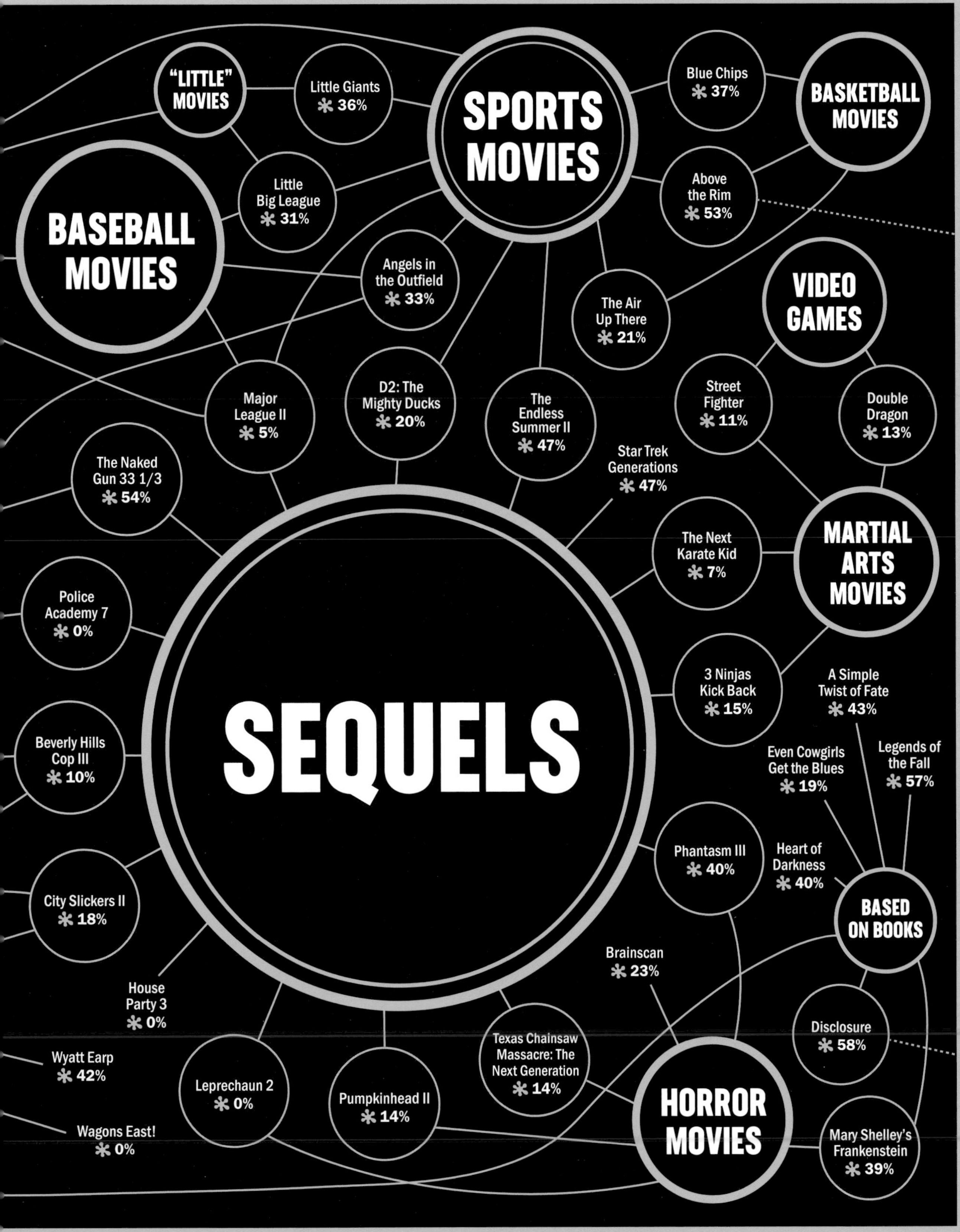

SEQUELS

SPORTS MOVIES

BASKETBALL MOVIES

BASEBALL MOVIES

"LITTLE" MOVIES

VIDEO GAMES

MARTIAL ARTS MOVIES

BASED ON BOOKS

HORROR MOVIES

Little Giants
✳ 36%

Blue Chips
✳ 37%

Little Big League
✳ 31%

Above the Rim
✳ 53%

Angels in the Outfield
✳ 33%

The Air Up There
✳ 21%

D2: The Mighty Ducks
✳ 20%

The Endless Summer II
✳ 47%

Street Fighter
✳ 11%

Double Dragon
✳ 13%

Major League II
✳ 5%

Star Trek Generations
✳ 47%

The Naked Gun 33 1/3
✳ 54%

The Next Karate Kid
✳ 7%

Police Academy 7
✳ 0%

3 Ninjas Kick Back
✳ 15%

A Simple Twist of Fate
✳ 43%

Even Cowgirls Get the Blues
✳ 19%

Legends of the Fall
✳ 57%

Beverly Hills Cop III
✳ 10%

Phantasm III
✳ 40%

Heart of Darkness
✳ 40%

City Slickers II
✳ 18%

Brainscan
✳ 23%

Disclosure
✳ 58%

House Party 3
✳ 0%

Wyatt Earp
✳ 42%

Leprechaun 2
✳ 0%

Pumpkinhead II
✳ 14%

Texas Chainsaw Massacre: The Next Generation
✳ 14%

Mary Shelley's Frankenstein
✳ 39%

Wagons East!
✳ 0%

NOT THEIR BEST WORK (OR SO THEY SAID)

Rare Rottens for Big-Name Fresh Directors

Steven Spielberg has directed just three Rotten movies in his incredibly Fresh five-decade career: 1979's rarely spoken-of *1941*; shark-jumping *Jurassic Park* sequel *The Lost World* (lucky pack!); and *Hook*, the story of the titular pirate and his nemesis, Peter Pan, who for some reason went and joined the real world and grew up. That last film is the Rottenest of the director's movies, with a Tomatometer score of just 26%, and widely considered—at least among critics—a big misstep for one of our great filmmakers. (Even Spielberg himself has essentially disowned it, as you'll read in this chapter.) And yet *Hook* remains beloved by so many of us who grew up wearing out our *Hook* VHS tapes screaming "Ru-Fi-Yo!" at our TV screens. It's also typical of the films we're looking at here: rare Rotten "off days" for some of the biggest names in movie-making. They're films that ended incredible hot streaks (Ridley Scott's Rotten fantasy epic *Legend* came on the heels of *Blade Runner* and *Alien*) or showed us that hot-shot newcomers weren't infallible after all (Sofia Coppola hit

her first snag with *Marie Antoinette* after the critical success of *The Virgin Suicides* and *Lost in Translation*). They show directors over-indulging their signature excesses (Wes Anderson's only Rotten film, *The Life Aquatic with Steve Zissou*, or Michael Mann's *Miami Vice*, which *Vanity Fair* critic K. Austin Collins defends in these pages), or being too smart for their own good, or at least a bit too smart for the critics (see critic Jessica Kiang's salute to Jane Campion's misunderstood *The Portrait of a Lady*). Like *Hook*, though, each has its defenders and fandoms, particularly those that bear the marks of their singular makers' idiosyncrasies. And like *Hook*, most of these were risks—big and bold and thrilling in their ambition. They're the foul balls hit as some of Hollywood's most talented people swung for the fences, and those at bat mostly learned from them before stepping back up to the plate. (Spielberg's next two films after *Hook*? *Jurassic Park* and *Schindler's List*, both released in 1993.)

> THEY'RE THE FOUL BALLS HIT AS SOME OF HOLLYWOOD'S MOST TALENTED PEOPLE SWUNG FOR THE FENCES.

THE WIZ 1978

 **44%** | **Directed by** Sidney Lumet
Written by Joel Schumacher
Starring Diana Ross, Michael Jackson, Nipsey Russell, Lena Horne, Ted Ross

Critics Consensus

This workmanlike movie musical lacks the electricity of the stage version (and its cinematic inspiration), but it's bolstered by strong performances by Diana Ross and Michael Jackson.

Synopsis

In this psychedelic 1970s spin on *The Wizard of Oz*, Dorothy is a Harlem schoolteacher swept away by a cyclone—during a snowstorm!—and transported to a reimagined New York City, which has been redubbed the land of Oz. To go home, she must find the Wiz and help the friends she meets as she eases on down the road to the Emerald City.

Why We Love It

It's hard not to wince when reading contemporary reviews of *The Wiz*. It's not just the question of "How did these critics get this so wrong?" (because they really, really did) but also, "Why did they have to be such assholes in the way they went about it?" While some critics took issue with the garish sets and some took aim at the quality of the songs, many also took an almost unseemly delight in slamming Diana Ross for being "too old" for the role of Dorothy, the twenty-four-year-old who's never been south of 125th Street.

But before we do away with that sort of nonsense and pay our due respects to the queen, we'll pay respect to the film that she—through incredible willpower and forceful behind-the-scenes negotiations—was instrumental in making happen.

The Motown-Universal co-production is constructed like a trip you never want to end, with one indelible image blurring into another: "munchkins" emerging from body-shaped graffiti on the walls of the fluoro-punk Munchkinland; Lena Horne singing in front of a floating flotilla of babies dressed as stars (really); a red-drenched sweatshop manned by monsters and overseen by the Wicked Witch of the West (Mabel King, who also played the role on Broadway). *Serpico* and *Dog Day Afternoon* director Sidney Lumet stages the epic set pieces with verve—some 650 dancers reportedly feature in an Emerald City number shot at the base of the World Trade Center—and keeps things moving between songs at a quick enough pace that we mostly don't register Joel Schumacher's clunky believe-in-yourself dialogue.

Of the performers, a then nineteen-year-old Michael Jackson is the standout of the supporting cast, managing to register doe-eyed emotion beneath thick layers of Stan Winston's unflattering scarecrow makeup. (Jackson met Quincy Jones, the film's music supervisor, for the first time while shooting, kicking off one of pop music's great partnerships.) But as *Oz* was Garland's movie, *The Wiz* is Ross's, and she's dynamite.

Ross radiates explosive joy in the climactic "Brand New Day" and is heartbreaking for the show's most beloved number, "Home," for which Lumet holds his camera tight on her face, never moving, never cutting away. The director had clearly fallen for his star, and you'd need to be missing a brain or a heart not to fall right along with him.

> " THE MOTOWN-UNIVERSAL CO-PRODUCTION IS CONSTRUCTED LIKE A TRIP YOU NEVER WANT TO END, WITH ONE INDELIBLE IMAGE BLURRING INTO ANOTHER. "

A CHORUS LINE 1985

 40% | Directed by Richard Attenborough
Written by Arnold Schulman
Starring Michael Douglas, Yamil Borges, Alyson Reed, Jan Gan Boyd, Terrence Mann

Critics Consensus

On stage, *A Chorus Line* pulled back the curtain to reveal the hopes and fears of showbiz strivers, but that energy and urgency is lost in the transition to the big screen.

Synopsis

A group of hopeful dancers audition for a mysterious new show, showcasing their talents and revealing intimate details about their lives over the course of a day that could change their lives.

Why We Love It

A Chorus Line was always going to be a tough film to pull off. Hollywood had successfully adapted stagey musicals before (*Cabaret, Hair*), but *Chorus* was an entirely new beast. Taking place over the course of a one-day audition, with sixteen hopefuls competing for a handful of paid gigs, the 1975 Broadway hit's action never leaves the theater. Instead, the actors face the audience, kicking and singing and jazz-handing in real time for an acclaimed director, played by Michael Douglas in the film as a chain-smoking Svengali sitting somewhere in the shadows of the orchestra section. The musical is a claustrophobic experience at times, designed to put us in the tap and ballet shoes of the desperate (and mostly aging) dancers. Save for a few radio-friendly ballads from composer Marvin Hamlisch and lyricist Edward Kleban, it wasn't exactly a sure-fire formula for a movie-musical smash.

And it wouldn't be. The movie grossed just $14 million of its $25 million budget and was mostly savaged by critics. Many reviews noted that proceedings felt too stage-bound and complained that the filmmakers had essentially made a recording of the live show. It was too rigid, too uncinematic, too contained. Fans of the musical, meanwhile, complained about the remix the show had been given, with certain songs excised and two new songs added: the random, puberty-focused "Surprise, Surprise" (awful, but energetically led by Gregg Burge) and "Let Me Dance for You" (less random, no less forgettable). The decision to transform the show's biggest hit, "What I Did for Love," from an ode to the dedication of dancers to a basic love song, was for some a kind of sacrilege.

The things the film got right, though, are too often ignored. The movie is deftly cast, with Vicki Frederick a standout as Sheila. And, working within the limitations of the show, director Richard Attenborough, fresh off of his Oscar-winning *Ghandi*, uses every trick in the book to bring cinematic energy to the film. His camera swirls, the stage plunges dramatically into sudden darkness, and the opening number—cutting expertly between dozens of on-stage dancers, backstage mayhem, and the chaotic New York streets for more than twenty minutes—is thrillingly virtuosic. Editor John Bloom was rightfully nominated for an Oscar for his work.

The opening is matched thrill-for-thrill by the finale, in which mirrors, tight choreography, and stunning gold costuming combine to create a kind of swarming kaleidoscope on the screen. *A Chorus Line* may struggle to feel fully formed as a movie at times, but at these bookending moments, it's as if you're right there next to Douglas in the theater, ready to stub out your cigarette and give a standing ovation.

HOOK 1991

 **26%**

Directed by Steven Spielberg
Written by Malia Scotch Marmo and Jim V. Hart
Starring Robin Williams, Dustin Hoffman, Julia Roberts, Maggie Smith, Bob Hoskins

The look of *Hook* is lively indeed, but Steven Spielberg directs on autopilot here, giving in too quickly to his sentimental, syrupy qualities.

Synopsis

What would happen if Peter Pan grew up, had kids, and proceeded to become a glued-to-his-flip-phone corporate lawyer who couldn't make their baseball games? And what would happen if Captain Hook had not died and was hot for revenge? Steven Spielberg has answers.

> *HOOK IS AT ITS BEST WHEN IT'S TOO SILLY, TOO SWEET, AND YES, TOO COLORFUL.*

Why We Love It

Production on *Hook* was as troubled as a leaky *Jolly Roger* stuck smack-dab in the middle of a mammoth squall. Do yourself a favor one day and go down a Wiki-hole on this one: during the 1980s, Steven Spielberg was attached, then not attached, then attached again; there were multiple storylines being explored (old Peter, young Peter, live Hook, dead Hook); the movie was at one stage going to star Michael Jackson as the boy who never grew up; and the eventual script, penned after Hoffman signed on to play the titular villain, underwent many rewrites, with none other than Carrie Fisher doing uncredited work polishing Tinkerbell's dialogue.

When filming began, things didn't get better. Spielberg went weeks over schedule and millions over budget, working more slowly than usual on three huge sound stages at the Sony lot in Culver City, Los Angeles. Rumors flew that Julia Roberts and Spielberg were butting heads—something neither party has denied with any particular vehemence. Recently, the director admitted to *Empire* magazine that he felt like a "fish out of water" making the film and that he had no confidence in the script, particularly the "body" of it, set in Neverland (he feels more fondly towards the real-world family stuff). "I didn't quite know what I was doing and I tried to paint over my insecurity with production value," he told the magazine. "The more insecure I felt about it, the bigger and more colorful the sets became."

Interestingly, those disowned Neverland segments of *Hook* and those garish sets (the ornate pirate ship, the Lost Boys' Nickelodeon game-show–style HQ) are among the real pleasures of Spielberg's uneven film. Does anyone remember the early scenes in which Peter Banning (Robin Williams), the real-world, grown-up Pan, runs around office corridors closing business deals on his flip phone? They do not. But do they remember Rufio ("Ru-Fi-Yo!") wheeling through the Lost Boys' home on some sort of skateboard-pirate-ship hybrid thing? Very much. And that every-kid's-fantasy food fight? Indeed. And the extraordinary scenery-chewing of Hoffman as Neverland's premier pirate, whose very eyebrows are curled into hooks? Of course.

Hook is at its best when it's too silly, too sweet, and yes, too colorful. Spielberg may not much like it, but he made a great film for boys and girls who never want to grow up.

THE PORTRAIT OF A LADY 1996

 **45%**

Directed by Jane Campion
Written by Laura Jones
Starring Nicole Kidman, John Malkovich, Barbara Hershey, Mary-Louise Parker

CRITIC: Jessica Kiang

Jessica Kiang is a freelance film critic with regular bylines at *Variety*, ThePlaylist.net, *Sight and Sound*, and BBC Culture. She has served on juries at the Zurich and Ljubljana Film Festivals, Black Movie Geneva, and Cinekids Amsterdam.

I've always found the title ungainly: *The Portrait of a Lady*. That initial "The" irks me. Apologies to Henry James (for this, if not the sacrilege of preferring the film to his book: further apologies to anyone whose monocle of outrage has just plopped into their soup of disgust). It makes James's portraiture the thing and its subject just any old "A Lady"—priorities that are effectively reversed in Jane Campion's 1996 interpretation. That might be partly why Jamesian purists and "faithful adaptation" dogmatists hated it so much. It's a lot of why I think it's a masterpiece.

Campion's prior film, *The Piano*, won the 1993 Palme d'Or, and in the mute yet expressive Ada (Holly Hunter), it too tells an erotically charged, nineteenth-century–set story of a headstrong woman in a foreign land, trapped by marriage. But *The Piano* is made of mud and wood and worsted; *Portrait* of lacquer and onyx. Compared to the forgiving, melodic resolve of Ada's story, the hard portrayal of Isabel Archer (Nicole Kidman)—a young American in Europe who, on account of the inheritance designed to set her free, is lured into a toxic marriage—judges her very harshly indeed.

The film in turn was harshly judged. Jonathan Rosenbaum disliked how Campion "seriously mauls the novel." Todd McCarthy lamented that it "appeals to the head far more than to the heart," while Janet Maslin missed literary-Isabel's "brilliance" and complained that "without [the novel's] intellectual dazzle . . . it risks being reduced to a quaint nineteenth-century *Dating Game*." The *New Yorker*'s David Denby got so caught up measuring the shortfall in descriptive power between James's pages-long paragraphs and Campion's seconds-long close-ups, which "cannot tell us everything," that he failed to examine what those lingering shots, those eyes and mouths and pinched expressions *do* tell us.

> "*THE PIANO* IS MADE OF MUD AND WOOD AND WORSTED; *PORTRAIT* OF LACQUER AND ONYX."

When she embarked on writing *Emma*, Jane Austen famously announced her intention to create a central character that no one but she would like. She failed, of course: Austen cannot resist the temptation to charm us through her heroine. Campion refuses to do the same; her Isabel doesn't win us over with extraordinary talent (like Ada's musical skill in *The Piano*). She gets few of the witty rejoinders of the idealized plucky period heroine. Her repartee happens offscreen, if it happens at all, a calculated absence in a film about the bitter, brittle lie of brilliance and the inadequacy of accomplishment, good taste, and charm to the needs of a fulfilled life.

It's not just a refusal to flatter. In Campion's portrait of Isabel—coauthored by screenwriter Laura Jones and a revelatory Kidman—the tragedy is that her fate is not set by social restrictions nor the deviousness of others. She is ultimately the architect of her own downfall, and she knows it. The one true thing that her horrible husband says is that one

must accept the consequences of one's actions, and Isabel does just that, with a self-imposed severity that makes me love and pity her as she refuses to do for herself. So Campion's feminism shows itself not in the condemnation of a bygone era's patriarchal values but in the creation of an excitingly, uncompromisingly imperfect female protagonist who has agency over everything she does, *especially* her gravest mistakes and the misery to which they condemn her.

Campion can only have such confidence in this characterization because she is somehow describing herself. In interviews she was fond of declaring "I *am* Isabel," something Henry James is unlikely to have claimed. Some elements are lost in Campion's personal approach (James's social satire, his New World/Old World culture clash), but look at what we gain: one of the most complex, self-compromised screen heroines ever, delivered in an un-self-pitying semi-confessional manner that makes it less a portrait *of* Isabel Archer than a portrait *from* her.

Read this way, the film's erratic expressivity feels earned. John Malkovich's maligned portrayal of Osmond makes sense if he's not playing a real man but a representation of Isabel's impressions, first a literal mesmerist, twirling a parasol to stupefy her into suggestibility, and later her sadistic tormentor. To Isabel, his mocking laugh might well sound like the braying of a donkey, and his unwanted touch might well feel like the abrasion of his beard against her face.

Madame Merle—a career-high Barbara Hershey —is at first pristine and fascinating because of Isabel's fascination with her and, by the end, pathetic and desperate in the rain of her detestation. Everything around Isabel is haloed in pathetic fallacy: when she is herself, there is always a stray hair floating loose from her head, and when she is estranged from her nature, buttoned into someone else's idea of her, her coiffure is immaculate. With her darkening destiny, her light, simple gowns morph into heavy, oily taffetas that cinch around her like the armored carapace of an insect, her waist so shrinkingly waspish it's as though she may snap herself in two. Her palazzo home is gloomy; she is rarely outdoors, and when she is, Stuart Dryburgh's immaculate photography makes the chill, gray English winter seem more welcoming than the Italian sunshine.

"I am Isabel," says Campion. At the risk of inciting a Spartacist uprising, I am Isabel too, though no one with a moat has ever proposed to me. But I am an Isabel who has had the benefit of Campion's caustic cautionary tale. I was riveted by its lessons about freedom: it might feel like my due, but it is only ever a gift, one that comes with an obligation and

> # "THE TRAGEDY IS THAT HER FATE IS NOT SET BY SOCIAL RESTRICTIONS NOR THE DEVIOUSNESS OF OTHERS. SHE IS ULTIMATELY THE ARCHITECT OF HER OWN DOWNFALL, AND SHE KNOWS IT."

can be revoked, lost, or squandered. *The Portrait of a Lady* may never be generally beloved because it, too, is difficult, prickly, and perhaps thinks too well of itself. But then, the ardor of us near-miss latter-day Isabel Archers out there should, like her cousin Ralph's deathbed admission of devotion, mitigate the disdain of so many: if it has been hated, it has also been loved—ah, but Isabel, *adored*.

Rotten Tomatoes' Critics Consensus Beautiful, indulgently heady, and pretentious, *The Portrait of a Lady* paints Campion's directorial shortcomings in too bright a light.

THE LIFE AQUATIC WITH STEVE ZISSOU **2004**

 **56%**

Directed by Wes Anderson
Written by Wes Anderson and Noah Baumbach
Starring Bill Murray, Anjelica Huston, Owen Wilson, Willem Dafoe, Cate Blanchett, Jeff Goldblum

Critics Consensus

Much like the titular oceanographer, *The Life Aquatic with Steve Zissou*'s overt irony may come off as smug and artificial—but for fans of Wes Anderson's unique brand of whimsy, it might be worth the dive.

Synopsis

A down-on-his-luck celebrity oceanographer and his ragtag crew try to hunt down the "jaguar shark" that killed one of their own for a comeback documentary.

Why We Love It

Just how much Wes Anderson is *too* much Wes Anderson? That's the question critics grappled with when the writer-director's fourth feature arrived at theaters. A paean to one of his childhood heroes, Jacques Cousteau, *Life Aquatic* is a feast of Andersonian flourishes, with intoxicating music-fueled sequences, scrupulous set designs, coordinated costumes, fanciful shots, and just about everything else in the Wes World bag of tricks. It's Wes Anderson, full throttle—which, for a film that tackles death, grief, fatherhood, failure, and other Big Dramatic Issues, came off to some as disingenuous or, to invoke the one-word slam often thrown at the director, "quirky." And to be fair, *Aquatic* can be cartoonish (literally, with animated candy-colored sea creatures like the appropriately dubbed crayon ponyfish), and the mishmash of dry humor, adventure, dramatic swells, and other tonal shifts is enough to unsteady any story.

So it's not a fully formed, tidy opus like *Rushmore* or a profile-raising ensemble picture like *The Royal Tenenbaums*, or a shaggy, endearing comedy like *Bottle Rocket*. For all its meticulousness, Anderson's fourth time around on the big screen is a structurally messier affair—but a really fun one. Uneven? Sure. Boring? Never. This is Anderson the errant artist making a big-budget movie in exotic locales with crazy gadgets and shootout sequences and a giant friggin' neon shark because he now has the clout to do so—and strikingly original *ways* to do so. Steve Zissou's introduction of his submarine, the *Belafonte*, is marvelous, tracking through the curious ship's nooks and crannies, creating an otherworld brimming with imagination. (Also marvelous: the boat was actually cut in half to make this happen.) The rescue-operation scene, too, keenly balances absurdity with honest-to-god fun bursts of action. The eye candy on display throughout is its own sort of achievement.

The Life Aquatic is more than mere visual bliss, though. Bill Murray, as the stoner semi-savant of a captain, dryly cranks out chuckle-worthy lines like "You know, cubbie's kind of a sucker-maker, but she's got some moves," referring to Cate Blanchett's character, a journalist once obsessed with Zissou who's writing a cover story on him. (She's great, by the way.) And smaller roles equally shine, particularly Willem Dafoe as a wounded-puppy-dog of a shipmate and Jeff Goldblum as Zissou's dapper competitor. The father-son story between Zissou and Ned (Owen Wilson) runs a little thin, its drama feeling a bit unearned and forced. But this is a seafaring, rock 'n' roll rollercoaster of a film, sountracked to Seu Jorge's kickass Portuguese covers of Bowie. Who can't get on board with that?

WILLOW 1988

 **50%**

Directed by Ron Howard
Written by Bob Dolman and George Lucas
Starring Warwick Davis, Val Kilmer, Joanne Whalley, Jean Marsh, Patricia Hayes

Critics Consensus

State-of-the-art special effects and an appealing performance from Warwick Davis can't quite save *Willow* from its slow pace and generic story.

Synopsis

Willow Ufgood, a farmer and would-be sorcerer, finds a baby who portends the end of the evil Queen Bavmorda's reign. Willow goes on a quest to return the child, teaming up with expert swordsman Madmartigan, sorceress Fin Raziel, and, eventually, Bavmorda's daughter Sorsha to keep the baby safe.

Why We Love It

George Lucas has cited Akira Kurosawa's *The Hidden Fortress* and Tolkien's *Lord of the Rings* as major influences on *Star Wars*; as the writer and producer of *Willow*, he brought those building blocks to bear on a more earthbound tale. Sure, like those aforementioned works, it's the story of a ragtag bunch who undertake an epic journey to stop the bad guys and rescue someone from an impregnable stronghold. And what's wrong with that? Plenty of fantasy stories recycle the same basic elements. But *Willow* was special for a couple of reasons.

First, its state-of-the-art digital morphing effects from Industrial Light & Magic. The revolutionary effects created the illusion of Fin Raziel (Patricia Hayes) transforming into a variety of animals before being changed back into a human (the technique would later be used to mind-blowing effect in Michael Jackson's "Black or White" music video). Second, and more importantly, its cast was terrific. Teenaged Warwick Davis was tasked with carrying the whole film, and he did so in endlessly appealing fashion. As Madmartigan, Val Kilmer swashbuckled with an easy, raffish charm that recalled both Han Solo and Kilmer's own work in *Top Secret*. And despite their limited screen time, Joanne Whalley, Patricia Hayes, and especially Jean Marsh managed to imbue their archetypal characters with heart and soul. (Even the baby actors are great!) Those kids who had only seen *Star Wars* on VHS (and who had yet to memorize every line from *The Princess Bride*) were utterly enchanted by *Willow* when it was released in 1988.

So why was *Willow* considered such a disappointment? Well, for one thing, the world expected a whole lot more from Lucas and director Ron Howard (who had already hit with *Splash* and *Cocoon*). Given the power that the *Star Wars* universe had on the collective imagination, it would be too much to expect Lucas to craft another fantastic tale with the same richness. But critics found the whole thing less classic than generic, a mishmash of familiar elements that lacked the magic and emotional pull of his famed trilogy, with a shortage of memorable dialogue and a pair of elven sidekicks who provided intrusive, incessant comic relief. (Lucas was famously stung by the bad reviews, but he probably didn't help himself by naming the main henchman "General Kael," after the legendary *New Yorker* critic Pauline Kael.) The public essentially agreed, and *Willow* was soon eclipsed at the box office by the likes of *Big*, *Who Framed Roger Rabbit*, and, uh, *Crocodile Dundee II*.

Willow failed to spawn the kind of cross-platform phenomenon Lucas and Howard probably hoped for, but it lingered in the hearts of a devoted cult that found it a guileless charmer rather than the soulless retread it was labeled in 1988. Those devotees may be rewarded in the near future, as Howard has said he'd love to make a sequel.

MARIE ANTOINETTE 2006

 **56%** | **Written and directed by** Sofia Coppola
Starring Kirsten Dunst, Jason Schwartzman, Rip Torn

Critics Consensus

Lavish imagery and a daring soundtrack set this film apart from most period dramas; in fact, style completely takes precedence over plot and character development in Coppola's vision of the doomed queen.

Synopsis

A stylized depiction of France's beautiful, pampered, and callous queen who was stripped of her riches and position and beheaded during the French Revolution that began in 1789.

Why We Love It

For her stylish rock 'n' roll directorial follow-up to Certified Fresh hits *Lost in Translation* and *Virgin Suicides*, Sofia Coppola once again tapped turn-of-the-millennium It-girl Kirsten Dunst, her *Suicides* star, to carry an exquisitely decadent film. The film was a triumph of style and auteurism. The daughter of a film dynasty, Coppola had rich examples for how to exercise artistic will, and boy did she exercise it. The outcome of her efforts on *Marie Antoinette* is vastly underappreciated.

In portraying one bold period, the film also captured a very specific moment and sensibility in film history: a time featuring the blasé swagger of Gen-X superstar film directors led by Quentin Tarantino, David Fincher, and Baz Luhrmann on the top end and snot-nosed punks like Spike Jonze, Wes Anderson, Edgar Wright, Paul Thomas Anderson, and Coppola herself on the upswing. These two groups were given almost free rein. (It's worth noting that though Coppola wasn't exactly in the very first wave of female directors kicking down doors, she was something of a unicorn in her own generation.)

Coppola again demonstrated her knack for casting and great taste in music. Along with Dunst, the film features Jason Schwartzman as Louis XVI, Jamie Dornan as the queen's lover, Tom Hardy as a member of court, Marianne Faithfull as Empress Maria Theresa, Rose Byrne as the Duchess of Polignac, Asia Argento as the Countess of Barry, the band Phoenix as court musicians, and the music of Bow Wow Wow, Siouxsie and the Banshees, The Cure, Aphex Twin, and The Strokes. Coppola showed her knack for collaboration in production, too: the film took home an Oscar for Best Achievement in Costume Design for the work of Milena Canonero (*Chariots of Fire*, *The Grand Budapest Hotel*).

Dunst tackled her character with aplomb, as you'd expect, portioning out naivete, insouciance, sexuality, and reverence for the queen's place in history as demanded by events unfolding on screen. With a flick of her brow, the talented young actress could telegraph all of the above at once. How critics didn't eat it up like so much delicious cake is beyond us.

LEGEND 1985

 **36%**

Directed by Ridley Scott
Written by William Hjortsberg
Starring Tom Cruise, Mia Sara, Tim Curry

Critics Consensus

Not even Ridley Scott's gorgeously realized set pieces can save *Legend* from its own tawdry tale, though it may be serviceable for those simply looking for fantasy eye candy.

Synopsis

Peasant boy Jack rallies an army of elves to stop an underworld prince from killing the last unicorns and plunging the world into eternal night. Jack must also rescue his great love, Princess Lili, from the demon's clutches.

Why We Love It

Ridley Scott's *Legend* was his own conception, which may explain the fantasy film's somewhat unmoored feel; it has no basis in mythology or classic fairy tales, and so it struggled to find an audience for the inhabitants of its magical realm.

In today's terms: it needed that bankable IP.

At the same time, the film offers an enchanting heroine in Lili, played by Mia Sara in her feature-film debut ahead of her career-defining role as Sloane Peterson in *Ferris Bueller's Day Off*. *Legend* was an intimate sword-and-sorcery tale that gave its damsel in distress almost as much responsibility for her own saving as her knight in, well, a grass-weave shorts set.

Donning the leafy pjs is twenty-two-year-old post–*Risky Business* Tom Cruise, which may have contributed to *Legend*'s negative reception. Critics (mostly male at the time) surely would have found it jarring that *Business*'s floor-sliding Joel, a.k.a. *The Outsiders*' Steve Randle and *Taps*' David Shawn, was now hopping around an enchanted forest, air filled with bubbles and dandelion fluff; spying on unicorns; keeping company with fairies, goblins, and leprechauns; and wearing glitter on his face and a skort. *This* was the actor's next choice?

How could anyone expect those graying critics to appreciate Scott's fairy tale and Cruise's sensitive charm in the heyday of Arnold Schwarzenegger and Sylvester Stallone, a time of *The Terminator*, *Rocky IV*, *Rambo: First Blood Part II*, and Scott's own *Blade Runner*? Where were the sixteen-year-old female YouTube stars who could have truly appreciated this iteration of Cruise?

Fantasy title *Ladyhawke*, from *Superman* director Richard Donner, also came out the same year but starred rugged Rutger Hauer as its male lead— Cruise was a skinny hipster by comparison—and buzzy *Scarface* moll Michelle Pfeiffer as his romantic interest. Critics gave it a big Fresh thumbs up, deeming it the superior of the two films. *Legend did* get nominated for an Oscar, however, for Best Makeup (Rob Bottin and Peter Robb-King). Fully deserved.

Tim Curry's at once bold and nuanced performance as demon Darkness is, alone, more than worth the viewing. One can only imagine what a remastered edition of the film, touched up with new-millennium credits and special effects, might look like. Fresh, most likely. Maybe even Certified.

MIAMI VICE 2006

 **46%**

Written and directed by Michael Mann
Starring Jamie Foxx, Colin Farrell, Gong Li, Naomie Harris, Ciarán Hinds, Justin Theroux

CRITIC: K. Austin Collins

K. Austin Collins is a film critic for *Vanity Fair*. His work has appeared in *Reverse Shot* and *The Ringer*.

Does Patti LaBelle know how essential she is to twenty-first-century American crime-movie auteurism? On the basis of one scene, no less. I'm talking about the sensual high point of Michael Mann's *Miami Vice*, a film that—for all its low-grade photography, cheese platter dialogue, and stilted action—is nevertheless a romance through and through, like much of Mann's work before it. It's a movie that I and many critics and filmmakers of my generation now love, which seems preordained: rewatching it even now confirms how purposefully it appeals to strange tastes, to people who can see through what makes it hokey toward the sad, soulful spirit at its core.

It's a strange film in that way—a sore sight, really, even to the most generous audience. And yet what's worst about it is also what's best. The Patti LaBelle scene in question—an impromptu detour to Cuba for mojitos undertaken by two would-be business partners who are about to embark on a risky affair that's even riskier than one of them realizes—is a case in point.

Moby's "One of These Mornings," sampling LaBelle's anthem of the same name, is the song that buoys the sequence and seems to summarize the entire movie. It is, like the men at the film's center, aspirational. Sonny Crockett (Colin Farrell) and Ricardo Tubbs (Jamie Foxx), detectives on Miami's vice squad, have gone undercover with a powerful drug organization after one of their former confidential informants was compromised, his family killed. None of the other agencies involved in the operation (the FBI, the DEA, and ICE) can be trusted with this assignment; the leak that got the CI killed came from within the operation. So, in stride Sonny and Ricky, posing as a pair of supremely talented drug smugglers in order to dickswing their way into the employ of the cartel in question. Sonny, with more than gathering intel on his mind, snuggles up to the cartel's financial advisor, Isabella (Gong Li), and gains her trust.

It's a twisty plot, overburdened with details and side-stories (white supremacist drug dealers! Cop-on-cop romance!) but pocked as well with dreamy asides, moments when Mann's men—Sonny, especially—look out into the distance toward some indeterminate future. This being a Mann movie, that future is something that hangs over the entire film with more melancholy than promise; even though sparks fire and the thrills get going, there's an anxious sadness to it all, just as there was in *Heat*, just as there was in *Manhunter*, in *Thief*.

It's a film that rides the tide of blink-and-you-miss-them apertures like these—throughlines,

> ## "WHAT'S WORST ABOUT IT IS ALSO WHAT'S BEST."

stylistic tics that cut straight to the heart of the movie if you're paying attention. And "One of These Mornings" is one such aperture; it gives the movie's melancholy its own soundtrack. It also, unmistakably, makes this a film of the aughts, and maybe that's part of what makes it so alienating. This is a film that wears its early digital hideousness and its completely washed musical taste on its sleeve with a blunt sense of defiance. It doesn't care that you think Jamie Foxx can't act; it knows it is camp. It doesn't care that you think it's a fantasy; it knows it's a fantasy.

And it does not care that you've seen better-looking movies, in the classical sense. *Miami Vice* was one of our earliest digital blockbusters, and there's something to be said for how confrontational its grainy blurriness begins to feel after two and a half hours. But under the thumb of Oscar-winning cinematographer Dion Beebe, who'd worked with Mann on *Collateral*, Mann's preference for high-definition digital video announced itself as not a substitute for film but a complete alternative to it, equipped with its own fluid aesthetic language and possibilities.

What we get here is a style we associate with documentary, which puts the campiness of the acting at such a disadvantage that it's no wonder people didn't—and still don't—know what to make of the movie. If what digital photography seems to capture is reality, the artifice of camp isn't left much room to seem appealing. It's stripped of what makes it cinematic; the images become testaments to its essential goofiness.

Mann was more equipped than most to make an art of that goofiness, to instill it with strange longing. He was an executive producer for *Miami Vice*, the series, for its entire 111-episode run in the 1980s. The movie, though, is more of his own thing. *Miami Vice* is equipped with everything that makes Mann's greatest films great, and much else besides—you just have to work a little to see it. But the other elements are all recognizable here. You sense that some of Farrell's coolness has drifted into the twenty-first century by way of Don Johnson, and that Foxx, running off at the mouth on occasion, has Philip Michael Thomas on his mind. The cast overall is fine; Trudy (Naomie Harris) and Jose (John Ortiz) make for strong secondary characters, and Ciarán Hinds, Justin Theroux, Isaach de Bankolé, John Hawkes, and Eddie Marsan all make something of their short screen time (especially Marsan, whose accent has to be one of the great movie mysteries of the century).

Manohla Dargis wrote in the *New York Times* that the film "made me think more about how new technologies are irrevocably changing our sense of what movies look like than any film I've seen this year." It isn't a bad film. But it is unabashedly an experiment that has, over time, emerged as the historical curiosity it was always bound to be.

I've sometimes wondered whether, were it made in the early aughts instead of the mid 1990s, Mann's beloved *Heat* would be the muscular, pristine thriller that we all think it is, or whether—filmed digitally, with Mann's taste for icky yellow industrial lighting and the overbearing thwump of emotive rock—*Heat*,

> **"*MIAMI VICE* IS EQUIPPED WITH EVERYTHING THAT MAKES MANN'S GREATEST FILMS GREAT, AND MUCH ELSE BESIDES— YOU JUST HAVE TO WORK A LITTLE TO SEE IT."**

too, would be revealed for the cheese fest it is. *Heat*, like *Miami Vice*, leans into its corniness. Suffice it to say, then, that it got lucky. It may have gotten the 35mm, blockbuster-era treatment, but in so many ways, these films are the same, built of the same masculine melancholy. The times are what changed. The constant is Mann's willingness to reflect them.

Rotten Tomatoes' Critics Consensus *Miami Vice* is beautifully shot, but the lead characters lack the charisma of their TV series counterparts, and the underdeveloped story is well below the standards of Michael Mann's better films.

CULT LEADERS

Hard to Love for Many, Loved Very Hard by Some

Cult classics happen mostly by accident. When Faye Dunaway showed up to set back in 1981 and bellowed that now-infamous line—"No wire hangers!"—she was under the impression she was contributing to a serious-minded portrait of Joan Crawford; she didn't expect to inspire generations of drag queens. A decade and a half later, the filmmakers behind *Empire Records* made a movie they hoped would connect with disaffected mid-'90s teens, likely unaware that those kids would hold onto it tightly into adulthood. In 2001, as writers David Wain and Michael Showalter watched their goofy comedy *Wet Hot American Summer* tank with critics and at the box office, they never could have expected the film would become so popular one day that Netflix would ask them to make a prequel series. Cult films like these don't always find an audience immediately, but by some happy accident—or the serendipitous positioning of a VHS case on a Blockbuster shelf—an audience eventually finds them. It's a devoted audience, too, one often made of people whose tastes lie on the margins of the mainstream. (And finding a movie to love and others who love it as much as you do can be a reminder that you're not so marginal after all.) The films in this chapter range from the "cult classics" that defined the term (LGBTQ favorites like *Valley of the Dolls*, *Mommie Dearest*) to newer titles that have found their tribes online (like the Will Forte comedy *MacGruber*, which Chicago critic Nathan Rabin writes on, and teen witch flick *The Craft*, in which *Empire* editor-in-chief Terri White finds a thrilling feminist rage). These are the films that live on in yearly Halloween costumes and at riotous midnight screenings, in widely shared GIFs, and deep in the hearts of their cultishly devoted fans—regardless of how splat-worthy critics may think they are.

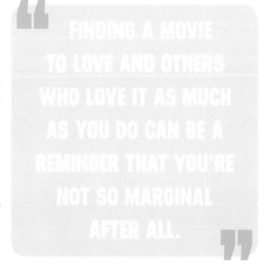

"FINDING A MOVIE TO LOVE AND OTHERS WHO LOVE IT AS MUCH AS YOU DO CAN BE A REMINDER THAT YOU'RE NOT SO MARGINAL AFTER ALL."

WET HOT AMERICAN SUMMER 2001

 36%

Directed by David Wain
Written by Michael Showalter and David Wain
Starring Michael Showalter, Janeane Garofalo, Michael Ian Black, Paul Rudd, Ken Marino, Elizabeth Banks, Marguerite Moreau, David Hyde Pierce, Amy Poehler, Bradley Cooper

Critics Consensus

Wet Hot American Summer's incredibly talented cast is too often outmatched by a deeply silly script that misses its targets at least as often as it skewers them.

Synopsis

It's the last day of camp in the summer of 1981, and a host of horny counselors try to hook up—oh, and save the planet from a space station barreling towards Earth—before heading back to reality.

Why We Love It

If you had told a fan of this flop upon its release that one of its stars would become an Oscar winner (Bradley Cooper), another a TV power player (Amy Poehler), and yet another a friggin' superhero (Paul Rudd), they wouldn't have believed you. (That those three *Wet Hot* alums would grace the same stage at the 91st Academy Awards? Also mind-boggling.) In fact, back in the early aughts, referencing this loopy spoof of randy camping flicks like *Meatballs* was something of a badge of honor, an indication to fellow devotees that you, too, dig fucked-up, askew comedy (at least when it's this good).

The culture did eventually catch onto *Wet Hot* (it spawned two Netflix series, and there was even talk of a sitcom spin-off for Fox). But in 2001, it was a cult film in the truest sense: misunderstood by many who saw it, unnoticed by everyone else (tons of people, with less than $300,000 in box-office pull), and an absolutely acquired taste. How acquired? Basically, if you don't find the idea of a can of mixed vegetables talking about sucking his own dick or children cheering on a grown man to hump a refrigerator funny, this movie is not for you.

Wet Hot's polarizing nature is by design. The comedy's director and cowriter, David Wain, said in an interview that film has an ethos similar to the one laid out in the lyrics of off-Broadway musical *[title of show]* (yes, that's the name): "I'd rather be nine people's favorite thing / Than a hundred people's ninth favorite thing." And despite nearly universal disregard upon its release, it eventually became a *lot* of people's favorite thing, including Kristen Bell, who gushed during a segment on NPR that the film is her all-time number one.

If *Wet Hot* is your cup of tea, the absurdist spoils are everywhere. There's a running joke about dead campers, complete with a bit where a kid drowns while counselors (Paul Rudd and Elizabeth Banks) make out; some crafty non sequiturs, including a gateway-drug montage where the gang (among them, Poehler, Michael Showalter, Michael Ian Black, and Janeane Garofalo) head to town only to graduate from sneaking smokes to robbing an elderly woman for heroin money; and did we mention the courtship between Molly Shannon's recent divorcee and one of her prepubescent students? What's more, Wain and Showalter's script is a veritable assault of quotable dirty lines (a brief sample: "I want you inside me," "I'm gonna go fondle my sweaters," and "my butt itches").

It's a weird, wonderful stew, with an ensemble comprising the cast of MTV sketch show *The State* and an impressive array of future comedic and dramatic big deals, the sort of dumb movie only very smart movie-makers could cook up. For proof, there's even a DVD audio commentary track that's *solely* composed of fart noises, a move that flaunts its own kind of silly-yet-brilliant defiance.

BUT I'M A CHEERLEADER 1999

 **39%**

Directed by Jamie Babbit
Written by Brian Wayne Peterson and Jamie Babbit
Starring Natasha Lyonne, Clea DuVall, Cathy Moriarty, Bud Cort, Eddie Cibrian, RuPaul

Critics Consensus

Too broad to make any real statements, *But I'm a Cheerleader* isn't as sharp as it should be, but a charming cast and surprisingly emotional center may bring enough pep for viewers looking for a light social satire.

Synopsis

Cheerleader Megan thinks she's straight, but her parents send her to a gay conversion camp, where she meets a strong-willed young woman and, ironically, only then begins questioning her sexuality.

Why We Love It

Long before mainstream America was aware that gay children were being sent away to be reprogrammed straight, Jamie Babbit *went* there with *But I'm a Cheerleader*. It had made a splash at film festivals because it was the rare queer film that dared to take a comic angle to the pain of being ostracized from your family, friends, and community because of your sexual orientation. For that reason, the film was put under the magnifying glass, expected to be representative of the gay community at large. But what piece of art can handle that pressure?

Critics wanted either a funnier or more dramatic movie but didn't understand Babbit's subversive style, which buried real, heavy trauma in cotton-candy colors to make it both more palatable for straight audiences and more cathartic for gay viewers who needed a light laugh after two decades of the AIDS crisis. Gemma Files writing for Film.com said the film was full of "ungainly sentiment and unnecessary stylization," while Owen Gleiberman writing for *Entertainment Weekly* went as far as to say, "Any self-respecting lesbian should rear up in horror." (Note: Gleiberman is not himself a lesbian.) Only Roger Ebert was able to nail just what would make this film so enduringly beloved: "*But I'm a Cheerleader* is not a great, breakout comedy, but more the kind of movie that might eventually become a regular on the midnight cult circuit. It feels like an amateur night version of itself, awkward, heartfelt and sweet."

Behind the scenes, Babbit was fighting an uphill battle just to get the film distributed; the MPAA gave it an NC-17 rating, and she had to cut out three innocuous shots whose hetero analogs would swim past the censors with no problems. Those who called for edgier humor in the film likely weren't aware how thin a line Babbit was walking to get any gay-centric content in the theaters at all. Still, what *is* there is memorable and even more affecting in hindsight because it's raw and honest; all the absurd things these characters are saying could have been said in real life.

Even now, twenty years after its release, *But I'm a Cheerleader* stands as a pioneering achievement in queer cinema, when other filmmakers are just feeling comfortable enough to create works that don't simply depict the pain of being gay but also the joy of knowing who you are.

48%

Directed by Jorma Taccone
Written by Will Forte, John Solomon, Jorma Taccone
Starring Will Forte, Kristen Wiig, Ryan Phillippe, Powers Boothe, Maya Rudolph

CRITIC: Nathan Rabin

Nathan Rabin is a former staff writer for The A.V Club and The Dissolve and the proprietor of Nathan Rabin's Happy Place. He's also the author of eight books, including *You Don't Know Me But You Don't Like Me* and *Weird Al: The Book* (with Al Yankovic).

Saturday Night Live may be a prestigious, awards- and accolades-strewn cultural institution, yet it has often served as a critical and popular punching bag. No aspect of the show has endured as much derision as its once-prolific and now seemingly shuttered film division. True, without *Saturday Night Live*'s forays into cinema, there would be no *Blues Brothers* or *Wayne's World* movie adaptations, but Lorne Michaels's venerable comedy machine's movie wing is more often associated with the opportunistic, bottom-feeding likes of *It's Pat: The Movie* and *Night at the Roxbury*. When someone says something looks like it could be a *Saturday Night Live* movie, they rarely mean it in a positive way.

So it is not surprising that when the *Saturday Night Live* movie machine returned in 2010 with a feature-film adaptation of a series of micro-sketches parodying *MacGyver,* a TV show whose run ended in 1992, the critical response was less than ecstatic. A.O. Scott of the *New York Times* sneered that *MacGruber* was "a film that poses a philosophical question fundamental to our inquiry here, namely: 'Why does this exist?'" Andrew Pulver of the *Guardian* jeered, "Only the merest hint of amusement is to be found in this uninspired latest effusion from the conveyor belt that is *Saturday Night Live.*"

Great satire often has the misfortune to be dismissed and mistaken for what it's satirizing.

And so, from a critical—if not a creative— standpoint, *MacGruber* might have suffered from looking and feeling exactly like the explosions-filled, testosterone-poisoned Jerry Bruckheimer blockbusters that were just as much the targets of its parody as the Richard Dean Anderson television program about the Rube Goldberg of crime-fighting.

Director Jorma Taccone surrounds his co-screen-writer and star Will Forte—who is ultraconvincing as

> ## "GREAT SATIRE OFTEN HAS THE MISFORTUNE TO BE DISMISSED AND MISTAKEN FOR WHAT IT'S SATIRIZING."

the world's biggest, least likable douchebag—with fellow *Saturday Night Live* ringers Kristen Wiig and Maya Rudolph, who play women unfortunate enough to discover that the film's demented anti-hero is as terrible and selfish at making love as he is at doing everything else. Otherwise, though, Taccone's commitment to verisimilitude sees him stocking the film with the kind of stone-faced serious actors you would find in the non-satirical version of this story.

The great Powers Boothe brings craggy tough-guy authority to the key role of the stoic-but-trusting mentor who has absolute faith in our anti-hero (despite him being a lethal threat to anyone cursed to be in his orbit). Ryan Phillippe, meanwhile, makes for a terrific, understated straight man as MacGruber's second-in-command, a qualified super-soldier who quickly discovers that the throat-ripping titular maniac views the agents around him as, alternately, cannon fodder, human targets, and sexual objects. Val Kilmer is a smirking delight as the movie's villain.

Taccone mastered the art of parody and pastiche in multiple forms and mediums as one-third of Berkeley-founded comedy troupe Lonely Island. (The group, which also includes Andy Samberg and Akiva Schaffer, gave us the hit comedy song "I'm on a Boat," among others.) He brings that gift to *MacGruber,* a film that shares Lonely Island's genius for delivering sublimely scatological silliness in a deceptively smart, subversive way. So along with all of the lowbrow, screamingly vulgar, and laugh-out-loud funny gags involving ghost sex and celery being stuck in unconventional places, there is a scathingly satirical takedown of action cinema's deification of alpha males and cult of unexamined machismo.

MacGruber boasts a hero who is probably, when it comes down to it, worse than most villains as it relates to cowardice, pettiness, and needless deaths caused through carelessness and stupidity. Throughout the film, we get subversive little glimpses into MacGruber's fractured psyche that suggest he's not just unhealthily cocky in conventional action-hero terms but also deeply unhinged, and not in a benign, casualty-free fashion, either.

Still, *MacGruber* is blessed throughout with a joyful sense of play. The film is child-like in the best sense, even as its titular emotionally stunted man-child embodies the worst aspects of childhood with his inability to look beyond his own selfish immediate urges and needs. It's poetically apt that a movie about a guy who can theoretically make useful contraptions out of random detritus is defined by a deceptive, impressive level of comic invention.

As A.O. Scott suggested in his pan, *MacGruber*

"WILL FORTE IS ULTRACONVINCING AS THE WORLD'S BIGGEST, LEAST LIKEABLE DOUCHEBAG."

may not have much of a reason to exist. That only makes its existence even more of a sublime, improbably sustained cosmic joke. *MacGruber* probably never should have even made it to air on *Saturday Night Live* given the perverse untimeliness of its satirical subject, but thank God that ridiculous series of sketches did make it to prime time and that it led to an even more transcendently ridiculous film adaptation.

Critics and moviegoers (who overwhelmingly stayed home rather than pay good money for what looked like a one-joke movie from an entertainment institution not exactly known for quality control or consistency) might have deemed *MacGruber* Rotten upon its release, but to its ever-growing army of cultists, it gets Fresher and more hilarious every year.

Rotten Tomatoes' Critics Consensus It too often mistakes shock value for real humor, but *MacGruber* is better than many *SNL* films—and better than it probably should be.

VALLEY OF THE DOLLS 1967

 **33%**

Directed by Mark Robson
Written by Dorothy Kingsley and Helen Deutsch
Starring Barbara Parkins, Patty Duke, Sharon Tate, Paul Burke, Lee Grant, Susan Hayward

Critics Consensus

Trashy, campy, soapy, and melodramatic, *Valley of the Dolls* may be a dud as a Hollywood exposé but has nonetheless endured as a kitsch classic.

Synopsis

Three women take different paths to the entertainment industry in the mid-1960s, but an air of drugs, vanity, and desperation haunts them wherever they go. Each comes to a dramatic realization about the price of fame.

Why We Love It

Before there was John Waters or *The Room* or *Showgirls*, there was *Valley of the Dolls*. By the mid-1960s, women's power in Hollywood was waning. All those big, bright stars like Bette Davis, Joan Crawford, and Judy Garland (who was fired from *Valley* and replaced with Susan Hayward) who had buoyed the industry during the studio era had been tossed to the wayside as male-centric stories dominated the box office. *Valley of the Dolls* was a meta-statement on the disposability of women and also a vehicle for those women to tear down the walls in one last hoorah.

Buried in the camp is one of the more enigmatic performances of Lee Grant, who would go on right after this film to win an Oscar for *In the Heat of the Night*. Here, though, she's mysterious and manipulative, selling alluringly strange lines like, "At night, all cats are gray," taking a 1546 John Heywood proverb and turning it into a searing Dorothy Parker takedown.

Patty Duke as Neely O'Hara delivers the biggest performance of the film, goaded on by director Mark Robson, who encouraged over-the-top outbursts rather than more subtle line reads. She snarls and stumbles, hollering at her husband, whom she's just found cheating on her in a pool. And yet Neely's narrative is plummy compared to that of Sharon Tate's Jennifer North, a kind of version of Tate herself who's naïve and willing to please, ensnared in the drama of more powerful, cunning people. Because this film is supposed to be a cautionary tale, like an after-school special on crack, Jennifer's fate tends toward the seedier side of things, involving such taboo subjects as porn long before that topic had been touched in the mainstream.

This film is the definition of camp—a serious attempt at drama that moves from horribly awry to terrifically right. And its impact is lasting. Without this monstrously melodramatic adaptation, we might have been deprived of a generation of drag queens inspired by the scenery-chewing female stars who relegate their male counterparts to unmemorable, furniture-in-the-room roles.

DEATH BECOMES HER 1992

 **52%**

Directed by Robert Zemeckis
Written by Martin Donovan and David Koepp
Starring Goldie Hawn, Meryl Streep, Bruce Willis, Isabella Rossellini

Critics Consensus

Hawn and Streep are as fabulous as the innovative special effects; Zemeckis's satire, on the other hand, is as hollow as the world it mocks.

Synopsis

Madeline Ashton and Helen Sharp have been rivals since youth; their bitter feud reaches new heights when each comes across an elixir that restores their youth and makes them immortal.

Why We Love It

The biggest innovations in special effects usually come to us courtesy of blockbuster action and fantasy films: think of the liquid menace of the T-1000 in *Terminator 2: Judgment Day*, the car-crushing T-Rex in *Jurassic Park*, or the pioneering motion-capture work showcased in *The Lord of the Rings* films and *Avatar*. And yet one of the biggest effects game-changers of the 1990s—one that pre-dated *Jurassic Park* and whose innovations would impact that movie—was a simple black comedy in which the only monsters to be found were a glammed-up Meryl Streep and Goldie Hawn.

In *Death Becomes Her*, the two play bitter rivals: Streep, an aging movie star desperately clinging to youth, and Hawn, a famous writer desperately clinging to her beef with her more glamorous frenemy. Both, for some inexplicable reason, are drawn to a dweeby plastic surgeon named Ernest (Bruce Willis). Like a WWE wrestling match, though, the storyline is irrelevant; you come here for the fight, and Zemeckis and his stars deliver. The fact that the two women are, for much of the movie, immortal lets the director off the leash, and the images that Industrial Light & Magic conjure are unforgettable. At one point, Streep's head is twisted around to the back following a plummet down a staircase; later, having been shot at close-range with a shotgun, Hawn emerges from a fountain with a mammoth "hole in my stomach!" Streep bends down to take a peek right through her.

At the time it was never-seen-before stuff, and it holds up.

What also holds up are the performances, with Hawn and Streep having so much fun out-diva-ing each other, you can almost hear RuPaul somewhere on set encouraging them to "scenery chew for your life!" Unsurprisingly, the film has become a favorite among the LGBTQ community. It's not just the drag-ready glam and *big* diva antics (though it is definitely that). The story is also tinged with tragedy. Here are two sad and lonely women, outwardly glamorous and successful, still compelled to butcher themselves and each other for the world's approval. For men's approval.

They're fighting an unfair fight in an unfair world. For anyone who's been pinned down for most of their lives, that's a battle they've fought before.

XANADU 1980

 **24%**

Directed by Robert Greenwald
Written by Richard Christian Danus and Marc Reid Rubel
Starring Olivia Newton-John, Gene Kelly, Michael Beck

Critics Consensus

Not even spandex and over-the-top musical numbers can save *Xanadu* from questionable acting, unimpressive effects, and a story unencumbered by logic.

Synopsis

Sonny dreams of leaving the rat race to achieve fame as an artist. One day, he receives a kiss from a mysterious stranger on roller skates who is actually a muse and meets a clarinet-playing dreamer who becomes his new business partner. (Yes, it takes enormous effort to not think this is a fake summary.)

Why We Love It

Imagine a world where pieces of a shredded watercolor painting floating on the breeze are so powerful that they cause a sidewalk mural of alluring women to come to life and start dancing. Such is *Xanadu*. The story takes so many odd leaps—nay, pirouettes—one must drape themself in a flouncy pastel dress of suspended disbelief and enjoy the (roller skate) ride.

Instead of making a standard "boy meets girl" story, the filmmakers created a "boy falls in love with strange girl on roller skates, finds out she's Zeus's daughter, skates defiantly around Venice Boulevard, and opens a roller-skating rink/nightclub" fever dream. By throwing cinematic supernovas Olivia Newton-John and the legendary Gene Kelly into a plot as wild as this, the filmmakers didn't give us coherent, nuanced storytelling but rather a wildly unique journey—a completely bonkers blast.

Xanadu doffs its cap to musicals of yesteryear but douses them in glitter and animated neon accents to make it delightfully 1980s. Kelly gets his moment to do some old-fashioned soft shoe, but then the movie transitions him into roller skates and gives him a shopping montage focused mostly on peach zoot suits. With a hit soundtrack and a hero that launches himself headfirst into that magical mural on a hunch it will lead him to Olympus, *Xanadu* gives us an opportunity to let the madness of youth and dreams roll through our hearts.

GUMMO 1997

 **35%** | **Written and directed by** Harmony Korine
Starring Jacob Sewell, Nick Sutton, Jacob Reynolds, Chloë Sevigny

CRITIC: Eric Kohn

Eric Kohn is the New York–based executive editor and chief critic at IndieWire. He also launched the Critics Academy initiative, a series of educational workshops for aspiring journalists, and teaches film criticism at New York University.

Although 2012's *Spring Breakers* may have introduced new fans to Harmony Korine's unique combination of rebellious posturing and poignant imagery, *Gummo* got there a long time ago. Reviled at the time of its release, the movie has been validated with time and provides an essential backdrop to the inspired wackiness that Korine had in store. While *Spring Breakers* gangster Alien mused "Look at all my shit!" as a defiant celebration of his material goods, *Gummo* digs into the exuberant lives of people with nothing left.

It's also a beautiful mess, loaded with macabre and disturbing tangents designed to make viewers uncomfortable and maybe even a bit restless. Believe it or not, this controversial portrait of a small town and its eccentric locals has sincerity buried beneath its prankish surface. When it hit theaters in 1997, many critics found *Gummo* appalling, in part because they had never been exposed to the reckless oddballs it portrayed and considered them crass exaggerations. Many reviews ragged on the movie for gawking at lost souls. But who was really gawking? *Gummo* is a magical portrait of people living on the margins of society and displays a striking willingness to empathize with their insular existence.

Fifteen years before Korine's candy-colored Florida odyssey *Spring Breakers*, the screenwriter's directorial debut unleashed an extraordinary collage of diverse people enmeshed in surreal activities as they moved aimlessly through some ruined corner of a broken world. Nashville stands in for the film's setting of Xenia, Ohio, but it's really Anytown, USA.

While Korine's *Kids* script stood out for its realistic depiction of raunchy New York teens, *Gummo* depicts the same kind of outsider energy with a more liberating, scattershot approach. The result is an immersive mashup of heavy-metal samples and operatic rock, sloppy vaudeville performances, and meandering riffs on sexuality, race, even death. The movie careens from one offbeat moment to the next, as if cycling through social media clips all captured in the same distinctive locale. The director's lush depiction of colorful outsiders, with faces and attitudes unfamiliar in much of American cinema,

> ## "*GUMMO* DIGS INTO THE EXUBERANT LIVES OF PEOPLE WITH NOTHING LEFT."

has accrued more value as the country wakes up to its many underrepresented people. No matter how much it was shunned upon its release, *Gummo* was ahead of its time.

Korine does his part to orient viewers up top. The soft-spoken teen Solomon (Jacob Reynolds) recalls the destructive impact of a tornado that tore the town to bits; in its wake, weary young locals wander through the wreckage with casual indifference, as if liberated from the constraints of an adult society that left them behind. From there, *Gummo* barrels through a series of vignettes, some more fleshed out than others, assembled in a naturalistic setting tinged with absurdist flourishes.

These mini-adventures are alternately mesmerizing, tiresome, and transcendent—but also rich with sociological implications. Disaffected kids Solomon and his pal Tummler (Nick Sutton) roam the landscape with BB guns, casually murdering cats around the neighborhood and selling them to a local Chinese restaurant; elsewhere, a trio of sisters (including rising star Chloë Sevigny, Korine's girlfriend at the time) goof around in their bedroom and later deter the advances of a local pedophile; and a group of burly white men engage in drunken arm-wrestling, but the strongest of them finds himself defeated by the African American little person with whom they're hanging out! Each instance hints at intriguing ideas about the nature of these characters and the conditions that seem to mandate their behavior.

Korine could have been guilty of crude exploitation if the movie didn't exhibit a blatant affection for its ensemble. In one potentially upsetting moment, a man pimps his mentally handicapped sister to Solomon and Tummler, but rather than building to a grotesque punchline, Korine arrives at an unexpectedly sweet encounter between the scrawny, wide-eyed Tummler and the unnamed woman as they lock eyes and exchange pleasantries. The sordid conditions lead to the unexpected glimmer of warmth.

The wandering voiceover often lands on captivating observations. "I knew a guy who was dyslexic, but he was also cross-eyed, so everything came out right," muses Tummler, and the memorable line becomes the movie's mission statement. Watching *Gummo* is like gazing at a Magic Eye Puzzle: disorienting and inscrutable at first, until its underlying significance comes into focus. By the time it arrives at a dizzying conclusive montage, set to Roy Orbison's "Crying," Korine has invented a fresh rhythm for expressing the complex emotions at the center of each frame.

The movie's central figure doesn't say a word, but he's a visual for the ages: a young boy (Jacob Sewell) wearing giant pink bunny ears stumbles across grimy parking lots and peers at traffic from a nondescript bridge. In one beguiling sequence, he lazily toys with an accordion while sitting on the toilet. As the movie veers from one vignette to the next, it often returns to this silent witness, as he becomes a kind of mute Greek chorus for the movie's central motifs. With time, the Bunny Boy has become an iconic embodiment of America's grittier counterculture, at once eager to stand out in the crowd and exiled by the so-called adults in the room. (More than one *Gummo* acolyte sports a Bunny Boy tattoo; find them on Instagram.)

Despite its somber atmosphere, *Gummo* isn't afraid to have fun. In one of the movie's more endearing sequences, an energetic widow (the great Linda Manz) digs out her late husband's tap shoes and dances around her scrawny son while he attempts an exuberant workout routine with silverware. Later, she feeds him a messy plate of pasta while he sits in the bathtub. It's no wonder the sequence won over director Werner Herzog, who became a rare *Gummo* superfan at the time of its release: the movie feels like a spiritual cousin to the idiosyncratic character studies that define Herzog's earlier work (particularly *Even Dwarves Started Small*) more than anything in the American movie scene that found *Gummo* so off-putting when it emerged.

Alternately tragic, hilarious, and profound,

> # "THE DIRECTOR'S LUSH DEPICTION OF COLORFUL OUTSIDERS . . . HAS ACCRUED MORE VALUE AS THE COUNTRY WAKES UP TO ITS MANY UNDER-REPRESENTED PEOPLE."

Gummo is a transformative attempt to mine ingenuity from a medium that so often sags into conventionality. Korine's freewheeling assemblage of everyday malaise and rambunctious behavior encourages you to cringe, then contemplate the impulse behind that very response. It's a timeless lesson about tolerance dressed up in bad-boy clothing, and it only grows wiser with age.

Rotten Tomatoes' Critics Consensus *Gummo*'s bold provocations may impress more iconoclastically inclined viewers, but others will find it hard to see past Harmony Korine's overwhelmingly sour storytelling perspective.

THE LAST DRAGON 1985

 **59%**

Directed by Michael Schultz
Written by Louis Venosta
Starring Taimak, Vanity, Christopher Murney, Julius Carry, Faith Prince, Keshia Knight Pulliam

Critics Consensus

The Last Dragon is a flamboyant genre mashup brimming with style, romance, and an infectious fondness for Kung Fu, but audiences may find the tonal whiplash more goofy than endearing.

Synopsis

A young Kung Fu novice in New York City searches for the "master" to obtain the supreme level of martial arts mastery known as "the glow." Along the way, he must fight a villainous Kung Fu expert and rescue and woo a beautiful singer from a maniacal music promoter.

Why We Love It

Putting Berry Gordy's name before the title didn't do *The Last Dragon* any favors in 1985. The Motown Kingmaker had a reputation for authoritarianism, and placing a producer's name so prominently before the credits allowed contemporary critics to dismiss the film as a vanity project from a musician who thought he knew how to make movies. But, directed by Michael Schultz, who helmed *Cooley High* and *Car Wash*, this genre mashup of Kung Fu flick and rom-com was a passion project in the best possible way. The film tapped into the ethos of every successful martial arts film before it: heart.

In what has to be the most commercial version of "Blasian" cinema, *The Last Dragon* borrows from and pays tribute to *Black Samurai, Black Belt Jones, The Black Dragon*, and, of course, everything that Bruce Lee ever did on screen—all reimagined with a black protagonist. Our *Last Dragon* hero, Leroy Green, played by stuntman-turned-actor Taimak, had deadly fighting skills to match his charisma. Green walks directly into danger due to a sense of obligation, not for revenge or even for personal gain; his is a higher cause, and that's why we and leading lady Laura fall head over heels for him.

The film's many homages to older works, its at-times cartoonish acting, and its very quotable dialogue are the delightful foundations upon which cult classics are built. It rightfully still occupies a space in the pop-culture lexicon ("Whose house is this? Sho-Nuff! I said who's the baddest? Sho-nuff!") and is a favorite at midnight screenings. It is particularly cherished in the African American community: Busta Rhymes, Wu Tang Clan, *Insecure*, and Boots Riley's 2018 absurdist dark comedy *Sorry to Bother You* have all paid homage to *The Last Dragon*.

The ultimate product of the MTV generation—complete with an aging Cyndi Lauper wannabe—*The Last Dragon* intermixes music-video breaks between *occasionally* impressive fight scenes. Perhaps that mix of *Purple Rain* and B-movie *Karate Kid* is why many critics didn't think much of it, but the triumphant ending, highlighted by some unmistakably 1980s CG, makes it shine—or rather, *glow*.

EMPIRE RECORDS 1995

 **29%**

Directed by Allan Moyle
Written by Carol Heikkinen
Starring Liv Tyler, Ethan Embry, Rory Cochrane, Robin Tunney, Renée Zellweger, Anthony LaPaglia

Critics Consensus

Despite a terrific soundtrack and a strong early performance from Renée Zellweger, *Empire Records* is mostly a silly and predictable teen dramedy.

Synopsis

The music-loving employees of Empire Records band together to save their store from a corporate takeover, even as secret crushes and long-building resentments threaten to tear them apart. Oh, and it's Rex Manning Day.

Why We Love It

Video may have killed the radio star, but it saved *Empire Records*. Allan Moyle's movie was a theatrical bomb by any measure, released onto just eighty-seven screens and making $151,000 in its first weekend before disappearing from theaters fourteen days later. And yet speak to any nineties kids worth their salt, and they'll be able to quote multiple *Empire* lines ("Shock me, shock me with that deviant behavior!"), recite the soundtrack listing, and tell you the date of Rex Manning Day (it's April 8). At some point, they probably had the movie's iconic poster, with a be-skirted Liv Tyler front and center, stuck to their wall. And it's all thanks to the VHS.

The road to cult classic for *Empire Records* cut through the video store. In the "Comedy" aisles of Blockbusters across the land, many curious teens were introduced to the single-day story of Gina, A.J., Corey, and the rest of the crew's efforts to prevent a Towers Records–style company from taking over their shop and, of course, discover themselves in the process. Something seriously clicked about the movie. It wasn't necessarily the cool kids—the kind of music snobs who actually *worked* at Empire Records—who fell in love with it; instead, it was the kids who wanted to be like them, who thought that the Cranberries were still cutting-edge and that shaving your head Sinead-style was still the ultimate act of rebellion. Kids who thought the line "What's with today, today?" was profound. Kids who were playing catch-up.

They were also kids with taste, it turns out. Dismissed by critics at the time, *Empire* is as endearing a slice of teen life as some of its more celebrated contemporaries.

The characters are what we might call today (or five years ago, maybe) "totally adorkable," especially Ethan Embry's goofy Mark. The save-the-store plot gives everything a nice sense of urgency and optimism (this was the era in which Tower and Borders posed a greater threat to small business than cell phones and Kindles, and movies like *Empire* and *You've Got Mail* romanticized the struggle). And where the script wobbles, the performances elevate—particularly a young Renée Zellweger as Gina, who seems to have it all together until she really doesn't.

Writer Carol Heikkinen is apparently working on a Broadway musical version of her film. The cool kids might roll their eyes at the thought—musicals are as uncool as Rex Manning, right?—but we'll be there opening night.

BURLESQUE 2010

 36% | Written and directed by Steve Antin
Starring Christina Aguilera, Cher, Stanley Tucci, Kristen Bell, Cam Gigandet, Eric Dane

Critics Consensus

Campy and clichéd, *Burlesque* wastes its talented cast (including a better-than-expected Christina Aguilera) on a movie that wavers uncertainly between *bad* and *so bad it's good*.

Synopsis

Aspiring small-town singer Ali finds herself quickly leaping from cocktail waitress to lead performer at a burlesque club when she moves to L.A. While club owner Tess spies star potential in Ali, not everyone is happy there's a new girl in town.

Why We Love It

The *How Did This Get Made* podcast—Paul Scheer, June Diane Raphael, and Jason Mantzoukas's bi-weekly breakdown of a single and singularly "bad" film—chose *Burlesque* as the focus of its very first episode. Digging into the musical's particular brand of badness less than a month after the film was released in late 2010, the hosts wondered whether the movie might have been stronger had the filmmakers gone harder, leaned into its trashiness, and produced something R-rated rather than PG-13. Something a bit more like the so-bad-it's-revered *Showgirls*.

With respect to that trio, and with the benefit of nearly a decade's worth of hindsight, we're all in on *Burlesque* precisely *because* it took the earnest, rosy-eyed PG-13 approach, just like its singular protagonist. There's something hugely endearing about the wink-free way with which this L.A. dreamer story is told; the way the actors—a game Christina Aguilera as the plucky soft-focus heroine, Ali; Cher as the sassy den mother, Tess; and especially Kristen Bell as the bitchy and territorial rival dancer, Nikki—commit. It means that writer-director Steve Antin's ludicrous dialogue lands squarely in the zone of memorable camp, as when Stanley Tucci's Sean asks what "Ali" is short for and, upon hearing the answer, says with a Cheshire-cat–like grin: "Alice? Well, welcome to Wonderland."

It's moments like that for which you entered this darkened club, with its sequins and top hats and come-hither gyrations. And perhaps the most delicious moment comes from Bell's Nikki when she declares, "I will not be upstaged by some slut with mutant lungs." And to be fair, when you hear Aguilera belt out the finale, you'll see the latter part of that insult is not an ill-fitting description.

You also came to hear that voice and the music, of course, and the soundtrack has endured for good reason: just try to resist the urge to shimmy to closing number "Show Me How You Burlesque," cowritten by Aguilera. Perhaps unsurprisingly, it's Cher, though, who runs away with the movie, belting out the Diane Warren–penned ballad "You Haven't Seen the Last of Me" in the film's most somber moment as Tess battles with potentially losing her beloved club. Actress and character merge as the song builds and that deep Cher voice soars. It's enough to make even a trio of cynical podcasters weep. Or, at least, we would have thought so.

THE CRAFT 1996

 **57%**

Directed by Andrew Fleming
Written by Peter Filardi and Andrew Fleming
Starring Robin Tunney, Fairuza Balk, Neve Campbell, Rachel True, Skeet Ulrich, Christine Taylor, Breckin Meyer

CRITIC: Terri White

Terri White is the editor-in-chief of the U.K.-based film magazine *Empire* and launched the magazine *Pilot TV*. She was previously the editor-in-chief of *Time Out New York* and executive editor of *Life & Style Weekly*.

The nineties' teen movies were movies of very specific teens. More expressly: of very specific teen *girls*. Rich, pouty, selfish, draped in barely-there designer clothes, and parented from a distance by fifty-somethings with shared perma-tans and martini habits. If these teen girls were burdened by anything, it was their overwhelming popularity and abundance of hair. *Clueless*, released into cinemas in the autumn of 1995, exemplified this more than any other film of the ilk and of the era. But just seven months later came a movie that completely upended cinematic teen tropes. And more than just simply toying with the form, it tangled with the specific type of teen girl in movies that nineties audiences had come to know. That film was *The Craft*.

The blonde narcissists of *The Craft* aren't the lead characters; they're the enemies of the four girls at the heart of the film. And our protagonists are more than just teenage girls; they're witches: a name, an identity historically given to women who exist outside of society's rules and norms. Here it's a title reclaimed by Nancy (Fairuza Balk), Bonnie (Neve Campbell), Rochelle (Rachel True), and Sarah (Robin Tunney).

What draws them together initially is their status as outsiders, as freaks ("we are the weirdos, mister," says Nancy to a friendly bus driver). And these outsiders *aren't* desperate to be inside, to be the same. The slow-motion scene in which they walk through the school—which would, in any other movie, signpost a successful mediocre makeover—is instead sending a clear message: we're not like you and we love it. It's blatant, splashy, unrepentant. Their difference worn with a snarl and an arched eyebrow.

> **"IT TANGLED WITH THE SPECIFIC TYPE OF TEEN GIRL IN MOVIES THAT NINETIES AUDIENCES HAD COME TO KNOW."**

The friendship between the four girls is authentic and relatable—the warmth, insecurity, and volatility flows between them fast and all at once. They pass around liquor, smoke cigarettes, trade barbed comments. They reveal everything to each other. "When things were worst for me was before I tried to kill myself," confesses Sarah to Nancy. "I used to hallucinate things. I'd close my eyes and just see snakes and bugs everywhere." It's information that Nancy ultimately uses against Sarah in the movie's finale.

The film is as ferociously honest in its depiction of the dying days of female friendships as it is in capturing the hazy, yellow days of their birth. These aren't perfect girls trying to score perfect grades and keep the perfect quarterback boyfriend. *The Craft* shows the racism, poverty, abuse, body issues, and

mental illness that they battle through. They're imperfect girls trying in so many respects just to simply survive: survive themselves, each other, and the rest of the world. Not least, the men of their world.

We see the rampant misogyny that boxes them in tight, that brutalizes them. A misogyny that fuels young, white, privileged men, shown by fellow student Mitt (Breckin Meyer), who calls Sarah "that snail trail." The film precisely tracks how this toxicity brews and boils into slut-shaming, gas-lighting, and sexual assault.

The response to this—a revolutionary one, in fact—is a reclamation of female power by any and all means necessary. "Exorcise your rights" stated the trailer. It's a declaration of intent furthered by the opening seconds of the film: Nancy, Bonnie, and

Rochelle, in a circle, surrounded by Wiccan paraphernalia, chanting "Now is the time, now is the hour, ours is the magic, ours is the power."

When the four finally summon Manon, the creator of the universe, it's a mighty and potent scene. And it makes one thing very clear: women, who are for their entire lives set up as competition and as adversaries, are actually more powerful together than apart. They can achieve significant things, great things, *because* they're doing it without men, not in spite of it.

More controversially, *The Craft* presents a case for selfish power. Not for the greater good, but for an individual. To redress the balance—*their* balance. When Nancy attacks sexist jock Chris (Skeet Ulrich), she screams: "The only way you know how to treat women is to treat them like whores, when you're the whore and that's gonna stop." She is screaming for every woman who's been lied about, had their reputations smeared and set alight. Every woman who said no when all he chose to hear was yes. For while the four girls take revenge, it's a revenge based—at least initially—in fairness and justice.

And yes, they get justice through magic, but a magic turbo-charged and given meaning and shape by rage. One that is articulated with clarity and intent.

"THE FRIENDSHIP BETWEEN THE FOUR GIRLS IS AUTHENTIC AND RELATABLE."

That comes from a specific place and has a precise, linear consequence. It's justifiable and meaningful rage, but it's not pretty or apologetic. When Nancy finally takes her revenge on Chris, the scene is one of horror, of ugliness: her head thrown back, neck bared in anger, as she shouts maniacally.

The Craft is not, admittedly, note-perfect; someone has to pay for the bloodshed and the loss of life, and that's Nancy, who ends up strapped to a bed in a psychiatric ward rambling about her "powers." But as the film ends, Sarah is still full of power, arguably more than she ever has been. More in control of it. Of her life. Still proud and defiant in her difference. And without a designer skirt or vodka martini in sight.

Rotten Tomatoes' Critics Consensus *The Craft*'s campy magic often overrides the feminist message at its story's core, but its appealing cast and postmodern perspective still cast a sporadic spell.

MARS ATTACKS! 1996

 53%

Directed by Tim Burton
Written by Jonathan Gems
Starring Jack Nicholson, Glenn Close, Annette Bening, Pierce Brosnan, Danny DeVito, Martin Short, Sarah Jessica Parker, Michael J. Fox

Critics Consensus

Tim Burton's alien invasion spoof faithfully recreates the wooden characters and schlocky story of cheesy fifties sci-fi and Ed Wood movies—perhaps a little too faithfully for audiences.

Synopsis

A battalion of Martians with bug eyes and oversized brains do not come in peace, and a variety of government officials and regular folks—all played by really famous people—try to stop them.

Why We Love It

In 1996, two alien invasion movies hit the multiplex. Both featured hideous space creatures doing battle with scrappy earthlings (and destroying famous landmarks). Both borrowed heavily from a host of Cold War–era classics, including (but not limited to) *The Day the Earth Stood Still*, *War of the Worlds*, and *Dr. Strangelove*. But whereas *Independence Day*'s extra-terrestrials were a formidable, scientifically advanced, strategically brilliant fighting force, the invaders in *Mars Attacks!* were dumb and vulgar, slaughtering everyone (including the entire US government) with the gleeful malevolence of an overstimulated thirteen-year-old playing *Grand Theft Auto*. *Independence Day*'s message was that humanity is at its best when everyone works together; *Mars Attacks!* suggested we might not be any better than these ugly, mean little creeps.

Coincidental similarities notwithstanding, "rousing" tends to be a bigger sell than "cynical," and perhaps unsurprisingly, *Independence Day* got some decent reviews on the way to being the biggest box office smash of 1996, while *Mars Attacks!* was a commercial and critical disappointment.

It goes without saying that Tim Burton is in his element with this material. From his earliest days as an animator at Disney, Burton has made it a labor of love to ennoble the freaks, misfits, and lonely monsters that inhabited the movies he loved—namely, cut-rate sci-fi flicks with exclamatory titles and basement-level production values. Heck, he loved trashy 1950s B-movies so much, he made a sweet biopic of *Ed Wood*, the trashiest, least competent, would-be auteur of that era—and the Academy loved it!

However, the charm of something like Wood's *Plan 9 from Outer Space* is the wide gulf between its ambition and execution. While some critics enjoyed the irreverent tone of *Mars Attacks!* (especially when compared to the sporadic over-seriousness of *Independence Day*) many wondered if a star-studded, big-budget homage ran contrary to the spirit of its influences.

Others, however, embraced *Mars Attacks!* for many of those same reasons. (Like the Topps trading card set it's based upon, the film has developed a devoted cult following.) As with the overblown disaster movies of the 1970s, *Mars Attacks!* had a loaded cast (and that's not counting Jack Nicholson in a dual role) that seemed to relish the absurdity of the proceedings. The standouts include, but are by no means limited to, Rod Steiger as a trigger-happy general and Lisa Marie Smith in a wordless role as a very conspicuous Martian spy. Even with the blockbuster trappings, Burton's love of dusty pop culture detritus is very much on display: the war for Earth is won with the help of an unlistenable Slim Whitman song.

And despite its misanthropic rep, *Mars Attacks!* ends with one young couple finding love (Lucas Haas, the oft-tormented kid who discovers the Martians' Achilles' heel, ends up with former president's daughter, and now president for real, Natalie Portman), another rekindling it (Jim Brown and Pam Grier reunite and decide to give marriage another go), and yet another sharing it fleetingly (the disembodied heads of Nathalie Lake [Sarah Jessica Parker] and Professor Donald Kessler [Pierce Brosnan] kiss before they presumably perish in a spaceship crash).

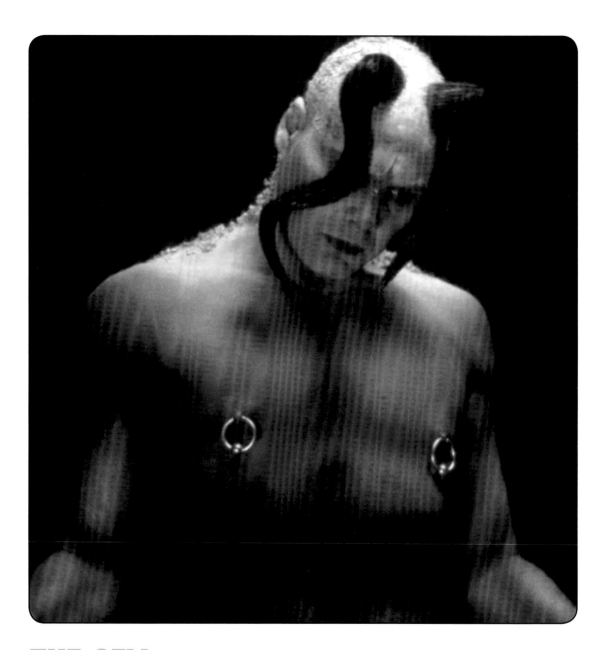

THE CELL 2000

 45%

Directed by Tarsem Singh
Written by Mark Protosevich
Starring Jennifer Lopez, Vincent D'Onofrio, Vince Vaughn, Marianne Jean-Baptiste, Dylan Baker

Critics Consensus

The Cell offers disturbing, stunning eye candy but is undermined by a weak and shallow plotline that offers nothing new.

Synopsis

A serial killer in a coma leaves detectives no clues as to where to find his latest victim, who will drown in one of his traps unless discovered. Desperate, they turn to an experimental new technology that will literally take a young psychologist into the serial killer's mind on a surreal search for answers.

Why We Love It

1990s cinema threw every kind of serial killer imaginable at us. There was the one who used your skin to make his clothes, and the one who used your sins to wipe you out. There was the guy who copycatted other serial killers, and the guy in the cab who collected bits of his victims' bones. There was even the guy who was actually possessed by the fallen angel Azazel. (That guy's in *Fallen*, with Denzel Washington, a totally ludicrous blast.)

Then, in 2000, we got *The Cell*'s Carl Rudolph Stargher (Vincent D'Onofrio), who likes to drown his victims in glass cells while he watches, suspended above them via hooks that he's dug into his own back.

This movie is what happens when filmmakers gather 'round and ask: "Serial killers are so in right now, but how do we take it to the next level?" So it is that our killer is a schizophrenic victim of child abuse who self-mutilates, builds elaborate torture devices, is a masterful plumber, and dreams of being a fabulously caped beast with horns made of hair. And so it is too that rather than just tracking Stargher down by searching for clues, testing DNA samples, and rummaging through databases, our heroes—the out-of-her-depth child psychologist (Jennifer Lopez) and cherub-faced detective (Vince Vaughn)—must literally enter his mind and do battle with him in his various incarnations to track down his latest victim.

Music video director Tarsem Singh, making his feature debut, gives them a very fucked-up mind to battle in. The imagery he creates is unforgettable. In the kingdom of Stargher's head, his doll-like victims are garishly made-up, mutilated, and unnervingly skittish (surely, the creators of *American Horror Story*'s credit sequences took notes), while Lopez is variously shrouded in bizarre face jewelry or cast as a Virgin Mary as her Catherine Deane starts to lose her will and ability to distinguish fantasy from reality. At one point, in a move inspired by Damien Hirst, Singh shows a horse cleaved into twelve segments by falling glass walls simply because—we think—*it looks cool.*

This everything-and-the-kitchen-sink-plus-the-diced-up-horse approach has earned the film a devoted fandom. But it wouldn't earn a place in this book without Lopez, who keeps things grounded as the singularly focused and sympathetic Deane. Even encumbered by outfits and makeup that the popstar J-Lo herself might deem a bit "much," she provides the human connection that gives the movie heart even as it loses its mind.

MOMMIE DEAREST 1981

 **50%**

Directed by Frank Perry
Written by Frank Yablans, Frank Perry, Tracy Hotchner, Robert Getchell
Starring Faye Dunaway and Diana Scarwid

Critics Consensus

Director Frank Perry's campy melodrama certainly doesn't lack conviction, and neither does Faye Dunaway's performance in the title role; unfortunately, it does lack enough narrative discipline to offer much more than guilty pleasure.

Synopsis

Based on her daughter Christina's scathing autobiography about her childhood, *Mommie Dearest's* Joan Crawford is portrayed as a complete monster whose career begins to decline despite her fighting tooth and nail.

Why We Love It

The essence of Faye Dunaway's unparalleled performance as Joan Crawford is perhaps best captured by one of the costumes she wears: a terry cloth bathrobe. Not to be confused with any nondescript, forgettable toweling agent, it is tailored to perfection and features shoulder pads of the kind usually found in only the fiercest awards-season gowns. Like the actress wearing it, it's *a lot*. And it hints at the camp joys to be found in *Mommie Dearest*.

When Dunaway's Joan casually ties this robe around herself, she's busy telling her young daughter that she's never going to be a good enough swimmer to beat her mother in a race. According to the memoir the movie was based on, it's just another Sunday with Joan.

Critics at the time wanted more than just vignettes from these terrifying Sundays (and Mondays through Saturdays) with Joan. They wanted conventional moviegoing pleasures like tight plotting and thoughtful dialogue. *Time's* Richard Schickel dismissed the movie as a "collection of screechy scenes." He wrote that: "Confronted by a movie without narrative tension or human interest, one is finally reduced to watching the paint dry—on Dunaway's face."

But what a face to watch it dry on. Dunaway's villainy in this movie is unique, bold, and unforgettable—which is why the film has endured as a cult classic, with devoted followers who watch it with eyes as wide as Dunaway's as she rages over those wire hangers. She's a classic and memorable monster, whether or not the portrayal is accurate. Diana Scarwid, as Christina, brings a measured rage against her over-the-top movie mom that provides the movie's only balance. Otherwise, it's all about watching Dunaway lose her marbles over improperly cleaned floors or her kid playing with her makeup.

While the narrative fails to portray Crawford as anything but a one-dimensional crazy-pants actress, the scenes director Frank Perry constructs to illustrate that characterization are the reason to tune in. If you pitted *Mommie Dearest's* Crawford against any of the classic horror movie monsters, we think she'd come out victorious, unscathed, and with her bathrobe not the least bit ruffled.

ROTTEN
HALL OF FAME

We celebrate random records with the Rottenest...

SUPERHERO MOVIE
MAX STEEL (2016)

✳ **0%**

OSCAR WINNER *THE SANDPIPER* (1965)

✳ **10%**

The Sandpiper won Best Original Song for "The Shadow of Your Smile."

MOVIE STARRING A MUSIC ARTIST
MADONNA IN

SWEPT AWAY (2002)

✳ **5%**

NUN MOVIE

✳ **7%**

SISTER ACT 2: BACK IN THE HABIT (1993)

MOVIE TO TOP ITS YEAR AT THE BOX OFFICE *FOREVER AMBER* (1947)

✳ **11%**

REMAKE BY THE SAME DIRECTOR
GÉLA BABLUANI FOR
13 (2011)

✳ **8%**

VIDEO GAME ADAPTATION
BLOODRAYNE 2: DELIVERANCE (2007)

✳ **0%**

✳ **0%**
with 29 reviews

MOVIE WITH AN EXCLAMATION POINT IN TITLE
WAGONS EAST! (1994)

GIANT ROBOT MOVIE

TURBO: A POWER RANGERS MOVIE
(1997)

❋ 16%

❋ 0%

'80S SLASHER

SILENT NIGHT, DEADLY NIGHT 2
(1987)

MOVIE STARRING "LARRY" FISHBURNE

Worst movie in which Laurence Fishburne was still going by "Larry" in credits.

❋ 0%

(1986)

AND THE ROTTENEST MOVIE OF ALL TIME IS...

BALLISTIC: ECKS VS. SEVER
(2002)

❋ 0%

with 117 reviews

MOVIE WITH TOMATO IN THE TITLE

RETURN OF THE KILLER TOMATOES!
(1988)

0%

SOPHOMORE SEQUEL SLUMP

The fall from *The Sting*'s 93% to *The Sting II*'s 0% is the largest Tomatometer drop between a movie and its sequel.

❋ 0%

THE STING II (1983)

SHARK MOVIE

❋ 0%

JAWS: THE REVENGE
(1987)

MOVIE STARRING A WRESTLER

HULK HOGAN IN

3 NINJAS: HIGH NOON AT MEGA MOUNTAIN
(1998)

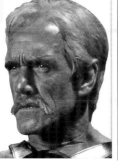

❋ 0%

MOVIE SERIES *ATLAS SHRUGGED*

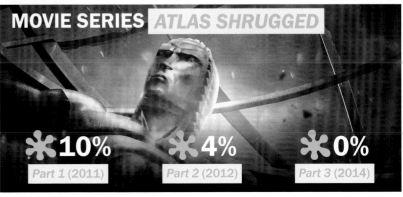

❋ 10%
Part 1 (2011)

❋ 4%
Part 2 (2012)

❋ 0%
Part 3 (2014)

AHEAD OF THEIR TIME

Oh, *Now* We Get It

Karyn Kusama's *Jennifer's Body*—released in 2009 and starring Megan Fox as a possessed high-schooler and Amanda Seyfried as the best friend who must confront her—has had quite a critical turnaround during its short life. Upon its release, *Jennifer's Body* was given the big green splat and dismissed by critics as a horror-comedy that couldn't quite get either genre right; today, it is the subject of countless reassessments that argue it's a genius dissection of toxic masculinity that neither its marketers nor its critics quite "got" when it was first released. (We're inclined to agree; turn to page 124 to find out why.) *Jennifer's Body* is one of what we're choosing to call "The Underestimated," those films that had a little more on their minds than perhaps critics gave them credit for at first. Sometimes, it seems critics had a hard time getting past surface flaws—as in *Practical Magic*'s seeming genre confusion, for example, or the cheap shock tactics of sci-fi/horror favorite *Event Horizon*, about which critic Bilge Ebiri writes here—to see the deeper joys to be found in these films. And sometimes time has been helpful in revealing how impactful these movies could be (witness the way *Blade* set the template for superhero and action flicks to follow, or *The Strangers* became a seminal and widely studied slasher). Sometimes, though, they're just plain masterpieces that the critics have slept on, as Australian critic David Stratton says of Julie Taymor's ambitious musical, *Across the Universe*. Whatever the reason these movies were underestimated, they've endured and stand today as reminders that Rotten scores shouldn't stop people from taking another look with fresh eyes.

> **THEY'VE ENDURED AND STAND TODAY AS REMINDERS THAT ROTTEN SCORES SHOULDN'T STOP PEOPLE FROM TAKING ANOTHER LOOK WITH FRESH EYES.**

THE STRANGERS 2008

 48% | Written and directed by Bryan Bertino
Starring Liv Tyler, Scott Speedman, Gemma Ward, Kip Weeks, Laura Margolis

Critics Consensus

The Strangers has a handful of genuinely scary moments, but they're not enough to elevate the end results above standard slasher fare.

Synopsis

A young couple staying in an isolated home find themselves under siege after a random knock at the door. Over the course of a night, they must try to outwit a trio of masked assailants determined to kill them—for no particular reason.

Why We Love It

Bryan Bertino's *The Strangers* was dismissed as a nasty little exercise in sadism when first released in 2008. While some critics paid grudging respect to the filmmaking craft, and many gave their due to Scott Speedman and Liv Tyler's lead performances, most wondered what any of it was in service of. It was a movie that was, apparently, about nothing. And on top of being empty, it was cheap. And schlocky. And twisted. And vile.

Cut to eleven years and one sequel later, and some folks—critics among them—talk about the film as *the* slasher classic of the 2000s. We think they're onto something.

Many of the critical reassessments of *The Strangers* cast an academic eye over the film, often reading it as a comment on post-9/11 America. Where once upon a time, slasher victims "invited" their demises by indulging in sex and booze and any of the other horror-movie "don'ts" that Randy Meeks lays out in Wes Craven's *Scream*, the two victims here are attacked by a masked trio of quiet psychopaths simply, and now famously, "because you were home." The violence is purposeless, untargeted—the exact kind of random attack that Americans as a collective had experienced just a handful of years before and now feared they would experience again.

We will leave that kind of dissection to the classroom. We love *The Strangers* because it succeeds so well as a horror film—that is to say, it's scary as hell. The movie is often compared to Michael Haneke's *Funny Games*, but it's true cousin, if you ask us, is John Carpenter's *Halloween*. (Folks forget, in the haze of lore-building sequels, that Laurie Strode was originally just a random and unrelated babysitter who, like Tyler and Speedman's couple in *The Strangers*, happened to be home.)

It's not just the cheap store-bought masks that both movies' killers wear, nor the knives they choose to use. Like *Halloween*, *The Strangers* is incredibly pared-back, a machine designed purely to terrorize. From the exquisitely framed "behind you!" reveals of the first half—so reminiscent of Michael Myers's slow materialization in the darkened doorway during *Halloween*'s climax—to the dread-heavy cat-and-mouse chase that fills out the second, the movie succeeds in its mission. And yes, Speedman and, particularly, Tyler are excellent.

A recent sequel, *The Strangers: Prey at Night*, is a worthy follow-up, switching out some of the original's moodiness for a fun, deliberately retro eighties slasher flair (complete with boppy soundtrack). The critics hated it, of course, but give them ten years and they may come around.

THE TRIP 1967

 **36%**

Directed by Roger Corman
Written by Jack Nicholson
Starring Peter Fonda, Bruce Dern, Susan Strasberg, Dennis Hopper

The Trip's groovy effects and contemporary message can't overcome the rough acting, long meandering stretches, and un-dramatic plot.

Synopsis

TV commercial director Paul is going through a divorce from wife, Sally. To find relief, he smokes reefer, meets free-love spirits, and embarks on his first acid trip.

Why We Love It

It's the sixties, and American independent cinema is swinging! John Cassavetes's pioneering Shadows had laid out the blueprint: interior films smaller than what the studios were interested in, with personal stories pawing at greater truths and fueled by raw method acting. And for The Trip, method research equaled LSD sessions with Peter Fonda, Roger Corman, and Jack Nicholson. The triad's quest: depict honestly the counterculture they were living, a sub-society that was letting subconscious desires flow onto the walls its members had painted, into the psych rock they danced with all night, and through the free love inflicted upon each other's bodies.

Fonda's Paul, his impending divorce affecting work, visits John (Bruce Dern), a gentle bearded shaman who plies people back to reality with apple juice. John procures the acid that Paul proceeds to drop, and soon he's off into the inner void, where questions of the self slumbered, now confronting answers. Cloaked and masked figures chase Paul around on horse. There are remembrances of carnal pleasure. Reality and fantasy begin to blur. Paul surrenders to the superorganism that he exists as a part of, that connects him to all life in the universe. He can feel the energy pouring off a piece of fruit. He laughs at a washing machine.

The journey is first merry and then nightmarish. It's told through kaleidoscopic effects, blasts of projected lights, avant-garde editing, and sequences of rapid-fire, loosely related imagery.

Some critics took significant displeasure in The Trip's garish, cut-up filmmaking, hackneyed performances, and wandering plot, and anyone watching the film today without the right frame of mind—ahem—might find it downright laughable. But for the common bohemian, this was a movie that came out at the right place, right time. In 1967, the nation's eyes were on San Francisco and its dawning Summer of Love, so the Los Angeles–set Trip is like a rambling postcard from southern California. American independent filming (now in full color!) was opening up our world, earnestly capturing the little dramas, victories, and setbacks that make up our day-to-day existence. And here, it's attempting to peer into the frontiers of the mind.

EVENT HORIZON 1997

 **27%**

Directed by Paul W. S. Anderson
Written by Philip Eisner
Starring Laurence Fishburne, Sam Neill, Kathleen Quinlan, Joely Richardson, Richard T. Jones

CRITIC: Bilge Ebiri

Bilge Ebiri is the former film critic for *The Village Voice* and currently contributes to *New York Magazine*, the *New York Times*, and *Rolling Stone*. In 2004, he released his first feature film, *New Guy*, which is Fresh on the Tomatometer.

Event Horizon is a ruthless, relentless film, which partly explains why it was so loathed by reviewers when it came out in 1997. Director Paul W. S. Anderson has never exactly been a critics' darling—his movies tend to be blunt, violent, and filled with cheap thrills—but the write-ups for this ambitious sci-fi horror picture, his third feature, were particularly dismissive: "A boring and blood-soaked mess," wrote Leah Rozen of *People* magazine. "I hear that the sound designer gets commission on every eardrum shattered," Ryan Gilbey wrote in Britain's *The Independent*.

It didn't help, of course, that *Event Horizon* at times evoked (or at least sought to evoke) some actual classics. You could describe Philip Eisner's script as a mash-up of *Forbidden Planet, Solaris, The Shining*, and *Alien* (with a dash of *Aliens* thrown in), but you'd have to overlook the inelegant dialogue and utter lack of subtlety, not to mention its wholehearted embrace of lowest-common-denominator shock tactics.

And yet it is perhaps for all these reasons that *Event Horizon* remains so unforgettable and upsetting and, yes, exciting. Anderson's directness of approach, hard-edged treatment of his characters, and general unwillingness to turn away from gore and grisly violence often lends his work a uniquely unforgiving, unsettling atmosphere. And on the *Event Horizon* itself—a possessed, murderous spaceship that has literally been to hell and back—he found the perfect setting.

Anderson's film starts off as another familiar sci-fi tale about a dangerous mission in outer space. The year is 2047, and the *Lewis & Clark*,

> ## "NOT ONLY IS HELL A REAL PLACE, BUT ONE CAN APPARENTLY REACH IT VIA SPACESHIP AND SOME FANCY MATH."

a search-and-rescue vessel commanded by the stoic but compassionate Captain Miller (Laurence Fishburne), has been tasked with exploring a once-lost ship that has mysteriously reappeared. Dr. Weir (Sam Neill), the scientist who designed the rediscovered vessel, joins the *Lewis & Clark* for the new expedition and informs the crew that the lost ship was in fact on a top-secret mission to create "a gateway to jump instantaneously from one point to another lightyears away" by bending space and time. Nobody knows how and why it's now returned—or where it's been all these years. All they have is an old, unearthed distress call from the *Event Horizon* with someone seemingly creaking, in Latin, "*Liberate me*" (*Save me*).

That cryptic message, combined with the ship's dark, chasmic interiors, conjures the essence of a gothic nightmare. Exploring the *Event Horizon*, our heroes find it empty of all crew save for a floating, eyeless corpse and thick, gory layers of blood along the walls. The vessel's interior looks at times more

like a massive, elaborate medieval torture device than a state-of-the-art spacecraft. Even the doors have spikes on them for some reason. The "gravity core"—the bizarre, giant device that powers the ship's space-and-time-bending gateway (the fake movie science here is truly impressive)—looks like a giant mace revolving inside two giant studded metal collars.

Soon, the crew of the *Lewis & Clark* are having troubling visions that reference their most sensitive memories. The already psychologically fragile Dr. Weir had started the film with a nightmarish vision of his wife, who committed suicide years ago, but now he seems to relive the night of her death. The ship's medical technician, Peters (Kathleen Quinlan), sees her disabled son with garish wounds on his legs.

We understand soon that the *Event Horizon* itself is prompting these visions—that with its journey into another dimension, the ship somehow became sentient or, maybe more accurately, possessed. "She tore a hole in our universe, a gateway to another dimension—a dimension of pure chaos, pure evil," says Dr. Weir. So . . . *hell*? "Hell is only a word. The reality is much, much worse."

The subgenre of sci-fi horror is an intriguingly conflicted one. It's a hybrid of two genres that, at least on the surface, often speak to different impulses, one to the scientific and the other to the supernatural. Of course, both turn on a fascination with the unexplainable, and science itself often makes for startling, monstrous creations. Space is indifferent; hell is cruel. There's a subtle difference between these two ideas, but in joining them together, *Event Horizon* conjures up a truly chilling conceit. Chilling, but ridiculous. Because in this film's conception, not only is hell a real place, but one can apparently reach it via spaceship and some fancy math.

How exactly does one tackle something like this with a straight face? Well, with a straight face: Anderson resists the siren call of camp or wink-wink self-consciousness. He takes the idea seriously or, to put it more plainly and colloquially: *he goes there.* When the crew of the *Lewis & Clark* finally sees what happened to the crew of the *Event Horizon*, what they (and we) witness is unusually disturbing, with flashes of torture, anguish, and bodily mortification. The glimpses are extremely brief, but they are many. Often, we're not even sure what exactly we're looking at, but we see just enough to fire our imaginations in entirely unsavory directions; it's hard to shake the image of a blood-soaked, grimacing man offering up his eyes to us.

Event Horizon is a uniquely, gloriously nutty movie. In one sense, the critics were right: it is filled

> # "IT'S A MOVIE THAT REFUSES TO PLAY BY THE TYPICAL RULES OF ITS CHOSEN GENRES. IN *EVENT HORIZON*, ANYTHING SEEMS POSSIBLE."

with jump scares and sudden shocks and unnecessarily loud noises, the tactics one often associates with unimaginative filmmakers who don't want to do the work of crafting inventive scares. But such elements also put us in a genuinely uncertain and uneasy state: we sense a consciousness behind the camera that might be as merciless as the ship itself—one unafraid to kill off major characters and to show us things from which most other films shy away. It's a movie that refuses to play by the typical rules of its chosen genres. In *Event Horizon*, anything seems possible.

Rotten Tomatoes' Critics Consensus Despite a strong opening that promises sci-fi thrills, *Event Horizon* quickly devolves into an exercise of style over substance, whose flashy effects and gratuitous gore fail to mask its overreliance on horror clichés.

JENNIFER'S BODY 2009

 **44%**

Directed by Karyn Kusama
Written by Diablo Cody
Starring Megan Fox, Amanda Seyfried, Adam Brody

Critics Consensus

Jennifer's Body features occasionally clever dialogue but the horror/comic premise fails to be either funny or scary enough to satisfy.

Synopsis

Jennifer is a pretty cheerleader, and Needy is an introverted nerd, but they're high school best buds whose childhood friendship is on its last legs. When Jennifer becomes possessed by a demon hungry for boy flesh, shy Needy must step up and battle for both the girls' souls.

Why We Love It

This groundbreaking film was so revolutionary that critics weren't yet clued in to how slyly subversive director Karyn Kusama and writer Diablo Cody were being. Instead, they assumed the filmmakers' divergence from—or awkward embrace of—horror tropes was merely accidental. Kusama's foray into big-budget Hollywood filmmaking had already been sabotaged when final approval over her sci-fi action film *Aeon Flux* was taken from her before the direction-less picture eventually flopped. *Jennifer's Body* was going to be her comeback, and Cody—having attained power seemingly overnight with her break-out hit *Juno*—hand-selected Kusama to helm the film. Unfortunately, *Jennifer's Body* was born into a world that was not yet enlightened to mainstream feminism, and its marketing was an embarrassment.

In interviews, Kusama explained that the marketing team wanted Megan Fox to do video interviews with sex workers to promote the film, despite the fact that her character is an underage teen and the movie has nothing to do with sex work. The final posters depict Fox clad in a sexy skirt and heels, lounging alluringly on a school desk, and while Fox is indeed a sexual being in the film, she also plays her character naïve, hopeful, hilarious, and vulnerable. Message boards lit up with disappointment when they realized Fox wasn't making a porno but an astute satire of high school femininity and horror villains. And some critics savaged her performance. Michael Phillips, writing for the *Chicago Tribune*, said, "in the middle of [the film] is a thinly conceived antagonist played by Megan Fox. Honestly, she's a pretty bad actress. She doesn't seem to get Cody's sense of humor. At all."

Respectfully, we disagree. To make it even worse for those who expected Fox to just sit and look pretty, she delivers an excellent, layered, comic performance—still her best yet.

The problem with this film is that people didn't *want* it to succeed and certainly didn't want Fox to succeed as a comic actress, forcing people to treat her with respect rather than as the easy butt of a *Transformers* joke (Fox has since spoken out about the pure meanness people threw at her at the time). Some genre fans wanted their negative opinions of Kusama and women directors confirmed, and Cody, who'd gotten so big so quickly, was an outsider woman with a little too much power for some people's comfort. *Jennifer's Body* has now become horror canon, having gifted a memorable and realistic depiction of relationships between girls and proven that high school is, indeed, hell.

THE FRISCO KID 1979

 **50%**

Directed by Robert Aldrich
Written by Michael Elias and Frank Shaw
Starring Gene Wilder, Harrison Ford, Penny Peyser

Critics Consensus

Not even a genial Gene Wilder or a dashing Harrison Ford can rescue *The Frisco Kid* from a monotonous procession of gently comedic sketches that never cohere into a memorable yarn.

Synopsis

A hapless Polish rabbi must travel across the Old West to deliver a Torah scroll for a new San Francisco synagogue. Along the way, he is beaten and robbed by a gang, befriended by a bank robber, and helped by a handful of unlikely allies.

Why We Love It

John Wayne was in his early seventies and a year away from death when he dropped out of *The Frisco Kid* and was replaced by a thirty-six-year-old youngin' named Harrison Ford, whose only bankable success was a little film called *Star Wars: Episode IV*. With Wayne playing the role of a cunning but kind bank robber, audiences would have known what kind of picture this was, but Ford was a wildcard who carried The Duke's wry humor but none of his cranky swagger—yet.

To confuse matters further, Gene Wilder was playing against type as well, as the wise fool rabbi in what he called the only Jewish film he ever made. Wilder, though uncredited for the work, also rewrote the script, mixing the tones of slapstick, black, and absurdist humor with heartfelt drama. Critics didn't know what to make of it. Roger Ebert said it was a movie for "nobody." Muddled as the tone may

be, *The Frisco Kid* is an anti-violence Western that contains the most nuanced and mature performance Wilder perhaps ever gave.

None of the actor's typical wild-man antics crop up in the film, tics that Wilder could occasionally lean on like a crutch. This is a stripped-down performance, one of complexity and vulnerability; he must often rely on subtle shifts in feeling being conveyed through his eyes alone, as when he's tied to a stake and questioned by Natives about this mysterious Torah book he carries. Surprisingly for the time of its making, the film doesn't depict the Natives as simplistic savages, and they and the rabbi connect over being outsiders in the white Christian man's new world. Yet Wilder's performance was seen as a disappointment for critics who were sorely missing the spontaneous comic genius he showcased in *Young Frankenstein*.

Director Robert Aldrich was best known for psycho-biddy fare like *Whatever Happened to Baby Jane?* as well as the cynicism of his noir films and then the ultra-violence of his 1967 hit *The Dirty Dozen*. Gary Arnold, writing for the *Washington Post*, said that Aldrich was "an awesomely inappropriate choice to direct an ethnic Western comedy." But Aldrich's entire career was founded on being awesomely inappropriate, reinventing himself every decade for a new wave of success. Here, he finds himself at his most restrained, allowing a gentleness in Wilder's performance to shine through for a film that is not quite great but consistently pleasant and sweet, something rare for a Western.

THE CABLE GUY 1996

 53%

Directed by Ben Stiller
Written by Lou Holtz Jr.
Starring Jim Carrey, Matthew Broderick, Leslie Mann, Jack Black

The Cable Guy's dark flashes of thought-provoking, subversive wit are often—but not always—enough to counter its frustratingly uneven storytelling approach.

Synopsis

A needy, cartoonishly energetic cable installer desperately tries to forge a friendship with a new client, an everydude whose life is quickly turned upside down and sabotaged.

Why We Love It

It's smart. It's dark. It's side-splittingly, stupidly funny. It's, dare we say, downright prophetic. So how did this Jim Carrey vehicle conjure a collective meh from American audiences upon release?

Let's call it too much of a good thing. When *The Cable Guy* hit theaters in 1996, comedy It boy Carrey was pretty much omnipresent at the box office. In the two years leading up to *The Cable Guy*, he starred in—deep breath—*Ace Ventura: Pet Detective*, *The Mask*, *Dumb and Dumber*, *Batman Forever*, and *Ace Ventura: When Nature Calls*. That's a lot of Carrey's rubber-face antics to endure in such a short amount of time, so we can forgive the groans from the public and the movie's reputation as a pricey dud in the years that followed. (During an episode of *The Simpsons*, Homer literally rips apart the screenplay at a Planet Hollywood–type restaurant, shouting "Stupid script! Nearly wrecked Jim Carrey's career!")

What we *can't* forgive, however, is writing off this gem decades later. Originally penned for fellow larger-than-life onscreen presence Chris Farley, the project went through several drafts, with director Ben Stiller, producer Judd Apatow, and Carrey (who nabbed a $20 million payday) eventually whipping the story into a comedic psychological thriller, a sort of *Cape Fear* with dirty jokes. Carrey's performance as a TV-addled stalker is nimble in retrospect: full-on adrenaline one minute, subdued (but equally ridiculous) sincerity the next. As the object of Carrey's bromantic affections, Matthew Broderick tempers the insanity with an always-straight-laced portrayal.

Well, *almost* always: during a scene in which Carrey does his best Hannibal Lecter from *The Silence of the Lambs*, you can see signs of Broderick breaking into laughs off-camera. The pop-cultural nods don't stop there: minutes after that *Lambs* riff comes a nifty recreation of a fight in a 1960s *Star Trek* episode. Elsewhere, references to everything from *Gimme Shelter* and *Midnight Express* to *My Three Sons* and *Ferris Bueller's Day Off* (very meta) abound.

It all adds up to a high-octane skewering of a generation lost in TV and technology, with a supporting cast (Jack Black, Leslie Mann, Owen Wilson, Bob Odenkirk, David Cross, Janeane Garofalo) that's like a who's who of about-to-break talent. So maybe folks didn't get what Stiller and co. were after back then. (Roger Ebert dubbed it "an exercise in hatefulness" while counting down his list of the worst films of 1996.) But twelve years later, Stiller may have had the last laugh: his satirical spoof *Tropic Thunder* was instantly beloved.

ISHTAR 1987

 38% | **Written and directed by** Elaine May
Starring Dustin Hoffman, Warren Beatty, Charles Grodin, Isabelle Adjani

Critics Consensus

Warren Beatty, Dustin Hoffman, and laughter itself get lost in the desert during a bloated spoof of classic road movies that's crippled by a pair of mismatched and miscast stars.

Synopsis

Two klutzy New York lounge singers book a gig in Morocco. In the midst of penning some truly awful songs, the two become caught up in a CIA plot and wander the desert on a blind camel, now the targets of a manhunt.

Why We Love It

Often when a female director is given a record heap of money, harsh criticism will follow. In this case, Elaine May had already made a short string of well-received comic dramas: *A New Leaf*, *The Heartbreak Kid*, and *Mikey and Nicky*. She'd already worked with some starpower, but *Ishtar* was her first big-budget picture, and after some longer-than-expected location shooting in the North African deserts, entertainment journalists were already exasperatedly reporting May needed *more* cash. The ways in which journalists talked about that need was akin to tsk-tsking a pretty wife for spending all her money on shoes. It's not like May could help it: real-life tensions in the Middle East halted much of the production.

But without all the hullabaloo about time and finances, *Ishtar*, evaluated on its own terms, turns out to be a pretty hilariously off-kilter comedy that features two of the biggest names of the time—Dustin Hoffman and Warren Beatty—in roles so unbecoming of them that you have to admire the guts it takes to ugly up the personality of a heartthrob for a laugh (think Brad Pitt and George Clooney's roles in *Burn After Reading*). These men are willfully unattractive, and May makes them perform the kind of slapstick comedy you'd see in a Three Stooges or Marx

Brothers routine. In fact, the story for *Ishtar* evolved from the classic road pictures starring Bing Crosby and Bob Hope, with the added oddball pleasure that neither character can actually sing.

Many critics mused that perhaps May was bored by the desert scenes she shot and so wasn't inspired while writing them, but they also conceded that her writing and direction in the booze-soaked night club portions were up to her usual par. Hal Hinson, writing for the *Washington Post,* said, "the bad song lyrics . . . and the lines that Hoffman and Beatty half-mutter under their breath are the shiny nuggets glistening in the creek bed" of an otherwise muddied film.

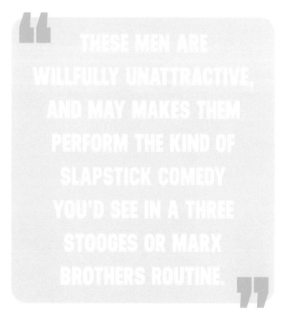

> THESE MEN ARE WILLFULLY UNATTRACTIVE, AND MAY MAKES THEM PERFORM THE KIND OF SLAPSTICK COMEDY YOU'D SEE IN A THREE STOOGES OR MARX BROTHERS ROUTINE.

Is this the best film May ever made? Probably not. But it didn't deserve the smug hatred spewing from the critics who made a meal out of her first big-budget movie. If anything, it's a must-watch because of May's daring to break all the rules of Hollywood pictures, dumbing down the heroes to imbecilic numbskulls and watching the actors lower themselves a few notches.

53%

Directed by Julie Taymor
Written by Dick Clement and Ian La Frenais
Starring Evan Rachel Wood, Jim Sturgess, Joe Anderson, Dana Fuchs, T. V. Carpio

CRITIC: David Stratton

David Stratton is a film critic at *The Australian* newspaper and was the co-host of the popular *At the Movies* TV show on the ABC, and before that, *The Movie Show* on SBS.

Across the Universe is a spectacular movie filled with the most enticing elements. For starters, it features thirty songs made famous by The Beatles. Then there's a screenplay by the talented British writing team of Dick Clement and Ian La Frenais, whose TV achievements included such peerless comedy series as *Not Only But Also, The Likely Lads*, and *Auf Wiedersehen Pet*, as well as feature films like *The Commitments*. In addition, there's the direction of Julie Taymor, whose *The Lion King* had been a phenomenon on Broadway and elsewhere and who had previously made the excellent and Certified Fresh feature film *Frida* (2002), a biography of artist Frida Kahlo, starring Salma Hayek.

That's an awful lot of talent, so what could possibly go wrong? I found myself wholeheartedly on Taymor's wavelength, but many others were clearly underwhelmed.

The original Beatles recordings aren't used in *Across the Universe*, and their connection with the film wasn't part of the original advertising campaign, although Revolution Studios is said to have paid $10 million for the rights to use the Lennon, McCartney, and Harrison compositions. Instead, the songs were re-imagined and re-invented in the Clement-La Frenais screenplay. And so, "I Want to Hold Your Hand," the cheerful boy-meets-girl song that, in 1963, was one of the mega-hits that propelled the four lads from Liverpool to international fame, is transformed into a soulful torch ballad sung by the isolated, bisexual Prudence (T. V. Carpio) as she gazes longingly at the beautiful Lucy (Evan Rachel Wood), a cheerleader at an Ohio college.

The film unfolds on two continents and opens in the mid-1960s, and its chief joy lies in the skill and invention with which the famous songs are used to drive the narrative across places and times. In

> **"TAYMOR HAS PRESENTED, WITH CONSIDERABLE CINEMATIC FLAIR, A PORTRAIT OF AMERICA IN CONFLICT WITH ITSELF."**

Liverpool, England, Jude (Jim Sturgess), a young manual laborer, sits on a chilly beach and introduces proceedings with "Girl": "Is there anybody going to listen to my story?" He lives with his single mother, Martha (Angela Mounsey), but is obsessed with the father he never knew, a US soldier who slept with his mother during World War II and returned to America without ever seeing his son. After a night in the dance hall with his girlfriend (Lisa Hogg) to the tune of "Hold Me Tight," Jude says goodbye to her ("All My Loving") and sails for New York.

Jude's investigations lead him to Princeton, where he believes his father is employed, but on arrival at the university, he discovers his dad, Wes (Robert Clohessy), is not a teacher, as he'd imagined, but a janitor. At Princeton, Jude meets Max (Joe Anderson), a cheerful rebel ("A Little Help from My Friends") who takes him home to share Thanksgiving with his family, including his sister Lucy, whose fiancé is fighting in Vietnam ("It Won't Be Long Now"). The fiancé is killed in action ("Let It Be"), and a connection forms between Jude and Lucy ("I've Just Seen a Face").

Opposition to Vietnam is on the increase, and Harlem is wracked by racial rioting when the principal characters all wind up in Greenwich Village. Jude and Max find accommodation with Sadie (Dana Fuchs), whose lover, Jo-Jo (Martin Luther McCoy), is a guitarist ("Come Together"). Lucy, an increasingly radical opponent of the war, tentatively begins a relationship with Jude ("If I Fell"), while Max is unwillingly conscripted into the military ("I Want You"). Until this point, Taymor has presented, with considerable cinematic flair, a portrait of America in conflict with itself, vividly staging the riots and divisions of the late sixties and employing a level of reality not often found in musical films.

There follows a long section, the most contested in the film, in which Lucy and Jude meet acid freak Dr. Robert (played by U2 frontman Bono) and become involved in an extended psychedelic trip ("I Am the Walrus") that includes an encounter with a bizarre showman named Mr. Kite ("Being for the Benefit of Mr. Kite," "Because"). In these scenes, Taymor's appetite for visual extravagance threatens to tip the movie into a variation of Roger Corman's

The Trip (1967) or maybe Milos Forman's film version of *Hair* (1979) but the use of the music and the film's sheer energy overcome the pitfalls of the trippy excesses.

Back in a wintry New York, Jude—now working as an artist—becomes jealous of the close relationship between Lucy, who is earning her keep as a waitress, and one of her radical friends ("Something"), and they argue about her commitment to the cause ("Revolution"). Jude gets into a fight and watches Martin Luther King Jr. on television ("While My Guitar Gently Weeps"); he is deported ("Across the Universe") and returns to Liverpool.

As the narrative arcs come together for a highly satisfying conclusion, the film makes deft use of other Beatles' classics, including "Don't Let Me Down," "All You Need Is Love," and "Lucy in the Sky with Diamonds." The "Hey Jude" sequence, in which two continents are linked, is a real show-stopper. The happy ending, improbable as it might seem (how did the deported Jude manage to obtain a visa to return to the States?) completes this breathtaking love story, with its vivid depiction of a politically and socially restless environment.

Yet with all that it had going for it—those unforgettable songs, the engaging characters, inventive direction, and stylish camerawork—the film failed to find a significant audience, making just shy of $30 million worldwide. The critics were deeply divided, with responses ranging from Roger Ebert's four-star rave ("Bold, beautiful, visually enchanting, audacious") to Owen Gleiberman's C- ("You wonder what they [The Beatles] did to deserve *Across the Universe*"). Melissa Anderson in *Time Out New*

"THE HAPPY ENDING COMPLETES THIS BREATHTAKING LOVE STORY, WITH ITS VIVID DEPICTION OF A POLITICALLY AND SOCIALLY RESTLESS ENVIRONMENT."

York suggested moviegoers "save your money for the *Help!* DVD." On *At the Movies,* the long-running Aussie TV show I cohosted with Margaret Pomeranz, I raved while she poured scorn.

But whenever I've shown the film to friends, they've loved it. I even presented it once on a cruise ship, where it was sensationally successful. I guess *Across the Universe* is just one of those movies you either love or loathe, but if the negative reviews originally put you off, still give the film a go, if only to see Prudence come in through the bathroom window and Max holding his (silver?) hammer.

Rotten Tomatoes' Critics Consensus Psychedelic musical numbers can't mask *Across the Universe*'s clichéd love story and thinly written characters.

THE WATCHER IN THE WOODS 1980

 **48%**

Directed by John Hough, Vincent McEveety (uncredited)
Written by Harry Spalding, Brian Clemens, Rosemary Anne Sisson
Starring Bette Davis, Lynn-Holly Johnson, Carroll Baker, Kyle Richards

Critics Consensus

The Watcher in the Woods boasts plenty of spooky atmosphere and a typically strong performance from Bette Davis, but it builds to a conclusion so dissatisfying that it undermines all that came before.

Synopsis

A family moves into a creaky manor house in the English countryside, where almost immediately the eldest daughter is haunted by visions of a girl about her age who went missing many years before.

Why We Love It

Disney has the Marvel Cinematic Universe, Star Wars, and Pixar as the jewels in its crown today, so it's hard to imagine there was a time when the Mouse House hit a bumpy patch. But such was the case in the late 1970s and early 1980s. In a bid to shed its squeaky clean image, the studio tested the waters with such diverse fare as special effects-laden sci-fi flicks like *The Black Hole* and *Tron* and the touching coming-of-age drama *Tex*. Hopes were high for *The Watcher in the Woods*—one exec reportedly said it could be the company's very own *Exorcist*—but after a disastrous early screening, the studio pulled the film from theaters for tinkering. Still, even a new ending failed to answer the question posed in the title: who (or what) *is* the watcher in the woods?

The answer they came up with was, to paraphrase History Channel host Giorgio A. Tsoukalos, basically "I don't know, therefore aliens"—or more specifically, what looks like a cut-rate version of the Xenomorph from Ridley Scott's *Alien*, which materializes with absolutely no warning and dissipates in a flash of mediocre special effects. Given this utterly bonkers conclusion, it's not hard to see why critics were less than enthusiastic.

But like an urban legend or a half-remembered ghost story, *The Watcher in the Woods* flickered in the memories of many a child of the 1980s. If you happened to be in that cohort, there's a decent chance that *The Watcher in the Woods* was the first horror movie you ever saw—and the first one that scared the dickens out of you.

Anecdotally, parents rented the film because the Disney logo was on the VHS box, and then unintentionally subjected their children to a tale rife with anguished spirits, possessed little sisters, and adults who are either absent, dismissive, or broken. The kids who stuck with it got a crash course in the language of horror movies, from credible jump scares and ominous POV shots à la *Friday the 13th*, to the eerie sound of a music box and the disquiet of things looming half-seen just beyond your line of vision. (Or right in front of you: the scenes in which the long-lost Karen tries to communicate through mirrors are downright terrifying.)

See it again in adulthood, and you might find that *The Watcher in the Woods* isn't bad at all, save for the botched ending(s); at the very least, it's a solid haunted house movie from director John Hough (who helmed *Escape to Witch Mountain*, another supernatural kid pic from Disney), and Bette Davis lends gravitas to the whole thing. But ultimately, the appeal of the movie might come down to its setting: every adventurous kid would love to root around in big old houses, dense forests, or abandoned buildings, and *The Watcher in the Woods* provides all three.

IN THE CUT 2003

 **33%**

Directed by Jane Campion
Written by Jane Campion and Susanna Moore
Starring Meg Ryan, Jennifer Jason Leigh, Mark Ruffalo

Critics Consensus

Director/cowriter Jane Campion takes a stab at subverting the psycho-sexual thriller genre with *In the Cut* but gets tangled in her own abstraction.

Synopsis

A writing teacher begins an erotic relationship with a detective investigating the brutal murder of a woman, but she begins to distrust and suspect every man she meets, even as her desire for the detective blooms out of control.

Why We Love It

This Jane Campion film was produced by Nicole Kidman, who'd dropped out of the starring role to tend to her personal life. That was fortuitous for Meg Ryan, who sports an eerily Kidman-esque haircut here. Ryan had spent her career playing pert if not pathologically likable people, and *In the Cut* offered the opportunity to be cold, distant, and inscrutable.

Ryan certainly rises to the challenge, even if critics were annoyed that the film was far more a character piece for her than it was an American erotic thriller. Male directors had dominated that genre in the nineties, and Campion was offering a more arthouse, slightly softer interpretation—sometimes in tone and sometimes in form, where the focus of the camera blurs dreamlike on the edges of the frame.

What's most striking about Campion's version of dangerous eroticism is that the director depicts sexual acts with a certain gentleness. In so many other films of the genre, the sex is sweaty and heavy, with an emphasis on domination and submission. Not here. Campion emphasizes care and protection, as Ryan's Frannie Avery is thoroughly pleasured by her detective lover. It's pretty hot. But that divergence in approach also makes the film more logical, explaining why Frannie would crave the detective's physical embrace, even if she might suspect him of murder: she's willing to sacrifice her body and life if it leads to a few sacred moments of bliss and safety.

Audiences may not have been ready yet for a seemingly normal female character who knowingly walks into annihilation and disaster. (Kidman would play a separate character with those traits in Jonathan Glazer's *Birth* in 2004, which was also summarily panned by critics who questioned the character's sanity and therefore didn't like her.) Richard Roeper was one of the first and few to praise Ryan's "compelling" performance, and Manohla Dargis, writing for the *LA Times,* called it "the most maddening and imperfect great film of the year," but others saw her foray into this arthouse world as almost a lark. Tom Long at the *Detroit News* wrote, "Ultimately the question people may ask about *In the Cut* could be, 'She took her clothes off for this?'"

Today, Ryan's portrayal of a disoriented and dissatisfied single woman living alone in New York City would be in the awards conversation.

BUFFY THE VAMPIRE SLAYER 1992

 **35%**

Directed by Fran Rubel Kuzui
Written by Joss Whedon
Starring Kristy Swanson, Donald Sutherland, Luke Perry, Paul Reubens, Rutger Hauer, Hilary Swank, *can you believe the list is this long?*, David Arquette, Stephen Root

Critics Consensus

Buffy the Vampire Slayer's supernatural coming-of-age tale is let down by poor directing and even poorer plotting, though Kristy Swanson and Paul Reubens's game performances still manage to slay.

Synopsis

Cheerleader Buffy must choose between her life as a sheltered high schooler or becoming the latest in a long line of slayers sworn to protect humanity from vampires.

Why We Love It

Let's just get this out of the way: the late-1990s TV show and this earlier movie share the same name and both center on a blonde high school student slaying vampires, but that's where the similarities end. And while both projects even have the same writer in Joss Whedon, he has gone on record saying that the movie doesn't reflect where he wanted to go. "I had written this scary film about an empowered woman, and they turned it into a broad comedy," he said. "It was crushing." His seven-season TV show, starring Sarah Michelle Gellar, has been read as a kind of correction. But Whedon might be being a bit hard on the film—and its slayer.

The movie version of Buffy is no slouch. Sure, she's a well-dressed Valley Girl who thinks that the ozone is something "we gotta get rid of," but she's also resourceful, ferocious, and funny. Kristy Swanson, as Buffy, is surrounded by top-tier talent, including the late Luke Perry as Pike, the heartthrob with whom she can share a dance and a stake. Rutger Hauer is here, too, playing to the back row as Lothos. And somehow they got Donald Sutherland to agree to be in the film as Merrick. Swanson's Buffy asks him for gum in the middle of a stakeout (haha, get it—*stake*out?), and he hurls a knife at her head in the girl's locker room, making them the greatest odd couple of the nineties.

Buffy primed modern audiences for ditzy gals who ended up being not so ditzy after all, most notably Cher in *Clueless*, which would come three years after this. In a sense, Buffy set the template for an average-seeming young woman who should not be underestimated. And her journey of discovery from ditz to powerhouse slayer—one that parallels more traditional comic-book narratives about geeky guys finding the heroes within—was almost revolutionary when applied to a typical American teenage girl and given a bloody twist.

Hollywood may have interfered with Whedon's original plan, but it couldn't snuffle out the power of his message.

HARLEM NIGHTS 1989

 **21%**

Written and directed by Eddie Murphy

Starring Eddie Murphy, Richard Pryor, Redd Foxx, Della Reese, Danny Aiello, Michael Lerner, Arsenio Hall, Jasmine Guy

An all-star comedy lineup is wasted on a paper-thin plot and painfully clunky dialogue. The production has a bit of style but not enough to distract you from the director's obvious limitations.

Synopsis

A 1930s New York nightclub owner battles rival operators, crooked cops, and bickering employees all while trying to protect and mentor his quick-on-the-trigger adopted son. When a larger outfit wants a piece of the pie, the club owner comes up with his next, and possibly his last, play: to beat the competition at its own game and walk away with a hefty payday.

Why We Love It

If you're 1980s Eddie Murphy and could cast Richard Pryor, Redd Foxx, and Robin Harris (your own idols) in your first directorial outing, wouldn't you do it? Regardless of what you think of *Harlem Nights* the movie, you can't knock the hustle. At the height of his power, Murphy took a big swing here, directing, producing, writing, and starring in his take on the black gangster movie. *Set It Off*, *New Jack City*, and *Hoodlum* would all score better with the critics, but they all owe a little something to Murphy's pioneering film.

Clearly inspired by Francis Ford Coppola's *The Cotton Club*, Murphy said he wanted to appear in a period piece, and with the actor dominating the box office with hits like *Coming to America* and *Beverly Hills Cop II*, Paramount saw no reason not to give him $16 million for his vanity project. Critics saw the eventual product as all style over substance, with a stale story only worsened by Murphy's pedestrian dialogue; Dolores Barclay from the Associated Press quipped, "Murphy's writing is about as snappy as a Sunday school lesson."

Spending too much time nitpicking some (admittedly) rough patches of the screenplay, however, is to ignore the strong chemistry between *Harlem Nights*' stars—especially between Della Reese and Foxx, who work together to generate big laughs and, ultimately, even bigger feels. It's also to ignore the movie's aim: as with any comedy, the goal here is to be funny, and *Harlem Nights* has plenty on screen that will have you doubled over with laughter, especially in the expletive-stuffed patter from Murphy, Pryor, Foxx, and Hall. (Even among that comedy royalty, though, it's Stan Shaw as the stuttering boxer Jack Jenkins who quietly steals every scene he's in.)

The costumes and look of the film were groundbreaking in their own way. This was not the first lavish 1930s period piece, but it was one of the first to feature a primarily black cast, and the care that costume designer Joe I. Tompkins takes with that distinction shows; Murphy's white suit and hat are the prime examples, along with any of Jasmine Guy's opulent gowns. Tompkins's costumes rightfully earned him an Oscar nomination.

The movie was released shortly after Spike Lee's *Do the Right Thing* (1989) and Robert Townsend's *Hollywood Shuffle* (1987), both of which were well received and earned enough money for some to wonder whether they heralded a resurgence of studio-backed black cinema. It was not to be at the time, but you can feel Murphy's earnest ambition here. He brought to the big screen black characters who existed in 1930s New York—the Civil Rights Movement decades away—and who weren't willing to accept their lot in life. They would be smarter and slicker than the people around them and ultimately pull off an epic heist, riding off into the sunset with the American Dream in their hands.

THE WAY OF THE GUN 2000

45%

Written and directed by Christopher McQuarrie
Starring Ryan Phillippe, Benicio Del Toro, Juliette Lewis, Taye Diggs, Nicky Katt, James Caan

CRITIC: David Fear

David Fear is a critic and editor at *Rolling Stone* and a former film critic for *Time Out New York*; his work has been published in the *New York Times Magazine*, *Spin*, *Esquire*, *The Village Voice*, *NY Daily News*, *Film Comment*, and other publications.

Let's say it's the beginning of the twenty-first century. Like a lot of people, you probably spent a good portion of the previous decade watching crime movies. Not just any crime movies, mind you—the kind with hip soundtracks, fast-talking wink-nudge dialogue, shocking violence, and a too-cool-for-film-school vibe. For a while, these jukebox versions of Jim Thompson–style stories (let's call the subgenre "pulp fiction," because y'know, give it a name) were everywhere.

So let's also say that, even though it's a totally different millennia, you notice there's a new crime film in theaters. Check out the poster, a lotta semi-recognizable character actors staring out, some old, some new, all of them looking stoic. One of them is holding a gun. No surprise there: *gun* is in the title. It's from the guy who wrote *The Usual Suspects*. You think, *I've seen this already, haven't I?*

Well, you have and you haven't. It helps to remind people of what the moment was like when Christopher McQuarrie released *The Way of the Gun* into theaters in September 2000. We'd seen countless diminishing returns regarding the Clinton-era template of crazysexycrime flicks, and audiences were suffering from what critic Scott Tobias called "an acute case of Quentin Tarantino fatigue." The assumption was that *Way* would just be more of the same old warmed-over Royale With Cheese.

And when you watch the first five minutes of McQuarrie's directorial debut, there's not a lot of reason to think otherwise. Two men walk out of a bar. Some colorful shit-talking ensues, courtesy of Sarah Silverman (!) and one of the guys, who's played by Ryan Phillippe. She throws around a particularly nasty epithet used to denigrate homosexuals; he offers to "fuck-start her head." We know punches are going to get thrown . . . though we don't expect that Phillippe will forego hitting Silverman's boyfriend and end up just clocking *her*. It's a toxic intro, followed by an even worse sequence in a sperm clinic.

Also, Phillippe and partner Benicio Del Toro's

> ## "IT'S CLEAR THE WRITER-DIRECTOR IS NOT INTERESTED IN BEING TARANTINO."

monikers are Parker and Longbaugh, the real sur-
names of Butch Cassidy and the Sundance Kid. This
is not going well.

All the more surprising, then, when McQuarrie
drops the majority of the cutesy meta touches so
characteristic of those second-generation reservoir
pups and settles into a groove that harkens even further back. Once the plot proper kicks in—these two
are petty criminals, and they've stumbled onto easy
cash by kidnapping a pregnant woman, only "easy"
never really enters into it—it's clear the writer-director is not interested in being Tarantino; he's after
bigger game. He's thinking of a different seventies
cinema, the kind where you can smell the whiskey
and weariness coming out of the characters' pores.
The touchstone is not *Pulp Fiction* here but Sam
Peckinpah.

McQuarrie has denied that *The Way of the Gun* is
his attempt to channel the spirit of Bloody Sam, and

you won't find the late, great filmmaker's signature
Grand Guignol set pieces here. We'll gingerly suggest
that he's missing the middle of the Venn Diagram
where their work meets. This is one of the very
few films to nail the mixture of lyricism and fatalism
that was Peckinpah's stock-in-trade. Combine that
with the film's singular blend of bruised masculinity
and by-any-means-necessary maternal protective-
ness, and you have the real tone of McQuarrie's
misunderstood, magnificent outlaw blues.

The bruised masculinity comes in the form of
nearly every male character on screen—primarily
in Phillippe's ragged, ferret-like killer and Del Toro's
high-caliber philosopher (more on the Notorious BDT
in a bit), but also in Parker and Longbaugh's counterparts, two slick-as-goose-shit bodyguards played
by Taye Diggs and *Dazed and Confused*'s Nicky Katt.
They've been hired to protect a surrogate mother
(Juliette Lewis, supplying killer maternal instincts),

who's having the baby of Scott Wilson's corrupt rich bastard, and to keep an eye on his son, the woman's OB-GYN (Dylan Kussman).

Their interactions go in ways you don't expect. Lewis's Robin is involved in a memorable shoot-out, one of several, but we barely get to see the gunfire. We do, however, see the bodies lying on the ground after, only one of which we recognize as a bad guy; the movie purposefully holds on the shot four times as long as you expect, all the better to linger not on the violence but on what violence leaves in its wake. A car chase that purposefully never seems to get to third gear follows.

Often, there's silence, like the scene in which Del Toro has to decide whether he's going to save his own ass or risk it to save Robin's, as she goes into labor and everyone else goes ballistic. Concentrate on the performance, the way Del Toro turns his head and puts one hand over his eye as he views a sonogram; watching again, you realize it's perfect. No big speeches, no heroic gestures. Exactly what a grandstanding star would *not* do.

The gist is: McQuarrie knows what you want. He's not going to give it to you, however, not really. He's admitted that he made this movie in a state of frustration with the movie business, which only wanted him to do crime movies, preferably something like *Usual Suspects Redux.* The writer-director decided, after some prodding from Del Toro, to put his rage on the page. The resulting movie is indeed filled with cinephiliac pleasures: Joe Kraemer's castanets-heavy score; its look, courtesy of cinematographer Dick Pope, going full-tilt retro seventies.

But it's really a movie about withholding,

> ## "IT'S REALLY A MOVIE ABOUT WITHHOLDING, SLOWING IT DOWN, MAKING YOU THINK ABOUT WHAT YOU'RE WATCHING."

slowing it down, making you think about what you're watching, why you root for who you root for. Yes, it's self-conscious, but it's also self-aware. It wasn't going to be just another video-store-cool movie—no wonder audiences didn't show up. It was occasionally going to get ponderous and plod even when it hit maximum pulpitude—no wonder many (though not all) critics blew a Bronx raspberry at it. And *The Way of the Gun* would prove that, even with a girl and a gun and photogenic guys playing tough, it could take the raw material of a million other films and make it feel like its own rough beast, slouching toward Tijuana and no man's land. No wonder we fans keep going back to it again and again.

Rotten Tomatoes' Critics Consensus Christopher McQuarrie may exhibit a way behind the camera in the stylish *The Way of the Gun,* but his script falters with dull characterization and a plot so needlessly twisty that most viewers will be ready to tune out before the final reveal.

PRACTICAL MAGIC 1998

 **21%**

Directed by Griffin Dunne
Written by Robin Swicord, Akiva Goldsman, Adam Brooks
Starring Sandra Bullock, Nicole Kidman, Dianne Wiest, Stockard Channing

Critics Consensus

Practical Magic's jarring tonal shifts sink what little potential its offbeat story may have, though Nicole Kidman and Sandra Bullock's chemistry makes a strong argument for future collaborations.

Synopsis

Two sister witches who possess the ability to cast love spells must also endure their family's love curse: any man they fall in love with will die an untimely death.

Why We Love It

What critics deemed *Practical Magic*'s biggest flaw—that director Griffin Dunne couldn't figure out if he wanted it to be a romance, a family drama, or a horror film—could also be *Practical Magic*'s greatest asset. Written off as a muddled adaptation and waste of star power, the film touched the hearts of many teen girls who'd already grown fascinated with witchcraft from 1996's cult hit *The Craft* (see page 103). But this was more mature fare and spoke to young women's need for depictions of more positive relationships between sisters, aunts, and daughters, and it hit serious notes about abusive relationships and grief. These were wholly accessible witches.

Dunne even made the decision to pull a moodier Michael Nyman score in favor of a more sparkling Alan Silvestri arrangement. (Nyman's score would show up later on in Antonia Bird's pitch-black horror comedy *Ravenous*.) It was as though Dunne had shot a horror film, then pulled back, bit by bit, until it was possible for the marketing team to release a trailer that could sell the film as a rom-com. You might call it Horror Lite, which was a risk back in the nineties, though now it's nearly standard, looking at hit television shows like *True Blood*, *Riverdale*, and the *Chilling Adventures of Sabrina*.

Still, at the time, even Roger Ebert couldn't suss out what Dunne was aiming at, saying, "The movie doesn't seem sure what tone to adopt, veering uncertainly from horror to laughs to romance." Others were harsher, like Mark Caro writing for the *Chicago Tribune*, who said, "The trio of credited writers exhibits a complete failure of imagination!" It does seem, however, the writers who concocted this mashup of genres may have been more imaginative than they were given credit for.

Though the movie's scenes of murder and possession certainly offer a jolt and a thrill, fans tend to connect most with one particular scene in which three generations of girls and women gather to dance and drink in the kitchen. Reportedly, Nicole Kidman had actually brought cheap tequila to the set for the night, and the actors were legitimately tipsy. But even without that authenticity, this scene exudes so much joy amid darkness that it's impossible not to be endeared to these lovelorn witches, misunderstood and feared by their community.

AMERICAN DREAMZ 2006

 **38%** | **Written and directed by** Paul Weitz
Starring Hugh Grant, Mandy Moore, Sam Golzari, Dennis Quaid, Marcia Gay Harden

Critics Consensus

A cheerfully silly satire with an unfortunate lack of focus, *American Dreamz* takes aim at numerous targets but isn't pointed enough for relevant social commentary.

Synopsis

Newly re-elected President Staton has signed up to be a guest judge on *American Dreamz*, a reality singing competition and national TV sensation that bears more than a passing resemblance to *American Idol*. Its creator and chief judge is scouting for fresh show talent—talent with an inspiring story—and finds just that in All-American Sally Kendoo and new-to-the-US showtunes fan, Omer.

Why We Love It

Perhaps no artifact more perfectly encapsulates mid-2000s America—when the country was as divided over Katharine versus Taylor as it was over Operation Iraqi Freedom—than this hammer-blunt satire from Paul Weitz. The *About a Boy* and *In Good Company* writer-director has called it a "cultural satire" rather than a political one, and that feels right, as his movie takes aim at, well, pretty much *everything*. It's as messy, broad, and all over-the-place as a bloated *Idol* finale, and just as fun.

George W. Bush appears here in the form of President Staton (a doe-eyed Dennis Quaid), whose mind is blown and spirit crushed when he picks up a newspaper for what might be the first time in forever. (Willem Dafoe is fabulous as the starkly bald Cheney-alike vice president trying to pep him up.) Simon Cowell appears in the form of Martin Tweed (Hugh Grant in slime-ball mode), the creator and only regular judge on *American Dreamz*. But we spend the bulk of our time with the ruthlessly ambitious America's sweetheart, Sally Kendoo (Mandy Moore), and Omer (Sam Golzari), who is tasked by his terrorist cousin with assassinating the president when he comes to guest judge, even though all he really wants to do is sing, dance, and win the competition.

Weitz's script is lighter on memorable zingers than you might hope, though he sticks the landing with some juicy nastiness thrown the industry's way: "[Agents] act greedy and mean for you so that you can seem like a nice person," explains Kendoo's mom, played by Jennifer Coolidge. And the sheer audacity of a studio movie going to the places *American Dreamz* goes is invigorating in and of itself. None of it would work, though, without the commitment of the cast, who find incredible levels of cartoon meanness throughout, without ever spilling into dull caricature.

Moore is particularly spellbinding as smarter-than-she-seems Kendoo. Skewering both her own teen-pop career and the cravenness of the wannabe stars moving through the *Idol* machine for their chance to emulate it, Moore is a terrifying fame monster. We'd definitely vote for her.

BLADE 1998

 **54%** | Directed by Stephen Norrington
Written by David S. Goyer
Starring Wesley Snipes, Stephen Dorff, Kris Kristofferson, N'Bushe Wright

Though some may find the plot a bit lacking, *Blade*'s action is fierce, plentiful, and appropriately stylish for a comic book adaptation.

Synopsis

Born of a woman turned into a vampire while pregnant, Blade has all of the benefits of vampirism with none of its downsides. Other vampires call him the Daywalker—they want his ability to face the sun; he wants to kill them all.

"ULTIMATELY, IT'S A VICTIM OF ITS OWN INFLUENCE."

Why We Love It

While critics wanted more substance, *Blade*'s style is its best feature.

The opening blood rave sequence is a great example of all the things this vampire superhero movie gets right. It's highly stylized, set to a killer techno remix of New Order's "Confusion," and features future *The Shield* costar Kenneth Johnson as the main course at a vampire bacchanal. The strobe lighting, jump cuts, sprays of rich red plasma, and Blade's (Wesley Snipes) entrance make for a near-perfect kickoff. It is no surprise that variations of the blood rave continued to appear in movies well after *Blade*'s debut.

With so many films imitating its style and story over the years, *Blade* reads a little been-there-done-that upon repeat viewing. The title character's personal war on vampires, the presentation of the creatures as a moneyed elite, and even the film's love of leather outfits cannot help but feel dated. That may be why it has been relegated to obscurity despite jumpstarting the Marvel film brand and convincing 20th Century Fox that there might be some sort of worthwhile project in the *X-Men* concept.

Ultimately, it's a victim of its own influence. The film's fight choreography, black leather, and desaturated colors set the tone for films that would go on to overshadow it—movies like *X-Men*, *The League of Extraordinary Gentlemen*, and more recent flicks like *Man of Steel* and *Batman v Superman: Dawn of Justice*. But few executed the look and vibe as well as *Blade* did. (Sadly, director Stephen Norrington never received the credit for his innovations.)

To watch *Blade* now is to see a film that exists outside of cinematic universes and reverence for the source material, which is the norm today. It stands on its own and defines its universe without the aid of Nick Fury, Iron Man, or even a character cameo from Ghost Rider. And it stands on the broad shoulders of Snipes, who ably anchors the world of *Blade*, giving the character a steely charisma as he and hematologist Karen Jenson (N'Bushe Wright) investigate a possible cure for vampirism.

Snipes's presence and the film's innovatively dark and stylish vision were enough to keep the series going for two more films. Reboot time, anyone?

SEQUELS WORTH
A SECOND LOOK

Follow-Ups That Recaptured the Magic —
Or Made Strange Magic of Their Own

It's long been held as moviegoing gospel that "sequels are never as good as their originals." When Rotten Tomatoes arrived on the scene, we were able to prove that to be true—with data to back us up. There are rare examples of superior follow-ups, of course: many consider *The Godfather: Part II* to be better than *The Godfather: Part I* (though the Tomatometer gives the edge to the original by a single percentage point), and Sami Raimi's superhero masterpiece *Spider-Man 2* earned a Certified Fresh 93% on the Tomatometer, beating the director's acclaimed first *Spider-Man* movie by 3%. More frequently, though, precipitous drop-offs are the order of the day. Critics often slap sequels around for carbon-copying their predecessors, failing to recapture a first film's magic, or for trying to do too much (even Raimi would fall into this final trap with his *barely* Fresh third *Spider-Man* movie). The Rotten movies in this chapter are guilty of

> THEIR FRANCHISES ARE ALL THE RICHER (AND WEIRDER AND WILDER) FOR HAVING THEM IN THE MIX.

some of these sequel sins—*Rocky IV*, about which critic Amy Nicholson writes, is guilty of all of them and truly wonderful because of it—but we're willing to forgive and even embrace them. Each, in its own way, does something to mark itself as more than just a retread: some take risks, like hot-footing it to Japan with an entirely new cast of characters (we're looking at you, *Fast and the Furious: Tokyo Drift*), and some take truly bizarre turns (remember the mutants in *Beneath the Planet of the Apes*?). Some make seemingly simple switches (a gender swap in *Grease 2*, a change of location for *Home Alone 2: Lost In New York*), managing to find new charms in gently tweaked conceits. They may not be Fresh, and most have achieved a certain "reputation," but their franchises are all the richer (and weirder and wilder) for having them in the mix.

HOME ALONE 2: LOST IN NEW YORK 1992

 32%

Directed by Chris Columbus
Written by John Hughes
Starring Macaulay Culkin, Joe Pesci, Daniel Stern, Catherine O'Hara, John Heard, Tim Curry, Brenda Fricker

A change of venue—and more sentimentality and violence—can't obscure the fact that *Home Alone 2: Lost In New York* is a less inspired facsimile of its predecessor.

Synopsis

They did it again: in a rush to make their flight to Miami, the McCallisters lose eight-year-old Kevin in O'Hare airport, leaving him to accidentally board a flight to New York City. At first, being not-at-home alone is a dream—Kevin checks into the Plaza and goes toy shopping—but soon he realizes that the same bandits he fended off a year ago are also walking the streets of Manhattan.

Why We Love It

For their sequel to their holiday smash *Home Alone*, writer John Hughes and director Chris Columbus were careful not to tinker too much with a very successful formula. In fact, save for the titular change in location, *Home Alone 2* is . . . *Home Alone* all over again. There's a chaotic airport scene, not one but two penny-dropping "Kevin!" screams, another scary-but-ultimately-lovely Boo Radley type, and, of course, plenty of slapstick violence directed at the Wet Bandits, now going by the "Sticky Bandits." For some, the change in setting wasn't enough to shake a dull sense of *déjà vu*; for others, especially kids who dreamed of a Kevin McCallister–style adventure, it was like a second helping of ice cream. In bed. With no pesky parents around.

The circumstances that place Kevin (Macaulay Culkin) in New York City for the sequel are ridiculous—a pile-up of gross parental neglect, airline oversight, and wild coincidence. The writers' work in these early scenes is as strained as one of Kevin's Rube Goldberg–like torture devices. And yet, once we get to Manhattan, the film takes off, largely because

Home Alone 2 absolutely nails the elements that it carbon-copies from the original. There's a wonderful sequence involving Kevin's cassette recorder that's lifted almost wholesale from the first movie, but no less funny because of it, and the "Pigeon Lady" (Brenda Fricker)—an at-first terrifying figure Kevin meets in Central Park—has a story arc that's every bit as sweetly moving as Old Man Marley's. Kevin's climactic showdown with the bandits in an abandoned Upper West Side brownstone feels more sinister than in the original, partly because he's on the offense: he's not defending his home this time; he's lured them here.

John Williams's memorably schmaltzy score, with a few new thematic additions, is excellent throughout.

Home Alone 2 does more than just rehash, though: it takes the thing that spoke to every kids' heart in *Home Alone*—the fantasy of having the house to yourself—and expands on it, providing audiences with the *Big*-like fantasy of having the greatest city in the world as your playground. Every nineties kid remembers living vicariously through Kevin as he explored a mega toy store, rang up wild room service bills in a fancy hotel, jaunted through Central Park, and made fools of a set of cartoonish big-city adults.

The movie also turns out to be a loving tribute to New York itself. The filmmakers could have played up the more sinister side of the city—this was pre-Giuliani and before the Disneyfication of Times Square—and yet they only hint at its darker corners, leaning instead into the excitement, hope, and sense of community for which the city is famous. This is a New York not just of muggings and porno theaters, but a city in which an eight-year-old can get by on his own just fine. A city in which he can stand atop a still-standing World Trade Center tower and gleefully imagine the many adventures that await below.

TEENAGE MUTANT NINJA TURTLES II: THE SECRET OF THE OOZE 1991

 **35%**

Directed by Michael Pressman
Written by Todd W. Langen
Starring Paige Turco, David Warner, Ernie Reyes Jr., Vanilla Ice

Critics Consensus

Not only is the movie's juvenile dialogue unbearable for adults, but the Turtles' dopey and casual attitude toward physical violence makes them poor kids' role models.

Synopsis

Picking up sometime after the first film, the Turtles search for a new home and learn about their mysterious origins. Meanwhile, the wicked Shredder sets out to re-establish the Foot Clan and get his revenge.

Why We Love It

Sometimes, a heavy swig of nostalgia and Turtle Power can overpower traditional film criticism.

In the first live-action *Ninja Turtles* movie, director Steve Barron opted for grittiness and dark lighting for his heroes, drawing inspiration from the characters' broody comic books. In the sequel, *The Secret of the Ooze*, director Michael Pressman goes brighter and far more comical, seemingly more inspired by the wildly popular nineties cartoon series. The Turtles are given broad lines to speak and dated vaudeville routines to perform, and under all the happy, bright lighting, it's hard to ignore the rather dubious lip articulation on those dodgy masks.

The quest for a more child-friendly film also means the Turtles largely refrain from using their weapons. The filmmakers wanted to tone down the violence, so the nunchucks, sai, katanas, and bo staff become decorative pieces as the Turtles instead use kitchen supplies and pratfalls to attack their foes. Also, Vanilla Ice makes an important cameo to deliver "ninja rap" to a generation of unsuspecting kids. (We still know every word.)

To put it another way, it's a little *too* Michelangelo. But deliberately so.

All of these changes indicate a very specific directive: make it fun. Many kids left the first film wondering why it wasn't like the cartoon, and the studio was not going to repeat that mistake. In changing the tone, the film does make plenty of mistakes. Jokes rarely land for anyone out of middle school. Tokka and Rahzar, the film's answer to cartoon baddies Bebop and Rocksteady, offer no menace, and even the showdown with a mutated "Super-Shredder" amounts to nothing.

And yet the film gets one thing very, *very* right— and it's a big one for true fans of these characters: it perfectly captures the essence of the early-1990s TMNT craze. In attempting to honor the feel of the cartoon and maintain *some* of the darker tone from the first film and the original comic books, it somehow portions out the history of the Turtles in the midst of all the cheese. It's fan service, *par excellence.*

The inexplicable "Ninja, Ninja, RAP!" has become for those fans the anthem of a simpler time before smartphones, mortgages, and an endless stream of TMNT reboots (which true fans, naturally, view with suspicion if not open hostility). Certainly a slight film, *Teenage Mutant Ninja Turtles II: The Secret of the Ooze* is a VHS version of a faded photograph taken in a roller rink: a perfect distillation of one very goofy moment in time. And one you love to pull out of the shoebox every now and then.

 **40%** | **Written and directed by** Sylvester Stallone
Starring Sylvester Stallone, Talia Shire, Dolph Lundgren, Burt Young, Carl Weathers, Brigitte Nielsen

CRITIC: Amy Nicholson

Amy Nicholson is a film writer and critic for *Variety*, *The Guardian*, and the *Washington Post* and the host of the movie podcasts *The Canon* and *Unspooled*. Her first book, *Tom Cruise: Anatomy of an Actor*, was published by Cahiers du Cinema.

In *Rocky IV*, Sylvester Stallone KO-ed communism in Moscow—on Christmas, no less!—but got battered by movie critics in his own country, aghast that the underdog they'd once championed all the way to an Oscar had turned into a Cold War bully. At one screening, a reviewer was alarmed to hear people in the audience get so riled up when Dolph Lundgren's Soviet boxer Ivan Drago accidentally kills Apollo Creed in an East-versus-West exhibition match that they spontaneously began to sing Bruce Springsteen's "Born in the USA." (The one eighties guitar anthem *not* shoehorned into the movie.) Stallone, who also wrote and directed the film, does try to smooth things over. After Rocky hammers the hammer-and-sickle in the climactic fight, he delivers a pacifist speech about healing the nuclear tensions with, er, fisticuffs. "In here, we're two guys killing each other," he bellowed. "But I guess that's better than twenty million." The real-life crowd wasn't having it. Hooted one ticket-buyer, "Yeah, but *we* won!"

Critics and moviegoers often square-off themselves—and this round, the audiences won. *Rocky IV* set a winter box office record, causing a journalist to fret that if "the *Rocky* saga is an indication of public opinion, it might be a good idea to check the location of the nearest fallout shelter." Lundgren was credited with bringing back the crewcut hairstyle. And Stallone, as ever, responded to success

> "**LUNDGREN WAS CREDITED WITH BRINGING BACK THE CREWCUT HAIRSTYLE. AND STALLONE, AS EVER, RESPONDED TO SUCCESS BY PRETEND-THREATENING TO QUIT.**"

by pretend-threatening to quit. "This is it for Rocky," he vowed. "You take on supposedly the greatest fighting machine ever built, a biochemically produced Soviet fighter. What can you do after that? Everything subsequent is anticlimactic."

Yeah, right. *Rocky IV* begat four more sequels, the most recent two of which, *Creed* and *Creed II*, wouldn't exist if Drago hadn't fatally clobbered Apollo. That alone is an argument for its inclusion in the pugilistic pantheon. But *Rocky IV* is a fascinating must-watch time capsule. It's at once simplistic and subversive, like a boxer who's taken so many knocks to the head that everything he says is dada-esque.

For all its jabs at cold-hearted USSR tactics, *Rocky IV* lands an equal number of blows on Ronald Reagan's America. If the Soviet Union is a frozen landscape of uniformed soldiers and doctors prodding Drago like a factory-made Holstein, the United States is rotting from decadence. Now that he's no longer breaking fingers for cash, Rocky struts around a mansion crammed with sports cars, then-state-of-the-art video cameras, and a six-foot talking robot programmed to be ex-butcher Uncle Paulie's (Burt Young) butler and girlfriend. For these modern-day Marie Antoinettes, life is so luxurious that Rocky finds an excuse to eat two different cakes in back-to-back scenes. "Party ain't over yet!" he grins to his wife. Sighs Adrian (Talia Shire), "It's Wednesday?"

Ego—not Drago—kills Apollo Creed. Instead of actually training to fight an undefeated ex-military gold medalist giant who dwarfs him by four inches and forty pounds, Apollo would rather put on a razzle-dazzle show with chandeliers and showgirls and James Brown swiveling on stage. When Drago walks into the ring ready to rumble, he sees Apollo Creed setting off fireworks in front of a giant animatronic goat head. What are these crazy Americans worshipping? Drago versus Apollo isn't even a contest. It's over in two rounds.

Lundgren's Drago barely speaks, except in catchphrases, most famously, "I will break you." His wife, Ludmilla (Brigitte Nielsen), does most of the talking, perhaps because the actress herself was about to marry Stallone. Yet, while audiences left quoting her husband—my personal favorite is his almost-Buddhist koan, "If he dies, he dies"—Ludmilla has the lines people should have remembered, which she delivers at a press conference in near-tears after her family receives death threats. "We are not in politics. All I want is for my husband to be safe," she insists. "You have this belief that this country is so very good, and we are so very bad—you have this belief that you are so fair and we are so very cruel."

Rocky IV mangles Russian accents. It even mangles Russian geography. (When Rocky yells at Adrian that his own ego is spurring him to Moscow, he angrily gets into a car and drives, as though if he hurried, he might still make it across the Bering Strait.) But in Ludmilla's big scene, *Rocky IV* holds

"LIKE BALBOA HIMSELF, IT'S NOT AS DUMB AS IT LOOKS."

up a mirror to Americans' self-conception that audiences weren't ready to see.

Now they are, and the film's punches hit more of their targets. The film itself is structured into twin fights that stare back at each other from opposite sides of the glassy Atlantic Ocean. Two foreigners, two hostile crowds, two hometown heroes defeated, and two very different reactions.

What matters isn't that Rocky wins—sorry to the random overexcited guy in the theater—it's the response of the fans within the film. The Americans boo Drago when he enters, about-face and cheer him when he starts to win, and hiss when he succeeds. The Russians boo Rocky when he enters, cheer when he holds steady in certain defeat, and slow clap when he survives long enough to pound Drago to the floor. We won, sure, but they were better losers. With the Russian-American relations once again at a deep freeze, today's audiences can have complicated feelings about *Rocky IV*. But like Balboa himself, it's not as dumb as it looks.

Rotten Tomatoes' Critics Consensus *Rocky IV* inflates the action to absurd heights, but it ultimately rings hollow thanks to a story that hits the same basic beats as the first three entries in the franchise.

DRACULA'S DAUGHTER 1936

55%

Directed by Lambert Hillyer
Written by Garrett Fort
Starring Gloria Holden, Otto Kruger, Marguerite Churchill, Edward Van Sloan

Critics Consensus

Dracula's Daughter extends the Universal horror myth in an interesting direction, but the talky script and mild atmosphere undermine its ambition.

Synopsis

Countess Zaleska carries the curse of vampirism inherited from her father. First, she tries psychiatrists to rid her thirst. Realizing what a sham that is, she resorts to the second-best option: kidnapping and feasting on luscious young women!

Why We Love It

The original *Dracula* ushered in the golden age of the Universal monsters, a time when Frankenstein experiments, the Invisible Man, the Mummy, and more shared not only screen time at the cinema but also a connected cinematic universe—decades before your Captain America and Wonder Woman. Universal was quick to churn out a *Frankenstein* sequel (and by "churn," we mean field another masterpiece with *Bride of Frankenstein*), though a follow-up to *Dracula* took longer for the studio to sink their teeth into.

When *Dracula's Daughter* released, five years had already passed in the real world, but in the movie, only mere minutes had lapsed. Van Helsing—sorry, VON Helsing—has killed the vampire and been taken into custody, where no one believes his batty story. That same night, a cloaked figure hypnotizes the guard and steals off with Dracula's corpse. Von Helsing's skeptical pupil, psychiatrist Jeffrey Garth,

is called to help. If you were wondering about the state of psychiatry in 1936, here's some sample medicine: Dr. Garth puts alcoholics in a room with a cup of liquor and punishes them if they touch it over the course of an hour. We trust him completely.

Dr. Garth has a new patient: Countess Marya Zaleska, a woman with a problem of supernatural nature that she cannot fully divulge. She is Count Dracula's daughter, the one who stole her father's body and has burned it to cleanse her soul. Yet, still with a hunger for blood, she turns to the field of psychiatry for help but soon will succumb to the dark ritual of vampirism. Gloria Holden, acting on contract and hating the horror genre, projects contempt by shutting down any flourishes of fun in the role. "Let them try adding any of *this* to my highlight reel," you can almost hear her gnashing between takes. But her hopelessly ambiguous acting had the opposite of the desired effect: it made the performance memorable, as witness to a vampire in roiling conflict with its own existence.

Anxiety and discomfort ooze beneath Zaleska's regal surface. Her moment with an undressed Nan Grey, modeling vulnerably for a painting, is so sizzling, it launched a million eyebrows and essays over the film's lesbian undertones. Cloaked in black velvet covering all except her searching, penetrating eyes, the Countess looks just as spooky as any of the evil-doers in the Universal monster camarilla. Holden made a horror icon without ever giving a shit.

DIE HARD: WITH A VENGEANCE 1995

 **52%**

Directed by John McTiernan
Written by Jonathan Hensleigh
Starring Bruce Willis, Samuel L. Jackson, Jeremy Irons, Graham Greene, Colleen Camp

Critics Consensus

Die Hard: With a Vengeance gets off to a fast start and benefits from Bruce Willis and Samuel L. Jackson's barbed interplay but clatters to a bombastic finish in a vain effort to cover for an overall lack of fresh ideas.

Synopsis

John McClane has been laid off the force for alcoholism and split from his wife. A psychopathic bomber begins taunting him, threatening to destroy New York City if John doesn't complete his tasks and collect his clues.

Why We Love It

Though Bruce Willis and Samuel L. Jackson both had roles in *National Lampoon's Loaded Weapon* (1991) and Quentin Tarantino's *Pulp Fiction* (1994), they'd never shared a scene together. *Die Hard: With a Vengeance* marked the beginning of their memorable cinematic partnership, leading to both *Unbreakable* (2000) and *Glass* (2019). Their comic timing and constant ribbing of one another brings to mind other classic duos, but specifically Mel Gibson with Danny Glover, and Richard Pryor with Gene Wilder, whose paired erratic deliveries dynamically played off one another. The magical element between Willis and Jackson, however, was their shared grumpiness. They are brother curmudgeons from another mother.

Just watch the scene in which McClane meets Jackson's Zeus Carver: McClane's hungover and (on the bomber's orders) standing in the middle of Harlem wearing a sandwich board with a racist message. Zeus approaches not with anger but exasperation and is surprised when McClane mirrors that right back to him. "You are about to have a very bad day," Zeus says. "Tell me about it," McClane replies with a resigned sigh.

The second installment of the franchise had already set up the premise that McClane could gain a helpful sidekick along the way, with janitor Marvin (Tom Bower) filling that small role. McTiernan predicted an audience might grow tired of McClane alone against the bad guys and, to ward off any franchise fatigue, writer Jonathan Hensleigh expanded the sidekick bit to become a fully fleshed-out character.

Some critics just weren't fond of a buddy for McClane. Rita Kempley, writing for the *Washington Post*, pointed out, "*Die Hard* movies are supposed to be one-man-against-impossible-odds, not the hero's chance to practice his social skills." But the setting of New York City actually lends itself well to a more communal approach to stopping a mad terrorist, where your friends and neighbors can begrudgingly band together to do what's right. Either way, it's rare that a franchise can completely reinvent itself, but with the addition of Jackson and a city setting that grounds the action in the real world with real people, McTiernan successfully reformed the series and gifted it and McClane new life.

Hensleigh would go on to rack up eight more Rotten scores for such beloved movies as *Jumanji* (1995), *Con Air* (1997), and *Armageddon* (1998).

GREASE 2  1982

38%

Directed by Patricia Birch
Written by Ken Finkleman
Starring Maxwell Caulfield, Michelle Pfeiffer, Lorna Luft, Maureen Teefy

Critics Consensus

Grease 2 is undeniably stocked with solid songs and well-choreographed dance sequences, but there's no getting around the fact that it's a blatant retread of its far more entertaining predecessor.

Synopsis

A new class at Rydell High sings and dances through a crazy senior year as British transplant Michael hides his identity to win the heart of Pink Lady Stephanie.

Why We Love It

Call it what you will—unnecessary, cynical—*Grease 2* is a campy gem that defies its reputation as a poor replay of the first movie.

Set three years after that film, *Grease 2* opens in much the same way that *Grease* did: with Principal McGee (Eve Arden) and secretary Blanche (Dody Goodman) anticipating a memorable school year. They are immediately ambushed by "Back to School Again," a big production number that introduces all of the new characters, reintroduces beauty school dropout Frenchy (Didi Conn) and acts as the opening credit sequence. It lacks the understated charm of the first film's animated credits—set to Frankie Valli's performance of "Grease Is the Word"—but it reflects the energy the sequel brings to the table and the valiant effort it is about to make to match its predecessor.

It also indicates the film's biggest problem for critics at the time: it feels like something's missing.

Losing the first film's stars (John Travolta and Olivia Newton-John, who both declined the invitation to return), *Grease 2* attempts to save itself by inverting the roles. Maxwell Caulfield's Michael is essentially Sandy, while Michelle Pfeiffer's Stephanie is a Pink Lady version of Danny. But even if that inversion seems cheap, the characters distinguish themselves in interesting ways. When we meet Stephanie, she is fed up with the Pink Lady/T-Bird dynamic and dumps T-Bird leader Nogerelli (Adrian Zmed) to spend her senior year single. We also learn she has aspirations greater than being a biker's girl when Michael begins tutoring her in school subjects. The polished Michael, meanwhile, adopts a de facto superhero identity to convince Stephanie that she should go out with him.

The ideas may be as light as air, but Caulfield, Pfeiffer, director Patricia Birch (choreographer of the first film), and the rest of the cast commit to the concept in a way that suggests far less cynicism on their part than the studio's when it rushed the sequel into production. The cast and crew's dedication leads to one dynamite song, "Cool Rider"—just try to get it out of your head—and at least two other great musical sequences.

Shameless cash grab? Sure. But sometimes you just wanna dance.

SCREAM 3 **2000**

39%

Directed by Wes Craven
Written by Ehren Kruger
Starring Neve Campbell, Courteney Cox, David Arquette, Parker Posey, Patrick Dempsey

Critics Consensus

Despite some surprising twists, *Scream 3* sees the franchise falling back on the same old horror formulas and clichés it once hacked and slashed with postmodern abandon.

Synopsis

Ghostface moves to Hollywood in this (allegedly) trilogy-ending installment of the nineties slasher sensation. When the cast of movie-in-the-movie *Stab 3* are picked off, franchise final girl Sidney Prescott finds herself once again having to fight the past . . . and her cell phone.

Why We Love It

Scream 2 was that rare thing: a horror sequel that many people thought was just as good as the original—and that the Tomatometer would tell you is actually slightly better. *Scream 3* was that much less rare thing: a horror sequel many fans felt was a cash-grabbing betrayal of the original and that the Tomatometer deemed a dirty, Rotten stinker. And given what was going on behind the scenes, it's no wonder this third outing for Ghostface, Sidney, Dewey, Gale, and Co. got splatted.

Late-nineties horror wunderkind Kevin Williamson didn't have time to write the full script for *Scream 3*, instead turning in a treatment that *Arlington Road* scribe Ehren Kruger would be tasked with adapting. What ended up on screen was very different from what Williamson had envisioned. Late 1999 was not a great time to make scary movies, especially ones set near high schools, given what

had recently occurred at Columbine; the studio pushed for the action to move to L.A., away from Woodsboro High, and for the filmmakers to lean heavily into comedy over gore. (Director Wes Craven apparently put his foot down when it was suggested the film feature no violence whatsoever.)

Adding to the drama: there were scheduling difficulties with the cast and script changes that would sometimes come in on the day of shooting. (The already meta horror series reaches Peak Meta when the actors in *Stab 3* complain about day-of rewrites.)

And yet if you know what you're getting into, the comedy actually works, particularly in the character of Jennifer Jolie, played by Parker Posey, making her first big indie-to-mainstream move. Posey is a twitchy delight as the actress cast as Courteney Cox's Gale Weathers in *Stab 3*, stalking Cox around the backlots and frantically unraveling when her costars' bodies start piling up. She also gets to take part in the movie's best moment, when Jolie and Weathers encounter cynical studio archivist, Bianca (Carrie Fisher in a fabulous little cameo that has interesting new shades in the post-#MeToo era).

There are solid scares here, too, and how could there not be, with Craven behind the camera? Particularly effective is the sequence in which Campbell's Prescott finds herself alone on the *Stab 3* set, exploring a recreation of the Woodsboro home she grew up in. When Ghostface inevitably shows up, it's a terrifying echo of the superior first film and a hint of what this trilogy closer might have been had Craven and Williamson been given the time and space to do their thing.

RETURN TO OZ 1985

52%

Directed by Walter Murch
Written by Walter Murch and Gill Dennis
Starring Fairuza Balk, Nicol Williamson, Jean Marsh, Piper Laurie, Matt Clark

Return to Oz taps into the darker side of L. Frank Baum's book series with an intermittently dazzling adventure that never quite recaptures the magic of its classic predecessor.

Synopsis

Concerned that her niece, Dorothy, can't sleep—or stop talking about a fanciful recent adventure to a faraway land—Aunt Em takes her to see a special doctor who, unbeknownst to the family, has an experimental plan. Aided by a mysterious young girl, Dorothy escapes the doctor's clutches and is swept away by a storm back to Oz, where she will face a new nemesis—the Nome King—and a perilous journey home.

Why We Love It

First-time director Walter Murch knew that returning to Oz was going to be risky. Not only was he making a sequel to arguably the most beloved movie of all time, but he was also going to ditch the things people loved so much about the original. That meant no songs, no dancing, no bright colors, and no munchkins. Adapting L. Frank Baum's second two *Oz* books—*The Marvelous Land of Oz* and *Ozma of Oz*—Murch, who cowrote the screenplay with Gill Dennis, hewed much closer to the author's dark tone than that of MGM's musical. And so it was that audiences entered the theater expecting another slipper-tapping trip down the Yellow Brick Road and were instead transported to a Victorian asylum where a preteen Dorothy Gale (Fairuza Balk) is strapped to a gurney and readied for a round of electroshock therapy. And that was just the first fifteen minutes.

The Guardian, in a thirty-years-later look back at David Shire's masterful and lyric-less score, called *Return to Oz* "the creepiest Disney film ever to grace the screen." We can't argue with that. This is not a movie that Internet meme masters would need to re-cut or re-score to turn into a horror flick; it does the work by itself. Dorothy escapes the asylum only to land in a desolate Oz populated by some of the most terrifying imagery the eighties fantasy genre had to offer. Witness, for example, the Wheelers, a troupe of Cirque du Soleil–styled meanies who patrol the deserted and destroyed Emerald City; or their master, Princess Mombi, who keeps dozens of alternate heads encased in glass cabinets along an almost endless hallway (she is primarily played by the fabulously evil Jean Marsh, who also played Queen Bavmorda in Ron Howard's *Willow*). The friendlier sidekicks Dorothy meets along the way—including a robot named Tik-Tok and a Jack Skellington–like figure named Jack Pumpkinhead—are inconsequential. This is an *Oz* where the nightmares linger much longer than the dreams.

No wonder Disney was nervous. At a certain point, with the shooting schedule delayed and dailies revealing the darkness of Murch's vision, the studio decided this risk was too large and briefly fired the director from the project. Murch told *Film Freak Central* that his close friend, George Lucas, flew from Japan to the United Kingdom to see the footage and then met with Disney executives, convincing them to re-install Murch and continue with production. He saw in this *Oz* movie the same thing that has gone on to make it something of a cult favorite: a film of bizarre, terrifying, and indelible delights. Murch, who would never direct another film following *Oz*'s commercial and critical failure, has called Lucas's intervention a "fantastic act of generosity." It was for him, and for us.

FRIDAY THE 13TH PART 2 1981

 **29%**

Directed by Steve Miner
Written by Ron Kurz
Starring Amy Steel, John Furey, Adrienne King, Kirsten Baker, Stu Charno, Warrington Gillette

CRITIC: Candice Frederick

Candice Frederick is a NYC-based freelance TV and film critic whose work has appeared in numerous outlets, including *Teen Vogue*, the *New York Times*, and *Harper's Bazaar*.

It's popular to turn up our noses at the very thought of a sequel to a hit slasher film. In this case, it was the follow-up to 1980's *Friday the 13th*, in which a masked villain (Jason Voorhees's mother) massacred a bunch of camp counselors similar to those who abandoned her son as a child, leaving him to drown in a lake. *Why would anyone ever return to Camp Crystal Lake to meet the same fate?* asked the critics. *What crude plot device will get them there? What been-there-done-that scenarios will we have to endure?* As DVD Town critic John J. Puccio noted in his review of 1981's *Friday the 13th Part 2*, which is set five years after the events of the first film, "The new camp counselors are interchangeable with the old ones. Different faces, same basic people."

He was right, of course. Yet while the characters (predominantly white, oblivious, and increasingly horny young adults) certainly follow a format, the film also does something subversive as it follows its familiar beats—something few generic slashers bother with. *Part 2* contextualizes the frightening state of mind of its legendary new villain, the resurrected Jason, and in doing so adds another chilly and fascinating layer onto its grisly premise.

Our first glimpse at this surprising depth, and the psychology of Jason, comes about three murders into the movie, well after our new group of doomed counselors has settled somewhere near Camp Crystal Lake. (They have yet to discover the dead bodies around them at this point—again, these fun-loving folks are completely oblivious.) Ginny (Amy Steel) is hanging out at a bar with Paul (John Furey) and a friend when she begins to wonder aloud whether Jason is in fact real and resurrected and if he will not rest until all of them are dead. After all, she says, it was camp counselors—just

> ## "PART 2 CONTEXTUALIZES THE FRIGHTENING STATE OF MIND OF ITS LEGENDARY NEW VILLAIN, THE RESURRECTED JASON."

like us!—who allowed him to die as they fornicated in cabins nearby. And it was a camp counselor who decapitated without remorse his own revenge-seeking mother in the first film's finale. Jason was just a boy when his life suddenly ended; could he have been stuck in that stunted little-boy mindset as he grappled with his mother's death? Ginny goes as far as to call him an "out of control retard" and "a boy trapped in a man's body." She follows that with a violent shudder, right before her friends have a good laugh about her fears. No points for guessing which of these three characters survives to the credits.

Jason's mental capacity hadn't really been examined or even referenced previously; it's also not pronounced in the follow-up films. Though the first film confronts Mrs. Voorhees's grief as she exacts revenge on those who stood idly by while her dear son flailed in the middle of the lake, only in this sequel are we compelled to consider how the trauma

impacted him—psychologically and physically. This adds a remarkable level of suspense for both fans of the franchise and for Jason's potential victims: the very thought of how a broken man—at once a victim and a maniac—will react once he sees people who dress and act the same as those who ignored him as a child romping around the grounds once again is terrifying. The same could be said about Jason's villainous counterpart, *Halloween's* Michael Myers, himself a prisoner of his own mind. But Jason has a vulnerability to him. He's not just out for blood; he's somehow managed to return to life, but the one person who made him feel safe is no longer there. He's not only enraged, he's in utter agony.

So when we finally see him for the first time in this franchise, in the third act of this sequel, he is every bit a horrifying manifestation of the trauma Ginny had feared. His face is almost completely decayed. He looks damaged as much as he looks terrifying.

He has a slow yet deliberate walk as he preys on the young camp dwellers, but he is not unflappable. In the film's final moments, Ginny—cornered by Jason in his broken-down shack—puts on Mrs. Voorhees's sweater, which the killer has propped up in a macabre shrine, and it stops Jason in his tracks. To a man whose own trauma and grief remain unchecked, the notion that his mother has somehow resurfaced and is once again by his side gives him pause. This scene is especially eerie if you consider Ginny's musings on Jason earlier in the movie. Her fears were laughed off, but she becomes the one who has to face him in the end. Jason may have been "just a legend" to her friends, but at this moment he is her worst nightmare fully realized: angry, damaged, unpredictable, and armed with a machete.

The fragility of this moment, which could have really gone either way (spoiler alert: Ginny's plan does get her out of that corner and temporarily out of Jason's sights), also resonates when you consider it through the hypersexualized lens of the franchise. Both the sequel director, Steve Miner, and the director of the first film, Sean S. Cunningham, have been rightfully criticized for the ways both movies exploit the female body; their cameras linger on bare breasts and zoom up close to the young women's butts. But before we meet Jason later in the film, we are forced into his perspective, sharing his view from behind his mask, and he does not appear to understand sexuality outside of its role in his death. These glimpses of flesh, then, are images of fascination and rage that hark back to his arrested development and his mother, who weaponized sex.

Yes, it's easy to write off *Friday the 13th Part 2*

> ## "THESE COMPLEXITIES ARE WHAT TURN A FACELESS, DERANGED VILLAIN INTO A SOMEWHAT SYMPATHETIC AND DEBILITATED MAN."

as just another teen slasher film. And worse than that: a teen slasher sequel! But that would neglect how effectively it confronts trauma and madness, legend and reality, grounding the film in a way that aligns with our own fears and sensibilities. These complexities are what turn a faceless, deranged villain into a somewhat sympathetic and debilitated man, one who could so easily be lurking around us, peering from a distance when we least expect it. It's why Jason continues to haunt Camp Crystal Lake in sequel after sequel—and in the darkest corner of our minds.

Rotten Tomatoes' Critics Consensus *Friday the 13th Part 2* sets the template for the franchise to follow with more teen victims, more gruesome set pieces, and fewer reasons to keep following along.

THE FAST AND THE FURIOUS: TOKYO DRIFT 2006

 38%

Directed by Justin Lin
Written by Chris Morgan
Starring Lucas Black, Bow Wow, Brian Tee, Sung Kang, Nathalie Kelley

Critics Consensus

Eye-popping driving sequences coupled with a limp story and flat performances make this *Drift* a disappointing follow-up to previous *Fast and Furious* installments.

Synopsis

In an effort to keep him out of trouble—and away from the fast cars that get him into it—Sean Boswell's mom sends him to live with his dad in Tokyo. It doesn't work. Once there, he finds himself drawn to the underground world of "drift" racing and the girlfriend of a local gang leader.

Why We Love It

Remember when the *Furious* franchise took a big sidestep—all the way to Japan? When Universal ditched Brian and Dom and the rest of the gang for a spinoff adventure about a young man finding himself in one of the world's wildest cities? *No?* Not ringing familiar? That makes sense: *Tokyo Drift* is the lowest-grossing entry in the mega-action franchise that has seriously revved up the global box office since it kicked off in 2002. And many who did see it have burned it from their memories. Their favorite movie franchise is about Vin Diesel and co. driving through skyscrapers and outracing nuclear submarines, and it's all about "family," not some young *gaijin* trying to navigate the Tokyo subway and the lunch line at his new Japanese school.

There is serious charm to this tale, though. Taiwanese American director Justin Lin was an inspired choice to lead the project. In indie breakout *Better Luck Tomorrow* (2002), Lin showed a knack for drawing natural performances from young actors and for portraying the allure of gang life in grounded ways, and he does much the same here. Lucas Black

is low-key and relatable as Sean, and Sung Kang (who starred in *Better Luck Tomorrow*) is magnetic as Han, the "good" gang member who extends a hand, and a set of car keys, to our out-of-place hero. The racial stereotypes are kept to a refreshing minimum, too, even in the early scenes of new-in-Tokyo confusion. Lin isn't interested in weird karaoke bars or ogling strange cuisines; his focus is on tending to that franchise hallmark: Lucas's entry into a new "family." A family of misfits that understands his driving passion.

> ## LIN'S SMART CUTTING BETWEEN PEDALS AND WHEELS AND DETERMINED FACES PUTS YOU RIGHT THERE.

Lin tends well to the franchise's other main priority, too: namely, those incredibly noisy, property-destroying car chases and races. The titular "drifting" doesn't add much to these scenes (a bit of sideways driving around corners, some slow-mo circling), but the action is heart-stoppingly staged nonetheless. It is also, like the drama in the film, more grounded than what you find in most *Furious* movies. The finale is essentially just a race down a hill—what, no glacier!?—but Lin's smart cutting between pedals and wheels and determined faces puts you right there. It's thrilling stuff and was enough for him to be given the keys to the franchise: Lin's fourth *Furious* movie—his third with Dom and the rest of the gang—releases in 2020.

BENEATH THE PLANET OF THE APES 1970

 **38%**

Directed by Ted Post
Written by Paul Dehn and Mort Abrahams
Starring James Franciscus, Kim Hunter, Linda Harrison, David Watson, Maurice Evans

Beneath the Planet of the Apes delivers more action than its predecessor; unfortunately, this is at the expense of the social subtext that elevates the franchise's best entries.

Synopsis

Immediately following the events of *Planet of the Apes*, a second spacecraft crashes in the Forbidden Zone, marooning another astronaut whose crew was tasked with investigating the fate of the first expedition. Brent, the only survivor, encounters a newly militarized ape population determined to infiltrate the Forbidden Zone and comes face to face with humanity's past.

Why We Love It

The original *Planet of the Apes* franchise didn't really begin to build its ongoing mythology until the third film in the series, 1971's *Escape from the Planet of the Apes*, which brought chimpanzee scientists Zira and Cornelius to present-day Earth and set the stage for future installments, including the recently rebooted trilogy. The second film in the series, *Beneath*, however, initially feels like a retread of the first movie (a tact that never impresses the critics) before it gets downright weird (which frequently baffles the critics), so plenty of folks are content to dismiss the entry as an unnecessary placeholder, even if its final scenes mark the chronological end of the saga. The biggest shortcoming of the film is that it was unable to secure Charlton Heston to reprise his role as Taylor for a second adventure across future-Earth (anyone who remembers the gas station scene in *Wayne's*

World 2 is aware how much of a difference his presence—and absence—can make). So the filmmakers chose instead to hire James Franciscus, and to his credit, he does a pretty decent job making you forget he's not essentially just "Discount Heston." Hell, when fully bearded, he looks just like him.

As Brent, Franciscus quickly speeds through the same story beats that Heston's Taylor encountered in the first film—the discovery of intelligent apes, the meet-cute with Linda Harrison's Nova, the request for assistance from Zira and Cornelius—but that's where *Beneath* takes a hard left into nightmare territory and gets *really* interesting. Brent and Nova eventually discover the ancient remains of the New York City subway system, all train tracks and decrepit turnstiles overtaken by centuries of calcification, and the sets are appropriately eerie and evocative. Then come the mutants. That's right: mutants. Specifically, they're human descendants who literally wear skin suits, possess extrasensory powers, and worship a nuclear bomb. It's an absolutely bonkers concept, but it's fascinating; it also makes perfect sense in the greater lore of the *Apes* series, and it leads to a terrifying, chaotic finish.

Unlike the sequels that followed it, *Beneath the Planet of the Apes* was less interested in exploring Important Ideas than it was in expanding upon the story of the first film and ratcheting up the existential dread. It can't hope to compare with its predecessor, but it doesn't have to, because it's got veiny albino telepaths who inspire apocalyptic terror with hymns about weapons of mass destruction. There's more to the film than just that, of course, but sometimes, that's all you need.

JURASSIC PARK III 2001

 **49%**

Directed by Joe Johnston
Written by Peter Buchman, Alexander Payne, Jim Taylor
Starring Sam Neill, William H. Macy, Téa Leoni, Alessandro Nivola, Trevor Morgan

Critics Consensus

Jurassic Park III is darker and faster than its predecessors, but that doesn't quite compensate for the franchise's continuing creative decline.

Synopsis

A reluctant Dr. Alan Grant finds himself on dino-filled Isla Sorna (John Hammond's Site B) after a bickering odd couple lures him there under false pretenses.

Why We Love It

Steven Spielberg opted to not direct *Jurassic Park III,* and it shows. There's little of the Spielbergian grandeur that defined the director's first two *Jurassic* films: gone are the goosebump-raising shots of the island's majestic giants, along with the endless close-ups of the wide-mouthed humans gawping up at them. There's little time spent chatting about the dangers of playing god and the ethics of genetic engineering. Taking the franchise reins, *Jumanji* director Joe Johnston wisely chose not to try to out-Spielberg the master and instead crafted a lean (it's barely an hour and a half) and very mean little monster flick.

Critics were mixed about the decision to go the pure B-movie route, with some missing the first films' more sweeping ambitions and others wanting a bit more story with their dino attacks. Lamenting what he called Johnston's lack of interest in the story's humans, *Rolling Stone* critic Peter Travers wrote that the movie "stinks worse than dino dung."

Maybe Travers's olfactory functions are keener than ours, but we'd respectfully disagree. *Jurassic Park III* is pretty good shit.

What's left when you strip away all that Spielberg "magic" is a set of inventive and suspenseful set pieces that play with our memory of the original film—we get a riff on the Jeep-versus-T-Rex scene, this time with our heroes trapped in the fuselage of a small plane that's just crash-landed—and expand upon threats only hinted at in the first two movies. A climactic sequence set in a mammoth aviary for Pteranodons is one of the best and most genuinely frightening things in any *Jurassic* movie, with Johnston fully capitalizing on all the potential menace of freaky-looking dinos attacking from the air. (An image of a gnarly Pteranodon emerging from the mist on a bridge could have come straight from a slasher movie.)

The primary threat in *Jurassic Park III*, however, is earthbound: the Spinosaurus, which is—according to some reports—even bigger than the Tyrannosaurus. And he's got a sail! He's got nothing on the T-Rex when it comes to screen presence, though, and by the time he's swallowed a phone and his stomach starts ringing, he's something of a hulking, scaly joke. Still, we appreciate the filmmakers' efforts to evolve the series, and the species one-upmanship introduced here would go on to heavily influence the future of the franchise once it was rebooted with *Jurassic World* and *Jurassic World: Fallen Kingdom*.

As for the humans in the movie, viewers are offered Téa Leoni's Amanda and William H. Macy's Paul, a quarreling divorced couple desperately trying to find their lost son. But the ace in the hole here is Sam Neill, returning as Doctor Alan Grant after sitting out the franchise's second movie, *The Lost World. Jurassic Park III* is a shaggy, go-for-the-jugular affair, but what little gravitas it conjures comes by way of the grizzled New Zealand actor. Bring him back for the next *Jurassic World* flick, please.

SPLAT STATS

NERD OUT WITH THESE (MOSTLY) ROTTEN DATA POINTS

AVERAGE NUMBER OF REVIEWS ...

4,787 ADDED PER MONTH

57,451 ADDED PER YEAR

OLDEST ROTTEN MOVIE
WITH 20+ REVIEWS

THE BROADWAY MELODY (1929)

✱ **35%**

MOST CRITIC-PROOF MOVIE
AT THE ALL-TIME DOMESTIC BOX OFFICE

TRANSFORMERS: REVENGE OF THE FALLEN (2009)

✱ **19%**

$402,111,870

TOTAL NUMBER OF REVIEWS ON ROTTEN TOMATOES

1,223,408

TELEVISION
103,743

FILM
1,119,665

THE AVERAGE TOMATOMETER OF ALL MOVIES

64%

9,996 ROTTEN MOVIES

TOTAL TOMATOMETER SCORES GENERATED

27,500

| TELEVISION | 1,578 |
| FILM | 25,922 |

NUMBER OF 0% MOVIES

597

125

NUMBER OF 59% MOVIES

LONGEST 0% STREAK

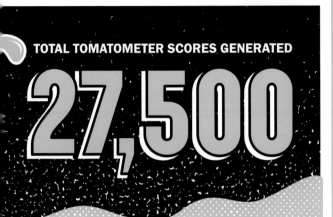

LIFE ON THE LINE (2016)

THE POISON ROSE (2019)

GOTTI (2018)

TRADING PAINT (2019)

SPEED KILLS (2018)

JOHN TRAVOLTA

BUT WE'LL LOVE YOU FOREVER FOR *PULP FICTION!*

*All data accurate as of print date.

BASIC INSTINCTS

Just Because They Make Us Laugh, Scream, and Pump Our Fists

We have included movies in this book the critics sorely underestimated—movies that were too smart for their own time or whose minor flaws distracted from genuine brilliance. Some, we'd go so far to argue, are masterpieces. This chapter is not about those movies. This chapter is about the films that "get the job done" and that we love because they do just that—comedies that make us spit-take, horror flicks that make us jump, action movies that slick our palms with sweat and quicken our heart rates. Admittedly, they're also movies that often don't do much else, and mostly they're not trying to. (You know when you're sitting in an Adam Sandler film—say, *Billy Madison*, featured in these very pages—and you're laughing really hard but you feel kind of silly for doing so because, well, it's pretty dumb? These are *those* movies.) Their appeal to basic human emotions is usually not quite enough to appeal to critics. At least, *most* critics. The following pages feature passionate defenses from seasoned critics who gamely make the case for dumb fun: *Time Out*'s Joshua Rothkopf stands up for Adam McKay's delightfully juvenile *Step Brothers*; the *Los Angeles Times*' Jen Yamato steps into the madhouse that is 1980s action flick *Road House* and never wants to leave; and April Wolfe, writer and host of the *Switchblade Sisters* podcast, demands cheesy horror flick *Dr. Giggles* be given its time in the sun. Meanwhile, we also go to bat for a bunch more movies that are as fun as they are Rotten and celebrate some of the masters of mindless thrills (The Rock! Jim Carrey! Chevy Chase! Van Damme!) who make them so damn rewatchable.

> THEIR APPEAL TO BASIC HUMAN EMOTIONS IS USUALLY NOT QUITE ENOUGH TO APPEAL TO CRITICS.

ROBIN HOOD: MEN IN TIGHTS 1993

 **40%**

Directed by Mel Brooks
Written by Mel Brooks, J. David Shapiro, Evan Chandler
Starring Cary Elwes, Richard Lewis, Roger Rees, Amy Yasbeck, Dave Chappelle, Tracey Ullman

Critics Consensus

Undisciplined, scatological, profoundly silly, and often utterly groan-worthy, *Robin Hood: Men in Tights* still has an amiable, anything-goes goofiness that has made it a cult favorite.

Synopsis

You want us to describe the plot? Seriously? Okay, fine: Robin Hood and his Merry Men go on a quest to save Maid Marian from King John. Hilarity ensues—along with occasional musical sequences.

IT'S A MOVIE IN WHICH A SWORDFIGHT IS BRIEFLY INTERRUPTED BY SHADOW THEATER.

Why We Love It

Robin Hood: Men in Tights is a deeply stupid movie. It frequently resorts to the lowest form of humor: the pun (as when King John declines to murder an entertainer, noting that "a mime is a terrible thing to waste"). *RHMIT* is also bereft of anything resembling a consistent tone: is it a parody of the overly serious *Robin Hood: Prince of Thieves*, or a satire of cinematic swashbucklers, or simply a canvas for Mel Brooks to riff on everything from (now-dated) pop culture references to his own body of work? (The answer is yes.) But as Roger Ebert wrote in his review of Brooks's *Silent Movie*, "Mel Brooks will do anything for a laugh. Anything. He has no shame." And it's that utter shamelessness that makes *RHMIT* such a goofy delight.

It's not hard to see why *RHMIT* bombed with critics (and grown-ups) when it hit theaters in 1993. They had grown up loving *The Producers*, *Young Frankenstein*, and *Blazing Saddles*, and found Brooks's later stuff didn't measure up. But the junior-high crowd didn't care: they loved *Spaceballs* and *RHMIT*, because, silly as they were, those two movies dropped references that made kids feel smart without sacrificing the obligatory flatulence jokes. "Mel Brooks films made me realize that adults could be funny in the same way kids could be," wrote Brad Becker Parton in *Vulture*, "that goofiness didn't go away with age."

It's that amiable, anything-goes goofiness that has made *RHMIT* such a favorite. It's a movie in which a swordfight is briefly interrupted by shadow theater; where what appears at first to be a witch's brew turns out to be a singularly unappealing omelet; where references to *The Godfather*, Arsenio Hall, and the JFK assassination mark this as a universe outside of time and space; and in which a musical number has the Merry Men singing, "We're men/We're men in tights/We roam around the forest looking for fights!"

A cast of game professionals do well to sell this nonsense: with his wry smirk, Cary Elwes is more Errol Flynn than Kevin Costner; Richard Lewis gives Alan Rickman a run for his money in the eye-rolling department; Tracey Ullman digs into a really gross character with relish; and in his film debut at the tender age of nineteen, Dave Chappelle delivers blasé observations on the ridiculous proceedings in the style we'd come to know and love. And if you think the movie has strayed too far beyond the medieval legend, Robin himself sets the record straight: "Unlike some other Robin Hoods, I can speak with an English accent."

FASTER 2010

42%

Directed by George Tillman Jr.
Written by Tony Gayton and Joe Gayton
Starring Dwayne Johnson, Billy Bob Thornton, Carla Gugino, Mike Epps

Critics Consensus

It's good to see Dwayne Johnson back in full-throttle action mode, but *Faster* doesn't deliver enough of the high-octane thrills promised by its title.

Synopsis

Released from jail after a robbery double-cross that left his brother dead, a getaway driver goes on a rampage after everyone involved.

Why We Love It

A tooth fairy clad in pink muslin, with frilly wings to match. A cabby who has to play daddy to some runaways. A player, on the football field and off, who gets suddenly saddled with an eight-year-old daughter. Do these sound like roles befitting a man who would one day be action king?

The second-half of the 2000s decade were a dark, dreary, laughter-filled (or, perhaps, laughter-attempted) time for fans of The Rock. Free from professional wrestling but making dreck like *Doom* (very Rotten at 19%), he utilized his brawn and appreciable acting chops in service of broad family comedies like *The Tooth Fairy* and *The Game Plan*. In essence: The Rock was, pardon the language, acting the jabroni.

But new decade, new you. In 2010, he executed a career U-turn like a Chevrolet Chevelle screeching on a desert road with *Faster*, a lean, mean revenge picture that left The Rock officially in rear view and starred, simply, Dwayne Johnson. Director George Tillman Jr. calls *Faster* a seventies throwback, going so far as naming Johnson's character simply "the Driver," referencing the 1978 Walter Hill movie, a year before Nicolas Winding Refn did the same in 2011's *Drive*. But *Faster* is less neo-noir, more blaxploitation with its sizzling soul soundtrack, gritty shootouts, and sermonizing moral center. The only crook who escapes getting perforated by the Driver is the one who cracks open the Bible. Jesus saves, folks!

Faster came out at a time when audiences were starting to fully grasp the dominating power of so-called cinematic universes, along with serialized, long-form television storytelling. A self-contained throwback revenge picture was simply an aberration in this pop culture landscape. There's no piece of plot development here you can't see coming, but *Faster*'s the kind of movie where more is less in this department. Plot is for people with brains, and most of the Driver's were blown out his skull during the double-cross. As an angel of death, he stomps through the underworld, dressing the scenery in red. There's a fired-up commitment to Johnson's nearly wordless performance, like he's paying penance for the sin of making movies kids could watch. Considering the blockbuster action turn his career would take after this, it seems all is forgiven.

BLOODSPORT 1988

39%

Directed by Newt Arnold
Written by Sheldon Lettich, Mel Friedman, Christopher Cosby
Starring Jean-Claude Van Damme, Leah Ayres, Donald Gibb, Bolo Yeung, Forest Whitaker

Critics Consensus

This is where it all began for the Muscles from Brussels, but beyond Van Damme's athleticism, *Bloodsport* is a clichéd, virtually plotless exercise in action-movie recycling.

Synopsis

Frank Dux is in Hong Kong, ditching the US army for a spot to compete in the Kumite, a mysterious and potentially life-ending martial arts tournament. With his superiors in chase and facing increasingly strong fighters, Dux must fight to survive inside and out of the ring.

Why We Love It

The first thing you'll notice about *Bloodsport*—besides the generous budget for glistening body oil—is how threadbare the plot is outside the ring. This, according to story/cowriter Sheldon Lettich, is by design. At a thirtieth-anniversary screening in Santa Ana, California, he cited *Enter the Dragon* among martial-arts films that used plot devices like undercover cop operations or slain loved ones to "justify" the action. Why can't a movie about punching men just be about men punching, *Bloodsport* asks. A scientifically proven majority of people don't join tournaments because they want to bust a drug ring operating inside the dojo or to avenge their murdered adopted Vietnamese little brother. It's the spirit of competition, where your mental fortitude and physical strength come together to try to demolish the opponent before you.

If *Bloodsport* is a movie that operates solely on the visual, it succeeds because the multiple martial arts depicted here keep the screen alive—and kicking. Each fighter has their own style, and the fun is in seeing how these bodies connect in sweat and sinew. This low-story, high-impact conceit was popular in the late 1980s and inspired creatives well beyond movies. Think of the revolutionary *Street Fighter 2* video game, which feels like a cousin to *Bloodsport*; thought about in those terms, Jean-Claude Van Damme is Ryu, Donald Gibb is Ken (though he looks like Zangief and acts like Guile), Bolo Yeung is M. Bison, and that one guy who fights on all fours? He's Blanka. You almost wish you had a joystick to play this movie.

Bloodsport breaks bricks and shatters bones, yet it maintains a curiously easygoing spirit throughout. It's the kind of B-movie that seeks maximum thrills on minimum budget and effort. The extinction of its type of movie really removed lots of character from the weekly box office, and the death of the companies that produced them—whether through bankruptcy (Cannon, Carolco) or consolidation (New Line)—signaled the end of an era when a studio could be run by weirdos with passion and gut feeling instead of spreadsheets, quadrants, and tracking.

Now, show us the Dim Mak.

STEP BROTHERS 2008

 **55%** | **Directed by** Adam McKay
Written by Will Ferrell and Adam McKay
Starring Will Ferrell, John C. Reilly, Mary Steenburgen, Richard Jenkins, Adam Scott, Kathryn Hahn

CRITIC: Joshua Rothkopf

Joshua Rothkopf is the global deputy film editor at *Time Out*, where he has worked since 2004. He has served on juries at the Tribeca Film Festival, the Sarasota Film Festival, the Hamptons International Film Festival, FearNYC, and others, and teaches at NYU's School of Continuing and Professional Studies.

Critics have a hard time praising immaturity. That's on us, not on *Step Brothers*, which arrived in multiplexes a little over a decade ago, made a decent amount of money (less than *Talladega Nights: The Ballad of Ricky Bobby*), and that now seems like a stealth comedy classic. Immensely talented actors behaving like sweaty, obnoxious twelve-year-olds for no good reason—that's difficult to defend. There are several reasons for this, some legit, some not. Being a critic sometimes imbues one with a certain professional sobriety, a willingness to dive into context, history, form, style. Being silly never helps our cause. *Championing silliness*, a fine distinction, can be dangerous.

Why is *Step Brothers* Rotten? It's only Rotten on Rotten Tomatoes—not at parties, job interviews, or in any situation that calls for somebody to rhetorically ask, "Did we just become best friends?" Mathematically, it's a close call at 55%, since there were a number of reviewers who got it right, including yours truly. But the naysayers held sway. Roger Ebert, usually the most unpretentious of critics, sniped, "In its own tiny way, it lowers the civility of our civilization."

Did it? One can only dream. The revulsion that met *Step Brothers* (Ebert wasn't alone) ignores what the film does well. It evokes with pitch-perfect clarity a certain age, just before adolescence, when a boy is more prone to cry than lash out. (In one standout scene, ugly-crying is exactly what happens.) Will

> "IT EVOKES WITH PITCH-PERFECT CLARITY A CERTAIN AGE, JUST BEFORE ADOLESCENCE, WHEN A BOY IS MORE PRONE TO CRY THAN LASH OUT."

Ferrell and John C. Reilly, as Brennan and Dale, characters pushing forty, are still somehow stuck in that younger moment; it's never explained. They collide when their separately divorced parents (Mary Steenburgen and Richard Jenkins) strike up a sweet middle-aged romance.

Ferrell and Reilly developed the surreal story with director Adam McKay in marathon sessions of improvisation. They found room for everything they could remember from junior high: getting dumb kicks from doing karate in the garage with pumpkins and a samurai sword; precariously stacking bunk beds into a tower, an accident waiting to happen ("So much more extra space in our room to do *activities*!" says Brennan, waiting for an elder's approval). There's a drum set that can't be touched, under pain of death.

(It will be touched, though, by a scrotum.) You can see the actors' physical prep work in Reilly's tighty-whities–clad rooster strut or Ferrell's slightly shy reservation, the delicacy of a kid who's used to being called gifted.

This isn't the feel-good magic of Tom Hanks getting *Big* or Jamie Lee Curtis morphing into a mopey teenager in *Freaky Friday*. *Step Brothers* has no deep moral to impart; its cross-generational wisdom is limited to Jenkins's "Don't lose your dinosaur" speech (i.e., hang on to those Chewbacca masks). Brennan and Dale just want to make fart jokes, watch *Cops*, and maybe get around to recording their rap album. Putting on a defiantly infantile spectacle is the film's *raison d'être*. Even more than *Anchorman*, it crystallizes Ferrell's shouty-man brand of comedy. Maybe that's why *Step Brothers* pissed off critics. There's nothing nourishing about it.

But in asking us to accept these awkward boy-men—and we do, through a stupefied veil of train-wreck magnetism and the distant recognition of our own twelve-year-old selves—*Step Brothers* ends up making a mockery of adulthood, and that's quietly radical. Is being a grown-up such a great thing if it means turning into an asshole like Brennan's older brother Derek (Adam Scott, the film's smarmy secret weapon), a Nazi-like jerk who conducts his family through an a cappella version of "Sweet Child o' Mine"? Should one's ultimate goal be making bank at the fucking Catalina wine mixer?

You either know these phrases or you don't, in which case I envy you, because you get to experience *Step Brothers* for the first time, a transformative experience. Brennan and Dale become our unlikely heroes, tugged down the road of phony maturity and nearly converted into stiff, inflatable versions of themselves before gloriously reverting in the film's final jaw-dropping minutes. Did Hollywood actually greenlight a scene in which Brennan finds himself on the toilet and out of paper, reaching for the bathmat? (The subsequent shot of him emerging from Costco with a brick of back-up rolls, triumphantly pumping his fist, is everything you need to know about this movie.)

And now, of course, *Step Brothers*—like Mike Judge's *Idiocracy*—has gained the additional resonance of being prophetic: a celebration of over-indulged, tantrum-pulling, developmentally arrested

> ## "BRENNAN AND DALE JUST WANT TO MAKE FART JOKES, WATCH *COPS*, AND MAYBE GET AROUND TO RECORDING THEIR RAP ALBUM."

boys who might be kings one day. "Is there any doubt Dale and Brennan would love Trump?" director McKay told Decider in 2017. "And their parents would hate him?"

McKay, meanwhile, has moved on to Oscar-friendly fare like *The Big Short* and *Vice*. *Step Brothers*' then up-and-coming producer, Judd Apatow, carries the mantle of socially sharp comedies best exemplified by *The Big Sick* and Lena Dunham's *Girls*. Will Ferrell and John C. Reilly have since reunited for *Holmes & Watson* (don't bother), but they still get asked about *Step Brothers* more than any other film.

Rotten Tomatoes' Critics Consensus *Step Brothers* indulges in a cheerfully relentless immaturity that will quickly turn off viewers unamused by Ferrell and Reilly—and delight those who find their antics hilarious.

SEE NO EVIL, HEAR NO EVIL 1989

28%

Directed by Arthur Hiller
Written by Earl Barret, Arne Sultan, Eliot Wald, Andrew Kurtzman, Gene Wilder
Starring Richard Pryor, Gene Wilder, Joan Severance

Critics Consensus

One of the weaker collaborations between Richard Pryor and Gene Wilder, *See No Evil, Hear No Evil* strands the comedy duo in a convoluted plot that generates precious few laughs.

Synopsis

At a New York lobby newspaper stand, a man is assassinated. The only witnesses are two employees: blind Wally and deaf Dave. This being the eighties, naturally the two are blamed for the murder and go on the run, hoping to prove their innocence.

Why We Love It

Richard Pryor and Gene Wilder. One guy was a profane stand-up comedian, the other a soft-spoken actor. Obviously, you put them together in front of a camera because of their potential *Odd Couple* quality, but the two had something you can never accurately predict: chemistry, legitimate but ineffable, like thunder and lightning working in comedic tandem—even in this boorish movie that critics deemed below their talents.

Sample joke from *Hear No Evil, See No Evil*: Wilder sticks up a naked woman with his concealed boner.

Another one: Pryor, recovering from a faked brain aneurysm and asked the first thing that pops into mind, screams: "Pussy!"

And yet "sweet," "good-natured," and "cute" may be the first things that pop into your mind when talking about this movie. Because the horndog and potty-mouthed habits may be totally eighties, but nothing could ever dim the soft, genuine, and generous twinkle in Wilder's eyes when he was on screen. In fact, it just made the filthy material coming out of him funnier.

Not that Pryor, still baby-faced in 1989 like some cherub of mischief, ever had issue filth-coating the jokes. Listen to any minute of his stand-up comedy and you'll get the sense Pryor was ever-ready to turn the comedy bluer, reveling whenever it did. Wilder seemed, by turns, amused and exasperated by the things people were paying him to say and act, and that was their magnetic magic as a duo—pulling in opposite directions but never in struggle.

And their comedies always had a buried social bent to them, like poking and prodding at mass incarceration in 1980's *Stir Crazy*, just before politics got a hard-on for jailing its most vulnerable people. Or in *Silver Streak*, an African American man teaching America's cuddliest Jew how to act the part in blackface—a masterclass in tightrope comedy-walking. This movie could make you wonder the last time a deaf or blind character got more than a few seconds of screen time in a movie or became the heroes in one. Who's to say they're not deserving of their own grubby comedies with dick jokes?

There's a manic dignity to these goofballs as they evade the fuzz, impersonate gynecologists, and yearn for love . . . or at least settle for lust. It's just another piece of that Pryor/Wilder magic: stripped of their senses, together they completed each other.

HOT ROD  2007

39%

Directed by Akiva Schaffer
Written by Pam Brady
Starring Andy Samberg, Jorma Taccone, Isla Fisher, Bill Hader, Danny McBride, Ian McShane, Sissy Spacek

Critics Consensus

Hot Rod has brazen silliness and a few humorous set pieces on its side, but it's far too inconsistent to satisfy all but the least demanding slapstick lovers.

Synopsis

Slacker and wannabe motorbike stuntman Rod is relentlessly mocked and tormented by his stepfather Frank. But when Frank falls deathly ill, Rod embarks on the probably possible: raising $15,000 to rehabilitate and then beat up Frank himself.

Why We Love It

A good movie's a nice way to pass the time. Bad movies are a waste of your time. But a movie that wastes your time on *purpose* and gets away with it while smelling like roses and motor oil? That's *Hot Rod*. At one point, after a fatally ill family member announcement gone sour, Rod flees to his "quiet place." In this remote, pine-lined glade, he engages in what could be described as a violent parody of the *Footloose* angry-dance scene. Booze and cigarettes are involved. Moving Pictures' "Never" blares through the forest. A log is rocked like a pommel horse.

Then Rod trips. And falls. And falls. And *falls*. The guy tumbles down for a solid minute screaming, flailing down the side of a rocky mountain. First it's funny, then only kinda, and then not. What's going on

here? And then you think about how all this tumbling looks really, honestly painful. This is honest old-fashioned stunt work, from guys whose calling in life is to throw themselves over cliffs and bounce off sharp terrain. In fact, all the stunts in *Hot Rod* are filmed in crisp, steady shots with minimal edits. You really feel the crunching impact of the stupidity on-screen. That's effort to be applauded. And then like a joke orbiting around the comedy sun, you notice Rod is *still* falling down this mountain. And it's kinda funny again. And then it is, and then it's hilarious.

It feels like the Lonely Island, the comedy troupe behind *Hot Rod*, made the movie completely unencumbered by any expectations—of studio executives, of box office projections, or even of what a movie "needs" to be. You can imagine the trio finding a couple million bucks between producer Lorne Michaels's couch cushions, who was just like, "Yeah, go ahead."

Hot Rod is at its best when it's squirming away from its own plot, in interruptions and asides like turning a *Footloose* parody into an endurance test, or in a singing montage that devolves into a street riot, or in remixing the phrase "cool beans" into an ad hoc rap during a teary reunion. Not since *The Simpsons*' Sideshow Bob getting hit in the face with a rake nine times in a row has filler material so gracelessly hit such soaring heights.

KING ARTHUR: LEGEND OF THE SWORD 2017

 **31%**

Directed by Guy Ritchie
Written by Joby Harold, Guy Ritchie, Lionel Wigram
Starring Charlie Hunnam, Jude Law, Àstrid Bergès-Frisbey, Djimon Hounsou, Aidan Gillen, Eric Bana

Critics Consensus

King Arthur: Legend of the Sword piles mounds of modern action flash on an age-old tale—and wipes out much of what made it a classic story in the first place.

Synopsis

King Arthur gets dumped in mud in this Guy Ritchie take on the legend that recasts the hero as a rough tumblin' brawler with street smarts and snarky dialogue and works all the other plot obligations of the story.

Why We Love It

There's no Euro classic Guy Ritchie has ever encountered that he couldn't hooliganize for modern audiences, from *Sherlock Holmes* to, um, *Swept Away*. Here, the director takes the same iconoclastic method to Arthurian legend. The result? Somewhere between *Sherlock Holmes* and, um, *Swept Away*. Gone are Lancelot and Guinevere; instead, here's Back Lack, Goosefat, and Chinese George. Out are reverence and notions of chivalry; in are brothel scraps, a menagerie of CG animals and monsters, and dialogue delivered with today's no-respectin' punch. David Beckham is there when Arthur pulls the sword out of the stone. It's nothing you would expect out of a movie called *King Arthur*. And that's a good thing if you thought the tale went stale centuries ago.

Not to be overshadowed by any legend besides his own, Ritchie declines to modify any of his crisply gritty filmmaking to respect a sixth-century story and instead makes his Guyest (!) Ritchiest (!) movie yet. It's got the trademarks: tough dudes and minimal women, accents everywhere, fast-forward and slow-motion action, those SnorriCam shots where the camera is rigged to the actor and the background becomes a jittery blur, and like, three instances of that thing Ritchie does where the characters stand in a circle explaining a plan with flashbacks and flashforwards and sideways talk.

Ritchie adds legitimate visual flair to epic fantasy action, the camera frequently swooping out for clear panoramas of battle, before crashing in to see up-close swords, arrows, and magical fire clash in intimate mayhem. If your main source of Arthur lore is the nineties miniseries *Merlin*, you'll recognize Vortigen, who's been promoted to main baddie with slither and sneer as given by Jude Law. And then there's Daniel Pemberton's pulverizing musical score, pounding away like it wants to wake up the Dark Ages.

A ye olde epic with vertiginous cameras swooping through computer-generated landscapes with a blatty soundtrack and modern attitude? Some critics (okay, perhaps a majority) would thumb their nose at it. For others (okay, just us), here's a movie that tears a page from history, rolls it, and lights up. We dig it.

TWO THOUSAND MANIACS! 1964

 **43%**

Written and directed by Herschell Gordon Lewis
Starring William Kerwin, Connie Mason, Jeffrey Allen

Critics Consensus

It didn't take much to thrill early splatter-film fans, and *Two Thousand Maniacs!* proves it with its shrill soundtrack, basement-level theatrics, and goofy flesh-tearing gore.

Synopsis

It's the centennial of Deep South town Pleasant Valley, and the citizens know how to celebrate. Not only is there a parade on Main Street, but they're luring, capturing, and killing Yankee travelers one-by-one!

Why We Love It

We go the theater and pay for horror movies to see fellow humans get tortured, slashed, crushed, stabbed, drowned, hung, mauled, electrocuted, hogtied, crucified, beheaded, degloved, and—in the case of two Jason movies—sleeping-bagged to death. You ever stop and think how that's weird? Well, don't, because it's totally normal and there's nothing wrong with it and we're definitely not implying a primal response to our world of decayed morals and deadening light, so knock it off, will ya!

They used to sing and dance to solve their problems in movies. People concluded stories with body parts intact—and thoroughly exercised. That changed in 1963 when schlockmeister Herschell Gordon Lewis released *Blood Feast*. Lewis had been making it as a director of nudie-cuties like *Boin-n-g!* and *Goldilocks and the Three Bares*, but with the market drying up, he needed a new hook. Guys ponying up to see naked women get off is a no-brainer, but would more pay to see people getting offed? *Blood Feast*'s runaway drive-in success proved it to be so, and from that was born a new kind of movie whose main purpose is to shock and excite audiences with blood and gore.

Blood Feast is the first splatter movie. Spiritual sequel *Two Thousand Maniacs!* is the first *watchable* splatter movie. It's a given that a Gordon Lewis production will play clunky and feel slapped together. That is, of course, part of its ugly and durable charm. *Two Thousand Maniacs!*'s natural state of disarray makes the flick feel like it was pulled from a bayou swamp. People who lived in the area were cast as the townspeople and dispense southern hospitality with extreme prejudice—arms are chopped off, horses split a guy apart, and a boulder smushes one victim via carnival dunk game.

Two Thousand Maniacs! gleefully plays up the emerging social splintering of America that would be bedrock to the later unrest of the sixties: it's one of the original movies to portray the South as a cauldron of unchecked fury toward the North. The movie delivered the knives and body parts to sate a violent appetite within that few had addressed before.

ORCA—THE KILLER WHALE 1977

 7%

Directed by Michael Anderson
Written by Luciano Vincenzoni and Sergio Donati
Starring Richard Harris, Charlotte Rampling, Will Sampson

Critics Consensus

Despite its all-too-obvious ambitions, the embarrassingly derivative *Orca* is definitely not *Jaws*.

Synopsis

After an Irish-born fisherman accidentally kills the mate of a killer whale, the orca chases him back to Newfoundland, where it creates havoc, leading to a perilous confrontation in the Arctic Ocean.

Why We Love It

In an era when every studio and independent producer was trying to recreate the success of *Jaws*, *Orca* managed to deliver a sometimes-impressive level of quality and craft—before its climax literally sinks the production. But there's fun to be had before disaster strikes.

Legendary producer Dino De Laurentiis tasked writer/producer Luciano Vincenzoni with finding a "deadlier fish" than a great white shark. Vincenzoni's solution was, of course, a mammal. The film takes great pains to assure the audience that although this creature doesn't have rows of sharp teeth, its threat lies in its intelligence, which may be equal to that of man.

If the claim is based on the intelligence of Richard Harris's Nolan, this may certainly be true, as he fails to heed the warning of a marine biologist (Charlotte Rampling) about the dangers of trying to capture an orca in the hopes of selling it to an aquarium. Once he accepts the orca's ability to seek vengeance—movie marine life can be very emotional—Nolan slowly goes mad from guilt and unresolved grief for his own similar tragedy earlier in his life. Harris successfully makes Nolan an interesting and charismatic character to follow; he also makes his descent into an Ahab-esque madness all the more compelling despite production issues in the film's final act.

The focus on Nolan sets *Orca* apart from its fellow *Jaws* knock-offs, which often neglected character development in favor of hiring lots of stars for brief cameos. And while Rampling's and Sampson's characters are not explored to Nolan's extent, their performances suggest a level of dedication rarely seen in *Jaws* wannabes.

Additionally, director Michael Anderson and his team maintain a certain craftsmanship unusual to this knock-off subgenre, with the death of the whale's mate—and the miscarriage it suffers early on—coming off as particularly gruesome and harrowing. Even when the filmmaking begins to fail the picture, *Orca* adopts Nolan's madness as its tone, offering both legitimate entertainment and silly thrills as the death toll starts to add up. Yes, the makeup and effects are as bad as the performances from some of the supporting cast, and a truly awful set that's meant to represent an ice floe is laughable, but it's chaotic and fun.

Critics may have dismissed it as a fishy tale, and many still do, but if you're in the right mood, *Orca* is—consider this line a tribute to the screenplay—a whale of a time.

TANGO & CASH 1989

31%

Directed by Andrey Konchalovskiy
Written by Randy Feldman
Starring Sylvester Stallone, Kurt Russell, Teri Hatcher, Jack Palance

Critics Consensus

Brutally violent and punishingly dull, this cookie-cutter buddy-cop thriller isn't even fun enough to reach "so bad it's good" status.

Synopsis

Hot-shot LAPD detectives Ray Tango and Gabriel Cash get results until a local kingpin frames them for the death of an FBI agent. Never exactly friends, Tango and Cash must team up to clear their names.

Why We Love It

Tango & Cash is a movie as much in a war with itself as the bickering title characters are with each other. That tension produces a fascinating, if failed, comedy/thriller.

Chasing the *Lethal Weapon* lucre, producer Jon Peters sought to make a film more over-the-top than Warner Bros.' buddy-cop success. Director Andrey Konchalovskiy, however, saw the movie differently and tried to strike a more realistic feel. The result is a clash of tones: actors like Jack Palance, Z-grade movie legend Robert Z'Dar, and Brion James reach for the B-movie rafters as Sylvester Stallone as Tango and Kurt Russell as Cash attempt—at least in certain scenes—to give their characters some depth.

The notion of realism disappears almost entirely once Tango and Cash end up on trial, though. From that point on, the film tries to outdo itself with each successive action set piece or alleged "comedy"

sequence. By the point Tango and Cash ride dump trucks through an exploding quarry to fight the bad guy, you may forget the grittier moments in the prison just forty-five minutes earlier. (A scene in which Tango overhears his sister, played by Teri Hatcher, tending to Cash's wounds and assumes they're having sex is as unfunny as it sounds. And more out of place than that.)

For their parts, Russell and Stallone are solid because they essentially play themselves. Yes, they start out the film delivering actual "performances," but at some point both actors accept that the audience just wants to see them escape explosions with the same spirit as Riggs and Murtaugh. It just about works whenever you can see their faces—they were some of the biggest movie stars in the world at the time—but an alarming number of scenes feature just the back of the characters' heads while the actors offer some unfunny quips added during post-production.

They also quip in close-up, with Russell doing his best to sell some seriously unfunny lines. The lead characters' love of yuks undercuts any of the jeopardy and tension Konchalovskiy hoped to create, but it also gives the film a giddy quality as it tries to force its audience into laughing. Humor finally happens, just not in the form Konchalovskiy or Peters intended. Instead, *Tango & Cash* leaves you chuckling from all the ways it fails to be what its creators wanted.

DR. GIGGLES 1992

 **17%**

Directed by Manny Coto
Written by Manny Coto and Graeme Whifler
Starring Larry Drake, Holly Marie Combs, Cliff De Young, Glenn Quinn

CRITIC: April Wolfe

April Wolfe is a writer, film critic, and filmmaker in Los Angeles. She hosts the *Switchblade Sisters* podcast on the Maximum Fun network.

Manny Coto's *Dr. Giggles* earned cult status in my childhood home. One night, my then stepfather had rented it from the video store and descended into the basement to watch solo, while the rest of us slept. But somewhere around midnight, my mother, sister, and I were awoken by the sound of thundering footsteps racing up the stairs. My big, burly stepdad—with a gun cupboard stickered with NRA logos—was so frightened by this movie that he had run up the stairs, afraid of the dark.

It was doubly wonderful when I then watched *Dr. Giggles* and fell in love with it, not necessarily because of its scares but because this slasher comedy was so unexpectedly funny, touching, and evocative of some of the most beautiful images of classic horror, particularly James Whale's *Frankenstein* (1931). A movie titled *Dr. Giggles* did not demand such exquisite cinematography and design nor Larry Drake's multifaceted performance as the eponymous medico, and yet, there it was.

Dr. Giggles tells the story of a boy with an eerie giggle. It's the 1950s, and his doctor father loses his mind when his wife grows ill. The father murders some townspeople, searching for a new heart for her, and the townspeople come for him, stoning him to death and tearing his home apart. But nobody could find his young son, whom they suspect snuck out through a secret passageway. Fast forward to the present, where a crazed man with an eerie giggle escapes from a mental hospital after performing "surgery" on the staff. Dr. Giggles (Drake) returns to his childhood home to avenge his father by punishing the townspeople with cheeky one-liners and horrifying medical tools that look like they were left over from David Cronenberg's *Dead Ringers* (1988). When Dr. Giggles finds out a young woman named Jennifer (Holly Marie Combs) has a heart condition, he focuses his attention on her, on the hunt to

> **" I NEVER KNEW A GIGGLE COULD MAKE ME CRINGE, THEN LAUGH, THEN TEAR UP IN THE SPAN OF A MINUTE. "**

capture her and give her the heart transplant of her nightmares.

Reviewers at the time totally misunderstood Coto's intentions. American horror was just coming out of the slasher boom of the 1980s, and critics mistook this outrageous yet strangely measured serving of medical gore as just the last gasp of a dying genre rather than the rebirth of a new one: the self-aware, meta horror-comedy. Keep in mind that *Scream* was still four years away, and Wes Craven's toe-dip into the well with *The People Under the Stairs* (1991) was already received poorly by critics. Coto was one of a handful of directors ahead of the pack.

The *Los Angeles Times* critic Kevin Thomas bought what Coto was selling, calling it a "fast and frequently hilarious collision of gore and gags, and a tour de force of smart, sophisticated exploitation filmmaking." Coto was clearly working within a cinematic tradition, his adoration of Whale apparent, especially in one scene where Dr. Giggles trudges through the forest in silhouette, backlit by a mysterious light, fog hanging low around him as he carries Jennifer's limp body in his outstretched arms. He is the monster. If one looks closely at every scene, you'll find production design mimicking those of the classics, too. But one scene in particular requires very little attention to realize it's expertly aping one of the most experimental moments in cinematic history: the mirror sequence from Orson Welles's *The Lady from Shanghai*.

Editing, cinematography, direction, and action in this particular sequence are stunning. Jennifer has wandered into a funhouse at a carnival. She's just caught her boyfriend making out with the school tramp and is trying to get away from him. Her boyfriend and the tramp follow Jennifer in, and unbeknownst to any of them, Dr. Giggles is not far behind. What follows is an atmospherically dazzling and dizzying showcase of Grand Guignol horror, which is punctuated by a comically bizarre murder that still somehow works inside the high art: the tramp is suffocated by a gigantic Band-Aid that Dr. Giggles just happened to have in his medical bag.

As the bad doctor, Drake's emotions oscillate and overlap: pain, fear, satisfaction, and insanity apparent in his voice, sometimes simultaneously. I never knew a giggle could make me cringe, then laugh, then tear up in the span of a minute. Add to this a sumptuously melodramatic score from Brian May, which borrows from all those torrid monster classics, and this film is irresistible.

To explain the plot of *Dr. Giggles* and see people's eyes glaze over when I tell them this was one of the most artful horror films of the nineties is a

> ## "CRITICS MISTOOK THIS AS JUST THE LAST GASP OF A DYING GENRE RATHER THAN THE REBIRTH OF A NEW ONE."

regular occurrence for me. But *Dr. Giggles* deserves revisiting. What's most interesting is that although Coto was never properly applauded in film, his talents found a home in television with *The Outer Limits*, *Strange World*, *24*, and *Dexter*. In 2018, he joined the team behind *American Horror Story*, which wasn't surprising; it's a show that traffics in the very brand of horror that Coto pioneered all those years ago.

Rotten Tomatoes' Critics Consensus Larry Drake's deranged performance as the titular doctor is just about all that distinguishes *Dr. Giggles* from its slasher brethren.

THE AMITYVILLE HORROR 1979

 **29%**

Directed by Stuart Rosenberg
Written by Sandor Stern
Starring James Brolin, Margot Kidder, Rod Steiger

Critics Consensus

Dull and disappointing, the best that can be said for *The Amityville Horror* is that it set a low bar for its many sequels and remakes.

Synopsis

Newlyweds ignore the fact that a murder occurred in their new home and move in anyway in this supposedly true story. Soon, they begin experiencing things going bump in the night *and* the day, until they discover the source of their woes is much more frightening than they thought.

Why We Love It

The Amityville Horror kicked off a prolific franchise by virtue of being one of the most memorable "haunted house torturing a family" flicks. The imagery from this film has given audiences the creeps for decades . . . or at the very least, become so iconic that other films in this overstuffed genre have trouble avoiding comparison. Just the house itself, with those two glowing eyes—er, *windows*—and its infamous bleeding walls is something modern audiences are likely to recognize without even necessarily knowing its origin. (Or perhaps they recognize it from *The Simpsons*' first ever "Treehouse of Terror" episode, which features a segment based on *Amityville*, with a little bit of *Poltergeist* thrown in for good measure.)

The plot is simple, as it often is in these kinds of movies, and it moves quickly. Right off the bat, Kathy (Margot Kidder) and George Lutz's (James Brolin) interactions with their realtor hint at a puzzling past for their new home in upstate New York. As that past—and its impact on the present—comes into focus, things go exactly as you expect they will, but it's done with a visual flair and inventiveness that most critics overlooked at the time.

Writing about the film, many focused less on its virtues and problems and more on its backstory. There was a real George Lutz, who claims that much of what is depicted in the film really happened to his family, and his story was told in a 1977 bestseller that studios were eager to adapt. *Did it really happen? Was it believable?* Critics asked the same questions America once obsessed about. The most pertinent, though, is "True or not, is the movie scary?" Critics were pretty split on that question, but those who dismissed *Amityville* as scare-free and plodding didn't have the benefit of hindsight to see how indelible some of its images would become.

While the script has some nice subtle touches, the actors' commitment is what makes this work much better than it might have. As George becomes more frightening, manic, and assumes a pallor rivaled only by South Korea's most famous cinematic spirits, Kathy fights harder against him to keep it together—even when her phone calls to the priest are overcome by static and her brother's wedding catering money goes missing, which are both enough to make any mom lose her marbles. Even a throwaway scene like the moment in which a babysitter is locked in a closet by a ghost named Jodi is so unsettling you have to wonder if the filmmakers went method to get that reaction.

When you add in some really gross and disturbing scares—glowing eyes outside second-story windows, flies swarming priests, windows slamming on children's hands, barfing nuns, and dinner guests who attack the basement walls with a pick axe—you've got a solid two hours on your hands and an experience that will make you look twice at the shadows in your own home.

POLICE ACADEMY 1984

54%

Directed by Hugh Wilson
Written by Neal Israel, Pat Proft, Hugh Wilson
Starring Steve Guttenberg, Kim Cattrall, G. W. Bailey, Bubba Smith, George Gaynes, Leslie Easterbrook, Michael Winslow

Critics Consensus

Unlike the spoofs that inspired it, *Police Academy* is a little too crass and derivative to leave a lasting impression.

Synopsis

As the result of a new policy enacted by a recently elected mayor in response to a shortage of police officers, a flood of ordinary, unqualified citizens enters the police academy and wreaks havoc, much to the chagrin of the veteran staff charged with training them.

Why We Love It

As far as R-rated comedies go, *Police Academy* is fairly tame, but that wasn't always the case. As originally conceived by producer Paul Maslansky, it was a much naughtier affair, full of gratuitous nudity, gross-out humor, and crude observations on race and gender. What audiences got was something of a compromise between his vision and that of *WKRP in Cincinnati* director Hugh Wilson, who did his best to tamp down the racier elements in the script. In retrospect, it's difficult to say whether a more vulgar version of *Police Academy* would have resonated better with critics, but its six (that's right, *six*) sequels all muted the adult elements even further and largely received far worse reviews—the last four entries in the franchise all earned zero-percent Tomatometer scores. In other words, taken as a whole, this is an abysmal collection of films full of juvenile, lowest-common-denominator humor, but it would be silly to dismiss the first installment outright.

Spoof comedies are traditionally hit-or-miss efforts composed of sketches and set pieces; *Police Academy* may bat a lower average with its jokes than classics of the genre, but those that do land do so because of the game cast. Leading man Steve Guttenberg is at peak smarm in his breakout role, doling out wisecracks and lighting up the screen with the same boyish charm we'd later see in *Cocoon*, *Short Circuit*, and *Three Men and a Baby*. As Lieutenant Harris, G. W. Bailey is so obnoxious that when he's launched headfirst into a horse's anus in one of the film's defining gags, we're too busy relishing the schadenfreude to question the stupidity of the moment. Leslie Easterbrook essentially plays a proto-Brigitte Nielsen as the ass-kicking maneater Sgt. Callahan, Michael Winslow is all blips and screeches in possibly the only appropriate outlet for his sound effect–based comedy, and George Gaynes's doofy Commandant Lassard is right up there with *The Naked Gun*'s Frank Drebin and *Airplane!*'s Steve "Looks Like I Picked the Wrong Week to Quit Sniffing Glue" McCroskey.

With all of its needless vulgarity, potty humor, slapstick, and off-color jokes about race and gender, *Police Academy* feels a bit like a children's comedy pretending to be grown up: it's kind of gross and a little offensive, and it doesn't always know where it's going. But then it does something hilarious, and once you've had a laugh and collected yourself, you want to lean over and say, "Aww, you made a funny!"

¡THREE AMIGOS! 1986

 46%

Directed by John Landis
Written by Lorne Michaels, Randy Newman, Steve Martin
Starring Steve Martin, Chevy Chase, Martin Short, Alfonso Arau, Patrice Martinez

Critics Consensus

¡Three Amigos! stars a trio of gifted comedians and has an agreeably silly sense of humor, but they're often adrift in a dawdling story with too few laugh-out-loud moments.

Synopsis

Three clueless silent-film stars head down to Mexico for what they assume is a big-budget shoot. What awaits them is a throng of villagers thinking they're real-life heroes who will save their town from a band of terrorists.

Why We Love It

"Does this remind you of your childhood?"

"It reminds me of ¡Three Amigos! *with Steve Martin and Chevy Chase."*

"Thank you, Oscar. That means a lot."

That exchange is from *The Office*, when manager Michael Scott throws a Mexican-themed welcome-back work party for one of his employees. And an oblivious-yet-likeable character like Michael Scott *would* love this movie (and take Oscar's not-so-subtle dig as a sincere compliment). It's broad, sunny, silly stuff, the kind of movie beloved by the sort of dude who makes cringe-worthy dad jokes.

Helmed by John Landis (*An American Werewolf in London*, *Animal House*, *The Blues Brothers*), *¡Three Amigos!* was a box-office (and critical) failure back in 1986 and is the first of an unofficial trilogy of movies about actors facing IRL danger that also includes *Galaxy Quest* and *Tropic Thunder*. It'd be easy (and, to be fair, pretty accurate) to deride *¡Three Amigos!*—which follows a triad of Hollywood stars going south of the border to revive their careers—as culturally insensitive. But keep in mind: these La La Land fishes-out-of-water are morons, and the joke is clearly always on them. (Just look to the stars' misunderstanding of "infamous," which leads to their ill-fated trip down south.)

Without its considerable comic chemistry, *¡Three Amigos!* would, indeed, be a forgettable misfire. But each of the three leads perfectly pinball off each other's sensibilities. Martin Short, in his second feature, is all wide-eyed and guileless, showing off his penchant for broad comedy and vaudevillian theatrics. Chevy Chase is at his dry-delivery best, throwing out lines like "Do you have anything besides Mexican food?" And Steve Martin, as the group's leader, is clearly having a blast playing the slow-on-the-uptake showbiz egotist. As icing on the cake, cowriter Randy Newman's songs give the project an additional dose of old-Hollywood charm.

In a bit of life-imitating-art silliness, Short was convinced by his castmates to show up at the film's premiere decked out in his bejeweled mariachi-esque getup. Of course, the joke was on him, and he was the only actor who dressed up. How appropriately hilarious.

REIGN OF FIRE 2002

 **42%**

Directed by Rob Bowman
Written by Kevin Peterka, Gregg Chabot, Matt Greenberg
Starring Christian Bale, Matthew McConaughey, Izabella Scorupco, Gerard Butler

Critics Consensus

Reign of Fire gains some altitude with its pyrotechnic action and a smolderingly campy Matthew McConaughey, but the feature's wings are clipped by a derivative script and visual effects that fizzle out.

Synopsis

A child awakens an ancient terror beneath the streets of London, setting off an apocalypse of dragon fire. Years later, the boy has grown to become the leader of a pocket of humanity, huddled in a remote, ruined castle. Then the gung-ho Americans arrive and all hell breaks loose—again.

Why We Love It

Reign of Fire brought a long cinematic history of dragons on film into the twenty-first century. Director Rob Bowman's film fully introduces the scaly pests to contemporary Western society as a biblical-sized world-killing plague of giant flying serpents. It answered the question: What if dragons were real and here, right now?

Everyone loves an outsized villain, and *Reign of Fire* more than delivers with its airborne menace. In an awesome first scene, the awakening dragon fills a drill site with hellfire and crushes a construction elevator, killing Alice Krige (as Karen Abercromby) as it escapes. It's a sit-the-bleep-up-and-pay-attention move—and you obey the command.

Bowman, a veteran of sci-fi TV hits *Star Trek:*

The Next Generation and *The X-Files*, also directed or codirected critical disappointments like the 1998 *X-Files* film and 2005 Marvel superhero super-bomb *Elektra*. *Reign of Fire* fits squarely in his sci-fi/fantasy wheelhouse but falls below the director's median Tomatometer score for feature films. And yet, it's probably his most thrilling—and certainly his most memorable—big-screen work.

In front of the camera, the movie feels like the perfect storm of talent at wildly different points in their careers. At the time of the film's release, star Christian Bale was riding a career uptick toward *Batman Begins*, while for costar Matthew McConaughey, this dragon tale would see the beginning of a string of Rotten films, including *How to Lose a Guy in 10 Days*, *Sahara*, and *Failure to Launch*, that would pre-date his famed McConaissance. Also, remember pre-*300*, when Gerard Butler wasn't really a thing? When he starred as the head bloodsucker in charge in—speaking of dumb, Rotten fun—*Dracula 2000*? Starry-eyed Butler is a different creature entirely in these Rotten romps compared to his *300*-and-on period, and in *Reign of Fire*, he completes the film's holy trinity of male hotness.

From Bale's sweaty, shirtless-mining scene and a sweet *Star Wars* stage play in the first fifteen minutes through to McConaughey's climactic sacrifice, *Reign of Fire* is a testosterone-fueled, fire-breathing thrill ride—right down the dragon's throat.

CLASH OF THE TITANS 2010

 **27%** | **Directed by** Louis Leterrier
Written by Travis Beacham, Matt Manfredi, Phil Hay
Starring Sam Worthington, Liam Neeson, Ralph Fiennes, Gemma Arterton, Alexa Davalos

Critics Consensus

An obviously affectionate remake of the 1981 original, Louis Leterrier's *Clash of the Titans* doesn't offer enough visual thrills to offset the deficiencies of its script.

Synopsis

After Hades, the callous god of the Underworld who killed demigod Perseus's beloved human family, threatens to unleash supersized sea monster the Kraken, Perseus steps up to save the city of Argos and Princess Andromeda.

Why We Love It

One of French director Louis Leterrier's first professional gigs was as a production assistant on *Alien: Resurrection* to director Jean-Pierre Jeunet. He went on to direct two of the *Transporter* films and 2008's *The Incredible Hulk*, starring Ed Norton—movies big on action spectacle. It should come as no surprise then that Leterrier's *Clash of the Titans* remake is a combustive love letter to the original 1981 film, its stars (Harry Hamlin, Laurence Olivier, Burgess Meredith, Maggie Smith), and legendary monster-maker Ray Harryhausen. The 2010 *Titans* takes a lesson from Desmond Davis's version by investing heavily in effects and putting an emphasis on cast, cast, cast, and cast.

Leterrier started with up-and-coming Australian actor Sam Worthington, who'd starred in—speaking of special effects—James Cameron's *Avatar* and McG's *Terminator Salvation* with Christian Bale. He then capitalized on an ensemble of names that, if they weren't already, would come to be familiar to international film fans. In addition to Worthington, Liam Neeson, Ralph Fiennes, Gemma Arterton, and Alexa Davalos, the cast includes Mads Mikkelsen, Liam Cunningham, Jason Flemyng, Polly Walker, Pete Postlethwaite, Luke Evans, Nicholas Hoult, Izabella Miko, Alexander Siddig, Danny Huston, Luke Treadaway, and Elizabeth McGovern. The mix provided at least one name for every moviegoer to get excited about. (That is, unless you're hoping to find a person of color in the film; *Titans* has been rightly criticized for white-washing a story that takes place primarily on the Aegean Sea.)

The only downside to such stellar casting is how underutilized some actors are in the final product: McGovern spoke only twenty words in the film. If she had any substantive lines, her primary scenes were left on the cutting-room floor—or, you know, in the editor's Final Cut Pro "DVD extras" project folder. Evans, Huston, Hoult, and Miko all suffered a similar fate.

But enough whining about who didn't get to do what. The spectacle that resulted provided enough gods and monsters to create an adventure story for a new generation of fantasy fans. *Clash of the Titans* may not be *Lord of the Rings*, but as thrilling homage, it more than works. *Release the Kraken!*

 **38%**

Directed by Rowdy Herrington
Written by R. Lance Hill and Hilary Henkin
Starring Patrick Swayze, Kelly Lynch, Sam Elliott, Ben Gazzara

CRITIC: Jen Yamato

Jen Yamato is a film reporter and critic for the *Los Angeles Times*. She has covered Hollywood and the entertainment industry for publications including *The Daily Beast* and *Deadline Hollywood* and formerly served as a senior editor at Rotten Tomatoes, where she began her career obsessing over film criticism and the movies.

Of the treasures of 1980s action begging to be unleashed from the vaults like a pumped-up bicep aching for a fistfight, none hold quite as special a place in movie history as *Road House*—a film filled to the rafters with brawls, boobs, rock 'n' roll, a safari-hunting sadistic land baron who loves to party, and the lithe, leonine Patrick Swayze at his Swayziest.

Arriving in theaters in the summer of 1989, *Road House* would go on to earn scorn from critics, modest ticket sales, and five Golden Raspberry nominations. Only time and robust home video rentals would prove its cache as a cult classic, thanks in no small part to Swayze's committed turn deconstructing hypermasculinity with cool-guy flair and that oiled-up beefcake bod, terrain he would revisit two years later in the seminal action bromance *Point Break*.

But those who only appreciate *Road House* from behind a "so bad it's good" veil do it a disservice. Because even when it misfires, the film cranks everything to eleven—an act that itself lays endearingly bare the mortal limits of the creative process.

And *Road House* is a prime example of just how human movies can get: while probing the precarious balance between peace and violence that lives within us, it is *also* a delightfully over-the-top picture (directed by a guy appropriately named Rowdy Herrington) about a hunky pacifist haunted by the fact that he just can't seem to stop ripping out the throats of his enemies. (Well, can you blame him? Sometimes you've got to rip a few throats to save a small town from ruthless, ascot-wearing crooks . . . *amiright?*)

> " **SOMETIMES YOU'VE GOT TO RIP A FEW THROATS TO SAVE A SMALL TOWN FROM RUTHLESS, ASCOT-WEARING CROOKS . . . AMIRIGHT?** "

That *Road House* can be many things at once is key to its unique poetry.

With nods to Wild West icons in a script by David Lee Henry and Hilary Henkin (*Romeo Is Bleeding, Wag the Dog*), *Road House* takes place in a flyover country hamlet caught in the economic crossfire of a changing America. It's here in Jasper, Missouri, that Tai Chi–practicing Dalton (Swayze), an uber-bouncer with a violent past and a philosophy degree from NYU, arrives from the big city to clean up the Double Deuce, a lawless roadside joint where brawling bikers, strippers, drunks, and corrupt bartenders are driving business into the ground.

Spouting pseudo-Buddhist aphorisms like "Be nice until it's time to *not* be nice," the preternaturally Zen Dalton trains a motley security crew, tosses out the bad eggs, turns the Double Deuce into a hot spot, and romances local doctor Elizabeth "Doc" Clay (Kelly Lynch), all while gazing upon the nightly crowd from his watchful perch, black coffee in hand, always one step ahead of trouble.

That is, until Dalton discovers the townsfolk are being terrorized by rich Chicago douchebag Brad Wesley (a delicious Ben Gazzara), which is when *Road House* turns into a *Mid*-Western showdown and our hero is put to the test: Can he stop Wesley and save Jasper—without tearing out *another* man's jugular?

The heightened, deadpan stakes are just a few of *Road House*'s many charms; hilariously convenient geography is another (evil Wesley lives right across the river from Dalton's converted barn bachelor pad, within peeping view of our hero's gravity-defying love-making sessions).

One must applaud the genius in assembling such a zesty cast, which includes pro wrestler Terry Funk and X punker John Doe as evil henchmen; blues rocker Jeff Healey as the leader of the Double Deuce's house band; and Missouri's own legendary Bigfoot monster truck, a beast that destroys its way through a car dealership in a scene that reportedly cost $500,000 to stage and could only be filmed once, for obvious reasons.

Meanwhile, bringing charisma to Jasper's exasperated band of townies are actors Kevin Tighe, Red

West, and Sunshine Parker, while Kathleen Wilhoite and a blink-and-you'll-miss-him Keith David help ground the ensemble around Swayze. Sam Elliott nearly steals the show as Dalton's charming mentor Wade Garrett, the O.G. cooler who breezes into town to help his protégé battle Wesley's goons.

Like catnip for muscular eighties action lovers, every fiery slo-mo explosion, massive bar brawl, and bone-smashing martial arts fight is lensed with a meaty vibrancy by cinematographer Dean Cundey (*Back to the Future, Jurassic Park*). Like all Joel Silver productions, it's the stuff thirteen-year-old boys' dreams are made of—for better and worse. Most fascinating is how *Road House* seems, at times, to be at war with itself.

After countless saloon scuffles and macho one-liners, despite unfolding at a rollicking pace through its first two acts, *Road House* careens off the rails once Dalton regains his taste for blood. As he becomes unmoored, so does the film. Few movies ratchet to such extremes as *Road House*'s over-the-top third act, which is when Herrington *really* turns on the gas.

You can track the shift in Swayze's increasingly frenzied face, in one of the fastest onscreen escalations of chaos committed to cinema. One minute, Dalton's a feathered-hair philosopher warrior reading Jim Harrison paperbacks in the moonlight—not terribly far removed from Swayze's *Dirty Dancing* heartthrob, if Johnny had a talent for breaking up bar fights instead of wooing divorcees. The next, he's a sweaty, shirtless maniac, tackling baddies off speeding motorcycles and doling out roundhouse kicks with the pointed-toe precision of a dancer. It's a role only Swayze could play, blessedly committed as

"IT'S A ROLE ONLY SWAYZE COULD PLAY, BLESSEDLY COMMITTED AS THE BODY COUNT SKYROCKETS AND DALTON'S MORAL COMPASS IMPLODES."

the body count skyrockets and Dalton's moral compass implodes. More shockingly unpoliced killings will plague this small Missouri town before Dalton, and the movie itself, will know the true meaning of "enough."

As he says early in the film: "Pain don't hurt." Then again, he might come to find that wisdom might not apply to the existential kind. With time, *Road House*'s zany flourishes have become battle scars it can wear with pride, a survivor of its own bombastic excess—not a film so bad it's good, but a film that dared to be so extra, it's great.

Rotten Tomatoes' Critics Consensus Whether *Road House* is simply bad or so bad it's good depends largely on the audience's fondness for Swayze—and tolerance for violently cheesy action.

I KNOW WHAT YOU DID
LAST SUMMER 1997

 42% | **Directed by** Jim Gillespie
Written by Kevin Williamson
Starring Jennifer Love Hewitt, Sarah Michelle Gellar, Freddie Prinze Jr., Ryan Phillippe

A by-the-numbers slasher that came out a decade too late, *I Know What You Did Last Summer* is a mostly tedious follow-up to Kevin Williamson's *Scream* that still might hook die-hard fans of the genre.

Synopsis

Four friends run down a mystery man on a road just outside their hometown and decide to dump him in the ocean instead of report the incident to the police. A year later, a mystery figure with a fondness for slickers and hooks shows up in their lives—and bedrooms, and locker rooms—to inform them that he knows their big secret.

Why We Love It

The problem for *I Know What You Did Last Summer* was that everyone—fans and critics alike—knew what writer Kevin Williamson had done the previous winter.

In December of 1996, almost a year before *I Know* was released, the Williamson-penned *Scream,* directed by genre master Wes Craven, had been a major horror hit—one of the decade's precious few. Critics loved that movie's super-meta take on a genre many of them reviled: loved that the kids in Ghostface's sites were wise-cracking horror-loving smartasses; loved the audacity of snuffing out big-name-star Drew Barrymore in the first ten minutes. Williamson was horror's Next Big Thing in 1996, and his follow-up film was always going to come splattered with high expectations: what would the guy who just revived the slasher genre do next?

When the answer turned out to be a conventional, almost irony-free slasher flick—the exact kind of movie he had just skewered—most critics shrugged it off as a disappointing sophomore slump. Fans, though, loved what they saw.

It had been a long time since Hollywood delivered an effective slasher aimed squarely at the teenage set, and, viewed away from the shadow of its over-achieving older cousin, *I Know* gets the job done. The Christopher Pike–style plot is just a flimsy string on which to hang some gleefully tense set pieces, the best of which sees Sarah Michelle Gellar's beauty queen, Helen Shivers, chased through what feels like every corner of the North Carolina fishing town in which the film is set. A scene in which the killer, shrouded under a plastic sheet, waits in perfect stillness for his chance to leap out at her is among the 1990s' most effective jump scares—seriously, put down your drink the *moment* Helen's clumsy-handed sister lets her in the shop.

Jennifer Love Hewitt and Gellar emerged from *I Know* as bona fide scream queens, and rightfully so; Hewitt's "What are you waiting for?" moment, in which she twirls around in a suburban street and screams pointlessly at the sky, has been heavily—and affectionately—parodied, and Gellar would go on to star in TV's *Buffy the Vampire Slayer*, *Scream 2*, and the US remake of *The Grudge*.

The movie falters mostly when it tries too hard to echo *Scream*; the whodunnit elements and bubbles of overly self-aware dialogue feel like they belong in a different and maybe more ambitious film. When Williamson and Gillespie pile on the violent hookings and double down on their eighties slasher vibe, however, *I Know* makes a killer case for repeat Halloween viewings.

ZOMBI 2 1980

42%

Directed by Lucio Fulci
Written by Elisa Briganti
Starring Tisa Farrow, Ian McCulloch, Richard Johnson, Al Cliver

Critics Consensus

Zombi 2 is an absurdly graphic zombie movie legendary for some gory scenes and pretty much nothing in between.

Synopsis

A boat is discovered drifting in the New York harbor, occupied only with zombies. The boat's owner has been missing for months and so his daughter departs for his last known location: a tropical island where voodoo research has been underway.

Why We Love It

If you grew up during the golden age of video rental shops, you'll remember the horror section and that palpable, seductive fear that came with it, going up and down the terrifying aisle. Walking that valley of death, the shelves lined with VHS cases—psychos and killers on one side, ghouls and the unspeakable on the other—each a clamshell tombstone, beckoning the impressionable to dig in for its R-rated secrets. "Not suitable for a general audience . . ." they whispered.

You begin hearing about what happens in these movies. The mythmaking starts. The hockey-masked killer who split a boy in twain with just a machete. A burn victim with a hat who literally haunted nightmares. Exploding heads in *Dawn of the Dead* and *Scanners*. The raw snuff of *Cannibal Holocaust*. Or the eyeball kill in *Zombi 2*. What soul would crave these punishing images?

Director Lucio Fulci had a lovingly gratuitous taste for gore, and so yes, this famed and cringe-inducing *Zombi 2* scene with the unfortunate eyeball is absolutely drawn out. The victim is a doctor's poor wife, who thinks she's home alone when a zombie punches through the door, grabs her head, and slowly pulls her to the shattered wood. Despite the struggle, her face glides straight towards a splinter, bursting the protective gel of her right eye before going through the socket and out the back of the skull. As a director, Fulci never met an orifice he didn't want to cover with corn syrup and red dye.

The rest of *Zombi 2* is a mix of island voodoo magic recognizing the genre's earliest origins and scenes set in gritty late-1970s New York—including scores of undead walking the Brooklyn Bridge among full traffic shot without permit. There's also a zombie punching a shark underwater. Excited descriptions of these images spread from video store to the playground and park, and before the over-exhaustion of trailers and marketing, this was how hype was built, and how a movie that was (falsely) marketed as a sequel to 1978's *Dawn of the Dead* in Europe moved from B-movie trash into legend.

ACE VENTURA: PET DETECTIVE 1994

 **47%**

Directed by Tom Shadyac
Written by Tom Shadyac, Jack Bernstein, Jim Carrey
Starring Jim Carrey, Courteney Cox, Sean Young, Udo Kier, Tone Loc

Critics Consensus

Jim Carrey's twitchy antics and gross-out humor are on full, bombastic display in *Ace Ventura: Pet Detective*, which is great news for fans of his particular brand of comedy but likely unsatisfying for anyone else.

Synopsis

A struggling private detective with unorthodox methods who specializes in missing animal cases is hired to investigate the disappearance of the Miami Dolphins mascot.

Why We Love It

Though he had appeared in a handful of films throughout the 1980s, Jim Carrey's over-the-top shenanigans were most familiar to American audiences through the Fox sketch comedy series *In Living Color*, thanks to fan-favorite characters like Fire Marshall Bill and Vera De Milo. *Ace Ventura* opened just as that show began to wind down its final season, and Carrey seamlessly transitioned into a monster year on the big screen that included *The Mask* and *Dumb and Dumber*. All three films relied heavily on Carrey's quick wit and knack for physical comedy, but *Ace Ventura* in particular had his fingerprints all over it, and it launched his career into the stratosphere.

When you consider what the film could have been, it becomes clear why it could only have succeeded with Jim Carrey in the lead. Before he was cast, the role was offered to Rick Moranis, and when he turned it down, the producers considered Alan Rickman, Judd Nelson, and Whoopi Goldberg—all terrific talents in their own right, but it's difficult to imagine any of them bringing the same kind of energy that Carrey brought. Can you picture Snape yelling at Tone Loc via his ass cheeks, for example? Yeah, we thought not.

Carrey also helped revise the script and insisted on a few changes to his character, namely that he should be portrayed in a slightly more intelligent (albeit still unhinged) light and that he should be as ridiculous as possible. The result is a larger-than-life performance that jumps off the screen and demands to be mimicked and parodied endlessly, which is exactly what happened. There's arguably no character Carrey has played that has endured the way Ace Ventura has. "Aaaaalrighty, then" is officially part of the pop culture lexicon, and his trademark Hawaiian shirt and red pants (or, alternatively, windswept hair and pink tutu) are Halloween staples to this day.

We get it. Jim Carrey isn't for everyone. On top of that, *Ace Ventura* makes a few outdated jokes at the expense of the LGBTQ community, and we recognize that's a non-negotiable thing for many viewers. But as a product of its time, when Carrey was ripe for mass consumption and eager to go balls-to-the-wall for his comedy, *Ace Ventura: Pet Detective* is one of the purest one-man shows around and one of the boldest announcements of fresh talent we've ever seen.

OVER THE TOP 1987

 27%

Directed by Menahem Golan
Written by Stirling Silliphant and Sylvester Stallone
Starring Sylvester Stallone, Robert Loggia, David Mendenhall, Susan Blakely

Critics Consensus

No movie about an arm-wrestling trucker should take itself as seriously as *Over the Top* does, and even Sylvester Stallone's raw star power is no match for the film's overly saccharine treatment of familiar themes.

Synopsis

At the request of his dying wife, long-haul trucker Lincoln Hawk escorts his estranged ten-year-old son Michael home from military school on the long road from Colorado to California. The two begin to form a bond along the way, even as Michael's grandfather does everything in his power to pull them apart.

Why We Love It

By the time *Over the Top* was released in 1987, Sylvester Stallone had carved out a nice career playing mononymous action heroes with a taste for violence (see: *Rocky*, *Rambo*, and *Cobra*). You can't blame the guy for wanting to branch out and showcase a bit of his softer side, albeit one that takes the form of a truck driver with a special skill for arm wrestling. *Over the Top* was Stallone's first true attempt to reach a family audience, and considering he cowrote the screenplay, it's understandable that it feels a little bit like a mix of the underdog story in *Rocky* and the father-son drama in *Rocky V*. If that combination sounds like a heaping helping of schmaltz topped off with enough cheese to build the world's biggest quesadilla, you're not wrong. But this is some gourmet cheese we're talking about.

Behind the lens, you've got Menahem Golan, who was nominated for a Best Foreign Language Film Oscar in 1978 for *Operation Thunderbolt*. He also happens to be the "Golan" in Golan-Globus, the producing team who took over Cannon Films and turned it into the notorious schlockhouse that gave us other cult gems like *American Ninja*, *Breakin' 2: Electric Boogaloo*, and *Masters of the Universe*. In the world of Golan's *Over the Top*, a nondescript truck stop becomes a grungy sweatbox where hulking men gather to challenge each other like so many silverbacks, and an arm-wrestling tournament is the most important thing in the world. It shouldn't make any sense, but thanks to Golan, who directs the film like an alien crafting its best approximation of American culture, it absolutely does.

Above all, the film is a remarkable time capsule that pulls together several disparate elements from the 1980s and blends them all into an exceedingly weird but earnest presentation. On one hand, you've got a glistening Sly Stallone mumbling platitudes like, "The world meets nobody halfway!", while Sammy Hagar belts out the film's theme song in the background. On the other hand, there's Robert Loggia sporting a perfectly caramelized bronze tan and acting the hell out of his "mean rich guy" role. If the film's ever-present soundtrack isn't broadcasting a pop hit from Asia, Kenny Loggins, or Eddie Money, you may find yourself grooving to synth master Giorgio Moroder's anthemic score (which is pretty great, by the way).

Over the Top isn't the best father-son bromance ever put to celluloid, but it does feature arguably the most eclectic fusion of cultural touchstones from the 1980s, and it's the only one engineered to tug at your heartstrings with an arm-wrestling match. That's the sort of singular oddness that warrants a viewing.

BILLY MADISON 1995

40%

Directed by Tamra Davis
Written by Tim Herlihy and Adam Sandler
Starring Adam Sandler, Bridgette Wilson-Sampras, Darren McGavin, Bradley Whitford

Critics Consensus

Audiences who enjoy Adam Sandler's belligerent comic energy may find him in joyously obnoxious form as *Billy Madison*, but this thinly-plotted vehicle surrounds its star with an aggressively pedestrian movie.

Synopsis

A spoiled twenty-something slacker must convince his hotelier father that he's worthy of inheriting his empire. How? By successfully completing grades one through twelve.

Why We Love It

In the one-season-and-done series *Undeclared*, college freshman Marshall corners Adam Sandler after a campus gig, saying that he's a big fan and that *Billy Madison* "was like punk-rock." Sandler laughs politely, then Marshall adds, "But like everything after that, though . . . I just didn't like, you know what I mean?"

We do. While Sandler had appeared on the big screen before, *Madison* was his cinematic arrival, chapter one in what we talk about when we talk about Adam Sandler Movies. That is, subsophomoric, loud, crude, dumb, and seemingly tailormade for prepubescent boys to quote to each other at recess. *Billy Madison* is all of these things. It's also very funny, with an absurdist bent that, while not nearly as incendiary as punk (to quote that aforementioned Judd Apatow show), has a rebellious spirit that makes it a sizable cut above Sandler's other manchild marquee efforts.

For the execs who greenlit it, *Billy Madison* was likely simply a big-budget canvas for Sandler to show off what was working so well for him at *Saturday Night Live*: the gibberish, the baby talk, the exaggerated facial expressions, the naivete, the macho outbursts—they're all there. But rather than just stacking these signatures against a cookie-cutter story about a manchild returning to grade school and finally maturing, the film gleefully veers off into dark and weird asides. Among the many non-sequiturs: a bus driver (Chris Farley) getting a handjob from a penguin, a family of bullies driving off a cliff to their death while shouting "O'Doyle rules!" in unison, Billy's nemesis (an excellent Bradley Whitford) burning alive, Billy receiving flirty valentines from his third-grade female classmates, and little kids laughing at a clown cracking his head open. Throw in some choice soundtrack moments (the Ramones' "Beat on the Brat," Electric Light Orchestra's "Telephone Line") and inspired bit parts (particularly a mild-mannered serial killer played by Steve Buscemi), and it's hard not to be amused.

In its own twisted fashion, at points anyway, "*Billy Madison* rules." (*Happy Gilmore* ain't too shabby, either.)

CLIFFORD 1994

10%

Directed by Paul Flaherty
Written by Jay Dee Rock and Bobby von Hayes
Starring Martin Short, Charles Grodin, Mary Steenburgen, Dabney Coleman, Richard Kind

Critics Consensus

Ill-conceived and desperately unfunny, *Clifford* stars (forty-year-old) Martin Short as a ten-year-old boy. You read that correctly. That's the joke.

Synopsis

A mischievous ten-year-old boy sabotages the life of his successful uncle in a quest to visit the amusement park Dinosaur World and win the affections of his uncle's fiancée.

Why We Love It

In his review, Roger Ebert called *Clifford* "profoundly not funny," "irredeemably not funny," and "a movie that should never have been made." Ouch. Although, as hilarious as we think this Martin Short vehicle is, the critic had a point with that last dig: *Clifford* put one of the final nails in the coffin of the already-bankrupt Orion Pictures. The *Chicago Sun-Times* scribe was hardly alone in his vitriol: people *hated* this movie. Part of what puzzled the public upon *Clifford*'s release was that it wasn't clear who this PG comedy was for. It's not really for children—pedophilia gags, body-shaming, and a generally icky and cynical vibe run throughout—and the levity Short brought to *¡Three Amigos!* and *Father of the Bride* is largely absent. It's . . . a weird one.

But *Clifford* is almost admirable in its unrelenting embrace of its weirdness. The title character purposefully dresses in a spiffy suit jacket, tie, penny loafers, and schoolboy-formal shorts, like AC/DC's Angus Young. In this getup, he tosses off antiquated phrases like "a kindly old priest gave it to me, Da" and "thank you ever so *kindly*, sir" with a gravitas and knowing wink no ten-year-old could ever muster. There's an odd (to put it lightly) quasi love triangle between a grown-up (Charles Grodin), his bride-to-be (Mary Steenburgen), and Clifford. And the titular character's father, a howl-inducing Richard Kind, is on the verge of a stroke (something Clifford callously pokes fun at), while his mother is a clear alcoholic (probably, we're guessing, because of her son). It's a lot of ugliness packed into what people probably took for a sunny problem-child comedy.

Without the comedic chops to back it up, *Clifford* would have just been a WTF-inducing curiosity. But the repartee between Short (having fun with the unflagging enthusiasm and eagerness he displayed on *Saturday Night Live* and *SCTV*) and Grodin (returning to the smiling-liar routine he nailed in Elaine May's *The Heartbreak Kid*) is incredibly funny and worth rewatching. Not surprisingly, the lambasted feature has since attained a cult status among some comedy fans. One such defender, Tom Scharpling, the host of the podcast *The Best Show*, regularly brings up its brilliance and even bought Clifford's outfit at auction. In Ebert's scathing takedown, he also noted, "The movie is so odd, it's almost worth seeing just because we'll never see anything like it again. I hope." We agree with everything but "I hope."

GLOSSARY

There are a few terms we use to talk about movies at Rotten Tomatoes that have very specific definitions, so we thought we'd help you out some with a little glossary. There's a bit of math involved, but don't worry—it's simple . . . *ish*.

Tomatometer: The Tomatometer score—based on the opinions of hundreds of film critics—is our measurement of critical recommendation. A movie's Tomatometer score measures the number of Fresh reviews against the number of reviews overall. Or, more simply, it measures the percentage of positive reviews for a movie. An example: A movie with 100 Fresh reviews out of 200 total reviews has a Tomatometer score of 50%. (See, told you the math was easy.)

Fresh: Can be used to describe both a positive movie review and a movie with a Tomatometer score of at least 60%. A Fresh movie is symbolized by a perfect-looking red tomato.

Certified Fresh: When a wide release movie has a stable Tomatometer score of 75% or above with more than 80 reviews, it is Certified Fresh. For limited release films, the threshold is 40 reviews.

Rotten: Can be used to describe both a negative movie review and a movie with a Tomatometer score of less than 60%. A Rotten movie is symbolized by a green splat.

Critics Consensus: A statement that summarizes how critics have reacted to a movie. It's written by the Rotten Tomatoes crew after synthesizing key points from multiple reviews.

Audience Score: Denoted by a popcorn bucket, this is the percentage of users who rated a movie positively.

Tomatometer-Approved Critic: We don't just count any critics' reviews in our calculation of a film's Tomatometer score. We have a growing pool of Tomatometer-approved critics who meet a set of criteria that you can find on our website.

Wide Release: A movie that is released in at least six hundred theaters nationally.

Limited Release: A movie that is released in fewer than six hundred theaters nationally.

ACKNOWLEDGMENTS

Rotten Tomatoes wouldn't exist without the world's movie critics, and neither would this book. It's their thoughts and words that help generate our Tomatometer scores and which help us offer credible and reliable recommendations for movie fans. For that reason, our first thanks go to those writers and broadcasters devoting their lives to enriching the conversation around entertainment.

Particular thanks go to the sixteen critics who are a part of this book, contributing insightful essays on Rotten movies they love. They are, in the order in which their work appears: Monica Castillo, Kristen Lopez, Leonard Maltin, Jessica Kiang, K. Austin Collins, Nathan Rabin, Eric Kohn, Terri White, Bilge Ebiri, David Stratton, David Fear, Amy Nicholson, Candice Frederick, Joshua Rothkopf, April Wolfe, and Jen Yamato.

The dedicated editorial staff at Rotten Tomatoes worked hard to narrow down the list of films that make up the book and to write the bulk of the entries. Jacqueline Coley, Debbie Day, Ryan Fujitani, Joel Meares, Tim Ryan, and Alex Vo all ensured the thing you're holding now is full of thoughtful recommendations and insights and passionate arguments about why you should explore the green end of the Tomatometer. We were aided enormously by Rotten Tomatoes contributors Erik Amaya, Tim Lowery, and April Wolfe.

The wider Rotten Tomatoes staff, too, helped shepherd the book into the world—everyone from the PR, marketing, and social media teams who have helped promote it to the tireless Curation team, which oversees aggregation and the generation of Tomatometer scores. The design team brought those scores to visual life with three fun infographics, which we hope you enjoy.

Finally, we want to thank two groups of people who, like the critics, are the lifeblood of what we do: filmmakers and film fans.

We love all kinds of movies at Rotten Tomatoes— Fresh and Rotten ones, big and small ones, those that make us think and challenge our perspectives, and those that make us cheer and pin us back in our seats. We *really* love those that do a little bit of all of that. We hope this book is a tribute to the incredibly diverse and talented filmmakers whose work is featured within, and to those whose work has been inspiring us for the twenty-one years we've been around. Special thanks to a specific filmmaker, the great Paul Feig, for writing the foreword to this book and reminding us of all that happens before a film is released and faces the critics, the Tomatometer, and fans.

For the fans—and we count ourselves in those ranks—we hope this book provides 101 more reasons to fall in love with the movies, and plenty of material to fuel future debate and discussion.

INDEX

ABOUT ROTTEN TOMATOES

Rotten Tomatoes is your go-to source for what to watch, packed with recommendations from critics and fans. It's the home of the Tomatometer (the world's most trusted measure of collected critical thought), Audience Score (which takes the temperature of fans), and tons of original editorial, video, and social content to help you discover, debate, and discuss the world of movies and TV.

Special Offer!

Want to watch the movies you've been reading about—with a discount? FandangoNOW has them all. To access that exclusive deal, see more great content, and continue the discussion, head to rottentomatoes.com/rotten-movies-we-love-book.

CONTRIBUTORS

Joel Meares | Alex Vo | Ryan Fujitani | Jacqueline Coley | Debbie Day
Tim Ryan | Grae Drake | Erik Amaya | April Wolfe | Tim Lowery